D1559935

THE Sixties

WITHDRAWN

THE Sixties

Edited by Peter Stine

 WAYNE STATE UNIVERSITY PRESS

Detroit

Originally published as a special issue of *Witness*, Summer/Fall 1988. Copyright © 1988 by *Witness*. Paperback edition copyright © 1995 by Wayne State University Press, Detroit, Michigan 48201-1309. All rights reserved. No part of this book may be reproduced without formal permission. Manufactured in the United States of America.

99 98 97 96 95   5 4 3 2 1

Library of Congress Cataloging-in-Publication Data

The Sixties / edited by Peter Stine
        p.   cm.
    ISBN 0-8143-2558-0 (pbk. : alk. paper)
     1. United States—History—1961-1969—Literary Collections.
    2. United States—History—1961-1969.   3. American literature—20th
    century. I. Stine, Peter.
    PS509.H5S45   1995
    810.8'0358—dc20   95-22000

ISBN 0-8143-2558-0 (pbk. : alk. paper)

Every effort has been made to contact the contributors to this volume to obtain their written permission to use material found in it. For the most part we have been successful, but in a few instances our letters were returned with no forwarding address. Those authors are asked to contact the volume editor or publisher, so proper acknowledgement to them can be made in future printings of the book.

Cover design by Doug Hagley

For identification key to cover photos, see page opposite inside back cover.

for my father, Zan and Nick

■ ■ ■ ■ ■ ■ ■ ■

Contents

Poetry

Fiction

■■■■■■■■■■■

Editor's Preface

Peter Stine

I f the curtain of amnesia and media distortion that descended upon the Sixties is any indication, that decade left in its wake some very disturbing memories. The Vietnam War still haunts us . . . the wasting of a tiny peasant country halfway around the globe . . . the wasting of 58,000 American troops, most of them teenagers from the ghettos and regions of poverty, shipped blind into a conflict so surreal, waged with such mendacity and naked ferocity that anywhere else was called the World. The civil rights movement changed race relations and the face of the South forever, forcing passage of the Voting Rights Bill of 1965 by a display of sheer courage in the practice of nonviolent resistance: yet one casualty was Martin Luther King, Jr.'s vision of brotherly love. The rebellious, high-minded energies of student activism unmasked the face of illegitimate authority everywhere, and would help stop the war, but eventually the movement lost its love of country and veered into Third World revolutionary fantasies in a nose dive toward self-destruction. The major utopian living experiment of the counterculture, the Haight-Ashbury district of San Francisco — a collective commune based naively on sharing, LSD, free love, and political quietude — quickly degenerated into a teenage bowery of runaways preyed upon by disease, hunger, false messiahs, and violence.

As if these traumas were not enough to inspire a disingenuous retreat, there was more. The bullets of assassins subverted electoral politics, striking down the Kennedy brothers and Martin Luther King, Jr., ushering in two decades of "accidental" presidencies. An entire generation was deprived, as John Lewis remembers, of "the type of leadership that we had all in a sense invested in, that we had helped to make and nourish . . ." The collective furies of the Sixties opened a painful fissure of consciousness between the generations, a rupture of blood ties. If the entire country was running, as Michael Herr reported about the effort in Vietnam, on "a dense concentration of American energy, American and essentially adolescent," then the subterranean theme of the decade was parricide.

It is not surprising, after this spirit of liberation and the war itself had forced so many inadmissible truths upon the country, that a period of "therapeutic" memory loss set in, the decade frozen in distortion and reduced to the foolish, yet manageable dimensions of a sitcom. By the mid-Seventies, cultural interference and political backlash allowed little that was serious and authentic about the decade to squeak through. Furthermore, the very trajectory of the Sixties — from idealism to nihilism, hope to rage, innocence to experience, life to death — left those who lived the times passionately feeling like refugees, with the taste of defeat in their mouths, a part of the aftermath of silence and willed forgetfulness.

It is important that this amnesia be lifted, especially for those young Americans, who, as Griel Marcus has observed, experience the Sixties "as an absence, like the itch of a limb amputated before they were born." The writers in this anthology are witnesses/participants who lived through that revolutionary atmosphere, and whose stories, recollected in relative tranquility, recapture the feel and complexity of events. They remind us there were many "spots of time" in a decade driven by an obsessive will to change. John Lewis's experiences with SNCC or Rosellen Brown's at Tougaloo College in the early Sixties are moral light years removed from P.J. O'Rourke's hilarious encounter with the Balto Congo in Baltimore in 1970. It requires some mind expansion to imagine Peter Najarian's first exposure to the counterculture in San Francisco in 1967 as contemporaneous with Richard Currey's initiation into killing in Vietnam. Maxine Hong Kingston's depiction of head-adventurers in the Bay Area forms an unlikely parallel with Tom Hayden's experiences in the streets of Chicago in 1968. Almost inconceivably, the New Left, whose lunatic demise Todd Gitlin records in his memoir on the Weathermen, had its start in what Casey Hayden recalls as "a holy time," the early voter-registration efforts in the South when "we were the beloved community." However, as Jim Miller's reconsideration of Bob Dylan's career and other essays make clear, all of these portraits of the Sixties must be hung on the same karmic wire. If no ultimate meaning emerges, the writings in *The Sixties* at least explode any simplifications about the decade and ought to rekindle in us a sense of wonder.

M y own experience of the Sixties was typical of thousands of young whites in America who, without any ideology or political affiliation in tow, were swept up in the tide of events. I entered graduate school at Berkeley in 1964, fresh from Amherst College and a year studying in England, so ignorant of politics that in Belgrade the previous spring I was attacked by a Serbian anarchist for not knowing who William Fulbright was. Yet within two weeks I was seated on a fender of an entrapped police car in the opening stage of the Free Speech Movement. If there actually *was* an apartheid system in the South, itself news to me, how could it be "illegal" to disseminate information about it on campus? As was true for so many back then, *the moral issues seemed obvious,* and it was simply a question of *putting your body on the line* — an existential mystique of exposing yourself to physical danger for a just cause, something I had first seen in Mario Savio and Bob Moses of SNCC, and in a fierce acceleration of time would see turn freaky/suicidal by the end of the decade.

But not before I was arrested with 700 other FSM demonstrators in Berkeley, nor until the mystique had drawn me into the South, first as a civil rights worker in Alabama, ending in the march on Selma in 1965, then as an instructor at a black college in South Carolina. The following year I returned to Berkeley to finish out the decade, now humming madly to the power transformer of the Vietnam War. And what changes there were — Haight-Ashbury, Black Power, acid everywhere, People's Park, a younger wave of war protesters now threatened by the draft, energized by their own vicarious death and also trapped in bad faith (as we used to say), realizing on the lower frequencies that their disadvantaged "brothers" were doing the real dying in Vietnam. The ensuing survival guilt whipped the New Left into a theatrical frenzy — political posturing called "bringing the war back home" — as if manhood could be reclaimed by mirroring the madness of Vietnam. The election of Richard Nixon as a "peace candidate" in 1968, followed by the "Vietnamization" of the war and its expansion into Cambodia in 1970, marked the exhaustion and defeat of liberal conscience in the Sixties. All the rest was helter-skelter.

Yet what an odyssey it was. And as the writings in this anthology bear witness, how rare and exhilarating to have shaped one's identity against such an epic tide of forces. The Sixties were charged with folly and tragedy, but also with fun, daring, creativity, and unacknowledged heroism on many fronts. Its achievements fell short of a dream, a very American dream of freedom and justice really, yet were real. Perhaps that generation is emerging from its Post Traumatic Syndrome to suggest that we have barely begun to understand our recent past.

T he writings in this anthology first appeared in a special issue of
 Witness (Volume II, Number 2/3, 1988), now published by Oakland
Community College in Bloomfield Hills, Michigan. An award-winning
literary journal, *Witness* has had special issues on Nature Writing and
Sports in America reprinted as books; the popularity of its issue on the
Sixties, and recognition of these contributors in *The Pushcart Prizes,
Best American Poetry,* and other honorary volumes led to this new edition
from Wayne State University Press. *The Sixties* offers college teachers
a fresh and creative text for courses in literature, history, or American
Studies. Of course, the independent reader will find literary pleasure
here too, as well as insight into an eruptive and formative decade.

■■■■■■■■■■■

The Prison Poems: #188

Paul Silas

He is frail. Already as he stands before us,
It is his absence that we see in him most clearly.
And that is why we love him, The Man of The Sixties.
Humanitarians representing all that is best in us
Elbow each other in the ribs for the chance
To grant him honors. In his leaving,
He is one of us at last. How delicately
The President guides him by the elbow
To address our nation from the Senate, which
Has taken this time from its urgent work on suppression.
The Medal of Freedom bounces on his bony chest.
It hurts to watch. We wonder if its ribbon
Feels heavy to his neck. He pauses before his text.
He pauses and pauses. We agonize
Over whether to rush up to catch him as he falls.
He does not fall. We made errors, he begins.
They were the necessary errors of our time.
It was only because of these that we could advance
To The Seventies, also long since repudiated.
Strange though it seems, even your decade
Will be found in error. Do not be disheartened.
This is our destiny. And our triumph. Life itself
Is an assumption — as you can see in my body
But not yet in your own — constantly being proved wrong.
Hands that in the next recess will junket off
To clasp torturers around the world dab at misty eyes.
Forget what the historians have written. This —
This man walking in humility to his grave —
This will forever be The Sixties for us.

John Lewis in Cairo, Illinois. Summer 1962.
(Photograph by Danny Lyon)

■ ■ ■ ■ ■ ■ ■ ■ ■ ■ ■

Two SNCC Interviews

Joan Morrison and Robert K. Morrison

JOHN LEWIS

Born into a black sharecropper's family in rural Alabama, Lewis grew up when total segregation was the rule of law in the South and blacks were routinely denied the right to vote. He was the first chairman of the Student Nonviolent Coordinating Committee (SNCC) and a participant in many of the civil rights struggles of the early Sixties. In 1966, he was ousted as chairman by Stokely Carmichael over the issue of whether whites should be allowed to remain in the organization. Recently a city councilman in Atlanta, Georgia, Lewis is now a United States Representative from the Fifth Congressional District in Georgia.

W hen I was a boy, I would go downtown to the little town of Troy, and I'd see the signs saying "White" and "Colored" on the water fountains. There'd be a beautiful, shining water fountain in one corner of the store marked "White," and in another corner was just a little spigot marked "Colored." I saw the signs saying "White Men," "Colored Men," and "White Women," "Colored Women." And at the theater, we had to go upstairs to go to a movie. You bought your ticket at the same window that the white people did, but they could sit downstairs, and you had to go upstairs.

I wondered about that, because it was not in keeping with my religious faith, which taught me that we were all the same in the eyes of God. And I had been taught that all men are created equal.

It really hit me when I was fifteen years old, when I heard about Martin Luther King, and the Montgomery bus boycott. Black people were walking the streets for more than a year rather than ride segregated buses. To me it was like a great sense of hope, a light. Many of the teachers at the high school that I attended were from Montgomery, and they would tell us about what was happening there. That more than any other event was the turning point for me, I think. It gave me a way out.

When I graduated from high school, I enrolled at the American Baptist Theological Seminary in Nashville, because there was an opportunity there for me to work my way through the college as a kitchen helper and janitor. While I was there I began attending these workshops, studying the philosophy and discipline of nonviolence: the life and times of Gandhi, the works of Henry Thoreau, and the philosophy of civil disobedience. And we began to think about how we could apply these lessons to the problem of segregation.

In February 1960, we planned the first mass lunch-counter sit-in. About five hundred students, black and white, from various colleges showed up and participated in a nonviolent workshop the night before the sit-in. Some of them came from as far away as Pomona College in California and Beloit College in Wisconsin.

We made a list of what we called the "Rules of the Sit-in"—the do's and don't's—and we mimeographed it on an old machine and passed it out to all the students. I wish I had a copy of this list today. I remember it said things like, "Sit up straight. Don't talk back. Don't laugh. Don't strike back." And at the end it said, "Remember the teachings of Jesus, Gandhi, Thoreau, and Martin Luther King, Jr."

Then the next day it began. We wanted to make a good impression. The young men put on their coats and ties, and the young ladies their heels and stockings. We selected seven stores to go into, primarily the chain stores—Woolworth's, Kresge's, and the Walgreen drugstore—and we had these well-dressed young people with their books going to the lunch counters. They would sit down in a very orderly, peaceful, nonviolent fashion and wait to be served. They would be reading a book or doing their homework or whatever while they were waiting.

I was a spokesman for one of these groups. I would ask to be served, and we would be told that we wouldn't be served. The lunch counter would be closed, and they would put up a sign saying "Closed—not serving." Sometimes they would lock the door, leave us in there, and turn out all the lights, and we would continue to sit.

After we had been doing this for a month, it was beginning to bother the business community and other people in Nashville. We heard that the city had decided to allow the police officials to stand by and allow the hoodlum element to come in and attack us—and that the police would arrest us—to try to stop the sit-ins. We had a meeting after we heard that, to decide did we still want to go down on this particular day. And we said Yes.

I was with the group that went into the Woolworth's there. The lunch counter was upstairs—just a long row of stools in front of a counter. My group went up to sit there, and after we had been there for half an hour or so, a group of young white men came in and began pulling people off the lunch-counter stools, putting lighted cigarettes out in our hair or faces or down our backs, pouring catsup and hot sauce all over us, pushing us down to the floor and beating us. Then the police came in and started arresting *us*. They didn't arrest a single person that beat us, but they arrested all of us and charged us with disorderly conduct.

That was the first mass arrest of students in the South for participating in a sit-in. Over one hundred of us were arrested that day. We were sentenced, all of us, to a $50 fine or thirty days in jail, and since we couldn't pay the fine, we were put in jail.

After we were sent to jail, there was pressure coming from people around the country. Parents of arrested students were writing letters to the city. There were telegrams from people like Harry Belafonte, Eleanor Roosevelt, Ralph Bunche. All the big schools in the North were sending telegrams in support of the students. Somebody asked Senator John F. Kennedy, who was campaigning for the Democratic presidential nomination, "What do you think about these young people sitting in at lunch counters and getting arrested?" And Senator Kennedy said, "By sitting down, they are standing up for the very best in American tradition." All of this put pressure on the officials in the Nashville city administration, and they let us out before the thirty days were over.

After we got out of jail, we continued the sit-ins, and more and more people got involved. In April, unknown people bombed the house of our attorney. It shook the whole area, and it shook us. How could we respond to the bombing, and do something that would channel the frustration of the students in a nonviolent manner? We decided to have a march, and we sent the mayor a telegram letting him know that by noon we would march on city hall. And the next day, more than five thousand of us marched in twos in an orderly line to the city hall. One of the students walked up to the mayor and said, "Mr. Mayor, do you favor integration of the lunch counters?" And he answered her, saying, "Young lady, I cannot tell these merchants how to run their businesses, but, yes, I do favor integration of the lunch counters."

The next day the *Nashville Tennesseean* had a headline saying, "Mayor Says Yes to Integration of Lunch Counters." We began negotiating with the merchants, and in less than two weeks most of the lunch counters of downtown Nashville were desegregated. We'd have people go in, a black couple and a white couple, and wait to be served, and we'd do it over and over again, making it appear that it was normal. There wasn't any trouble, and the merchants began saying, "Why did it take all this time? We should have done it a long time ago." And so Nashville became the first major city in the South to desegregate its downtown lunch counters and restaurants. That was the power of nonviolence.

T he next year, CORE (Congress of Racial Equality) decided to test the Supreme Court decision outlawing segregation in public transportation, and they settled on a "Freedom Ride" as the best way to test it. They were going to send groups of blacks and whites together to ride on buses in the South. I sent in an application to go along, and was accepted in the first group.

I'll never forget it as long as I live. I went up to Washington, and we got our orientation there, and I met the other people that were to go on the ride with us. There were two or three other college students, and some people from the American Friends Service Committee, a college professor and his wife, and a couple of others—altogether seven whites and six blacks. We stayed in Washington for two or three days getting our training and preparing ourselves. On the last night we went to a Chinese restaurant, and some of the people were joking, saying, "Eat well. This may be our last supper." We knew that we would be facing trouble as the ride went on.

We went south from Washington, testing the facilities. My seat mate was Arthur Bigelow, a tall, handsome white man from Connecticut, and we sat in the front of the Trailways bus when we left Washington, side by side. As we went through Virginia, we both used the so-called white waiting room and the toilets marked "White Men," and sat in restaurants in the so-called white areas without any problem. People would stare, but there was no outbreak of violence in that state.

When we got to South Carolina, the bus arrived in a little town called Rock Hill, and Arthur and I, walking together, tried to enter the white waiting room. Several young white men met us at the door, and when we tried to open it, they knocked us down in the street and began beating us with their fists. We both shed a little blood. The next day I had to leave the ride temporarily to be interviewed for a program I had applied for with the American Friends Service Committee, so I wasn't on the bus when it got to Anniston, Alabama. It was bombed and set on fire. One of the men had his skull opened up, and it took fifty-seven stitches to patch him up. At that point, Robert Kennedy, who was attorney general, suggested there be a cooling off period, and CORE dropped the ride. I flew back that night, and a group of us—three young women and seven young men—made a decision that we wanted the ride to continue . . .

We got to Montgomery on a Saturday morning. Just seconds after the bus stopped, a white mob came out of nowhere that grew to more than two thousand people. It was very angry and hostile—mostly young people. They had baseball bats, lead pipes, chains, bricks, sticks—every conceivable weapon or instrument that could be used as a weapon. I thought it was my last demonstration, really. I'd never seen anything like that. They were looking for blood.

First they jumped on the press. If you had a pencil and a pad, or a camera, you were in real trouble. Then, after they had beaten the press people, they turned on us as we descended from the bus. I was hit on the head with a soda crate and left unconscious on the street.

While I was lying there, according to a Montgomery paper later, the attorney general of the State of Alabama stood over me and read an injunction prohibiting white and black groups to travel together through the State of Alabama on public transportation. The mob was going around beating everybody at that point.

What saved the day was that the public safety director of the city showed up and fired a shot straight up, and said, "There will be no killing here today. There will be no killing." And the mob dispersed. Some white postal officials opened the basement door of the post office, which was right near the bus station, and allowed some of the Freedom Riders to come in there, and several white citizens in Montgomery assisted us in getting to the doctors' offices or hospitals.

During the night, we made the decision to continue the ride into Mississippi. I had some reservations, because Mississippi is supposed to be worse than Alabama. I didn't know what we were getting into, but I had a feeling that we had to go on, in spite of the fears, in spite of the beating. We had to continue the ride. We couldn't let a mob defeat us.

When we got to Mississippi, we got off the bus and walked into the white waiting room of the bus station. The police captain was standing there, and he said, "You're under arrest." One of the white men with us was arrested for trying to use the colored men's restroom, and one of the black men was arrested for trying to use the white restroom, and others were arrested for drinking out of the fountain marked for one race or another. We were all charged with disorderly conduct or failing to move on.

That summer we filled the Jackson city jail with people testing the segregation laws. Hundreds of people from all over the country came to Mississippi to go to jail. They poured into the state and got arrested at the airport, at the train station, and at the bus station.

Finally the ICC (Interstate Commerce Commission) issued a ruling banning segregation in all places of public transportation, and said that train stations and airports must place signs saying that "seating on this vehicle or in this station must be regardless of race, creed, color, religion, or national origin." They just banned it. [*Snaps fingers.*] And it was wrapped up.

I felt very good about that, because I thought I'd had a part to play in keeping the ride going. If we hadn't continued the ride that summer, I'm not so sure we would have received that ruling from the ICC. It was a real triumph of nonviolence.

Late that summer there was the March on Washington. In the beginning, President Kennedy had been doubtful about the march. He had told us he was afraid that some acts of violence or disruptive behavior might set the civil rights movement back. But when the day came, it all went well, and he had us back to the White House after the march was over, about eight of us, to have refreshments with him in his private quarters, and he was glowing. He said it was the right thing to do, and it had gone right. It seemed like the beginning of a new era for America. And then, not long afterward, President Kennedy was killed. It was shattering . . .

After President Johnson became president, we began to focus on a voter registration bill, because black people were being denied the right to vote or even register to vote in many places in the South, and we had a number of demonstrations in various places. A young black man, who was leading a demonstration near Selma, Alabama, was shot and killed by a state trooper while he was leading a peaceful, orderly, nonviolent march. And we made a decision—Dr. King, Reverend Ralph Abernathy, Andrew Young, and myself—that we should march to Montgomery from Selma to dramatize the need for a voter rights act, and to dramatize the violent climate that existed in Alabama.

A day or so before the march was to begin, Governor George Wallace made a statement that it would not be allowed. SNCC debated all night over it. Some were saying that the days of marching were over—someone might get hurt, someone might get killed. But people were coming from all over to join the march, and I felt that if people wanted to march, we should be there with them. Finally, the committee said to me, "You can march as an individual, but not as a chairman of SNCC." And I decided to do that.

We met outside the church to participate in the march. We lined up in twos, and Hosea Williams and I were the first two. I don't know what we expected. I think maybe we thought we'd be arrested and jailed, or maybe they wouldn't do anything to us. I had a little knapsack on my shoulder with an apple, a toothbrush, toothpaste, and two books in it: a history of America and a book by Thomas Merton.

It was a sunny afternoon. When we got to the top of the bridge crossing the Alabama River, we looked down and we saw this *sea* of blue. It was Alabama state troopers. The night before, Sheriff Clark had asked all white men over the age of 21 to come to the Dallas County Courthouse and be deputized to be part of his posse. So they'd all become state troopers. When we looked down we saw all these men with guns, and we thought, "Well, they're probably going to stop us or arrest us," so we kept on walking.

There was total silence. You could hear only a soft *stomp-stomp-stomp* of people walking. When we got in hearing distance of the state troopers, a major identified himself and shouted on a bullhorn and said, "This is an unlawful march. It will not be allowed to continue. I give you three minutes to disperse and go back to your church." We kept on walking, and in less than half a minute maybe, he said, "Troopers advance."

We stopped then. The only thing moving in our line was my trenchcoat flapping back and forth in the wind. I think I said to Hosea something like, "Shall we stand here in a proper manner or should we kneel?"

But before we could do anything, they came to us—men on horses, men on foot. The horses were trampling over the people, and the state troopers that were not on horses were hitting us with clubs and beating people down with bullwhips. We couldn't go forward, because if you tried to go forward, you were going into the heat of the action. You couldn't go to either side, because you would have been jumping over the bridge into the Alabama River. They came to us as if they were mowing down a big field, and they left a path of people lying down on the ground behind them, hollering and screaming.

I was hit in the head, and apparently I blanked out, because I don't know what happened after that. The doctor later said I had a concussion. Someone must have got me back to the church, and I remember saying, "I don't understand how President Johnson can send troops to Vietnam, to the Congo, to Central America, and he can't send troops to protect black people who want the right to register to vote."

The next morning, Dr. King came over to the hospital where I was, and he said something like, "John, don't worry. We're going to make it to Montgomery. I've issued a call for ministers and priests, rabbis and nuns, the religious community of America to come. We're going to make it."

The next day they tried another march, which I couldn't participate in, and several hundred religious leaders got as far as the line of state troopers on the bridge and were turned back. That night the Reverend James Reeb, one of the young white ministers who'd come down, was beaten by a group of white men in Selma. He died a few hours later in a hospital in Birmingham.

Afterward President Johnson went on nationwide television and made, to me, what was the greatest speech ever on the whole question of civil rights. He spoke from the soul about the point in history when fate and time come to a meeting of the ways. He said, "So it was at Lexington and Concord. So it was a century ago at Appomattox. So it was last week in Selma, Alabama." Then he went on to say that the most powerful nation in the world has heard the moan, the groan, the cry of an oppressed people, and we are responding. He said one good man, a man of God, was killed. Two or three times he said there was a need for a strong voting rights bill. At the end he said, "We shall overcome." I saw Dr. King cry that night. Tears came down his cheek, and I knew then that it was just a matter of time till we would have a strong voting rights act.

Then came the second phase of the march, and it was one of the most meaningful efforts of any demonstration that I participated in. It was black people, it was white people, it was Protestant, it was Jewish, it was Catholic. There were young people, old people, some very poor people, some very rich people, a senator's wife, a cousin of Governor

Rockefeller, a former attorney general. People came from all over. They blended together, and we all marched together.

I was still recovering from the concussion, but I marched, too. We had roadside tents along the way for people to stay in, and it took us four or five days to get to Montgomery. We had someone responsible for the preparation of the food, we had trucks to carry the food, and we carried toilets along the way.

President Johnson called out the United States military to protect us and at night they would shine these huge lights and light up the fields where we were staying. We would see the soldiers on the roadside inspecting the bridges, looking under bridges before we walked across them. It was as if we saw the government of America saying, "These people have a right to exercise their constitutional rights, a right to peaceful protest, to assemble." And President Johnson used the military to make it possible.

Along the way, people made up little songs, marching songs, you know: "Pick 'em up, lay 'em down, all the way from Selma town." There was such a sense of family and sense of community that you sort of wanted to keep on going. There was a sense that we'll get there, we'll make it, because the cause we were involved in was right. It reminded me of Gandhi leading his march to the sea.

The last night we made it to outside Montgomery and gathered together on a grassy field on the campus of Saint Jude's School and Church. There was a huge rally, and people like Harry Belafonte and Joan Baez, Pete Seeger, Peter, Paul and Mary, and others came and sang with us out in the open, to support our effort.

In the morning, we marched down the streets of Montgomery, up to the steps of the Capitol. People kept joining us and by the time we got there we had over thirty thousand people. . . . In October of that year the Voting Rights Bill was passed and we all felt we'd had a part in it.

I n the spring of '66, there was a movement in SNCC to get the whites out of it, and in the struggle over that my chairmanship came to an end. I understand the feelings of some of the blacks who didn't want to work with the whites, but if you're really going to be true to the discipline of nonviolence, you have to accept it as a way of living. It can't become a tactic that you turn on and off like a faucet. If we're struggling to bring about an open society, a beloved community, your tactics must be those of love. I think some of my colleagues in SNCC and some of the other organizations missed the boat in those days.

Because if you turn on the reservoir of nonviolence, where do you turn it off? Do you apply it only to your own ethnic group or people of the same color or class? No, you have to cut the chains of hatred and say, "No more."

I worked on civil rights for the Ford Foundation for a couple of years, and then in 1968 I campaigned for Robert Kennedy. I felt he was serious in his commitment to civil rights—you felt it was coming out of his gut, really—so I wanted to be involved in his campaign.

I was in downtown Indianapolis with him at the time we heard that Martin Luther King had been assassinated. He was to speak at a rally in a transitional neighborhood, and I guess his guards, the FBI agents, or somebody who was with him, were insisting that he not speak because it would be too dangerous. But Kennedy made the decision to speak, and he stood on the back of a car and gave one of the most moving speeches I'd ever heard. He announced to the crowd, who hadn't heard the news yet, that Dr. King had been shot, and the crowd just went sort of "Oooohh." And then he said something about his own brother being shot, and that we don't know who killed Dr. King, but let's be peaceful and pray for his family. The crowd was calm, and we were all crying. . . . I went home for a while after that and helped Mrs. King and her family in the funeral, and I sort of dropped out of the campaign for a week or so.

When I went back, I felt so terrible and sad because I had lost Martin Luther King, who'd been sort of a hero to me, and I felt a tremendous sense of loss. Then I said to myself, "Well, you still have Bobby Kennedy," and so I worked for him in Portland, Oregon, and then in the California primary. Campaigned all over Los Angeles and Los Angeles County.

I'll never forget the last day of the primary. On the evening of the election, a group of us were up in Bobby Kennedy's room on the fifth floor of the Ambassador Hotel before he went down to make his victory speech. Then he told us, "You can come down or stay up here with my sister and the other people." So we saw him on television making his statement, and then we heard that he had been shot, and we all just fell to the floor and started crying. To me that was like the darkest, saddest moment.

The Kennedy family invited me to come to New York to the Mass, and to stand as an honor guard there. I stood with Reverend Abernathy for an hour or so in Saint Patrick's, and the next morning I went to the service. After the service, we all boarded the train from New York to Washington to Arlington Cemetery. On the train you had the body of

Senator Kennedy, the family, a lot of friends, and the people who had
been involved in the campaigns and in the Kennedy administration. All
along the way, you saw people coming up to the train crying and these
handmade signs saying, "We love you, Bobby," "Goodbye, Bobby," "God
bless you, Bobby," and so forth. In a way, you didn't want the train ride
to stop. You wanted it to go on and on, because in a sense it was like
marching, and when you stopped at the train station, and then at the
cemetery, it was so final, you know . . .

There are people today who are afraid, in a sense, to hope or to have
hope again, because of what happened in 1963, and particularly what
happened in 1968. Something was taken from us. The type of leadership
that we had in a sense invested in, that we had helped to make and to
nourish, was taken from us when these three men, all very young, were
killed. Something died in all of us with those assassinations . . .

In 1970 I became head of the Voter Education Project. I helped
register hundreds and thousands of black voters and low income
white voters and Hispanic voters. I didn't have any desire to run for
public office, but I encouraged other people to run.

Then, in 1980, several friends and supporters said, "You should run
for city council in Atlanta," and I ran and carried all of the districts except
two. I got more than 69 percent of the vote, and I was reelected in 1985
with 85 percent of the vote. I like being in politics. I've always said the
ballot is probably one of the best nonviolent weapons that we have . . .

The civil rights movement that I was a part of has, in a short time,
changed this region. There are still problems, no question about it, but
when you go around this area, you see people working together in a
way that is simply amazing. It's a different climate.

You go back to some of these same communities where we had
marches, and you see some of the same people. I was in Selma not long
ago, and the mayor who was mayor then gave me the key to the city.
You go to lunch or dinner with some of the people who were in power
then, and the guy will say, "John, I was wrong. I was on the wrong side.
I tried to keep you all from marching. I had you arrested. We thought
you were an agitator. We were wrong. We made a mistake." In recent
years, I've met with Governor Wallace and with other officials. I met
with the son of the major who gave the orders for the troopers to
advance at Selma, and this young man said to me, "We're sorry about
what happened, and about what my father did."

I'm telling you, they are entirely different people now, and I think one thing the movement did for all of us in the South, black and white alike, was to have a cleansing effect on our psyche. I think it brought up a great deal of the dirt and a great deal of the guilt from under the rug to the top, so that we could deal with it, so that we could see it in the light. And I think that in a real sense, we are a different people. We are better people. It freed even those of us who didn't participate—black people, white people alike—to be a little more human.

■   ■   ■

BOB ZELLNER

The son of a Methodist minister, Zellner grew up in Alabama and attended Huntington College in Montgomery. During his senior year, while doing research on a term paper on "the racial question," he began going to meetings with local black civil rights organizations. As a result, the Ku Klux Klan burned crosses on campus, and he was pressured to resign from college. Zellner refused, and upon graduating in 1961, he became one of SNCC's first white staff members—and eventually one of the last. He now works as a building renovator and carpenter based in New York City.

I grew up in Alabama. Many people don't realize that twenty-five years ago, apartheid was the system in the South. Everything was segregated. It was just the way things were. You didn't think about it. Sometimes when you're inside a system, you can't see it very well. But children are not born racists. They are taught to have racial attitudes.

I remember I worked in a little country corner store, and one day the owner said, "You can't do that," after a black couple had left the store.

I said, "What do you mean?"

He said, "Well, you didn't treat those people right."

"Well, wasn't I polite and courteous and everything?"

"Yeah, that was the problem. It's okay with me, and it's all right if it's just you and I here. But if there are other white people here, you can't say 'yes ma'am' and 'no ma'am' and 'yes sir' and 'no sir' to a colored person."

"Well, why is that? They're older, and I was always taught to be respectful to my elders."

"Well, I know, but you can't. You're not supposed to say 'sir' or 'ma'am' to the black people."

I remember being very puzzled about that. "Why are black people different? Why should I do that?" And he said, "Well, I don't agree with it, and you don't have to agree with it either, but it's just something that you have to do, because people expect it." I remembered that later as a very poignant kind of a lesson. Here was a man who probably was not an unusually racist person, yet still having to pass on these racial lessons to a young kid.

For the first few months working with SNCC, I was in jail every other month. The first time was in McComb, Mississippi. What happened in McComb was that Herbert Lee, the local person helping in a SNCC voter-registration campaign, was murdered. A Mississippi state legislator shot Lee to death, right in the middle of town, because he'd gone to city hall and asked to register to vote. There were two black witnesses, who gave the whole story to the FBI, and the sheriff immediately confronted them with their testimony and broke one's jaw with a flashlight or a billy club. One of them left town immediately and the other witness was shotgunned to death in his front yard. So this was the situation in McComb.

We went there for a staff meeting, and about 125 black students walked out of the high school and said they were going to march to the county courthouse to protest the murder of Lee. I remember hearing in the far distance the soft strains of "We Shall Overcome," and it got louder and louder as the students came up to this SNCC meeting. And their question was: "We're going to the county courthouse. Who's going with us?"

My immediate response was, No, I can't possibly go, because I'm white and I'd be the only white person in the demonstration, and that would cause more violence. Plus, my parents would get in deep trouble. My mother would lose her teaching job, my father wouldn't be able to get a church, and so forth and so on. And the more reasons I gave myself for not going, the more I realized that these students were going to participate in the first march in Mississippi history since the Reconstruction. They were going to march in the open countryside and protest the murder of one of their fellow workers. And I said, What *they* have to lose is so much greater than anything I have to lose. Of course I have to go.

There were big mobs, the line of march was attacked, and it was stopped at the city hall. The mob surrounded me, and some of the SNCC people tried to protect me, but the cops came over and beat them with billy sticks and dragged them off and just left the white mob to get me. And then the mob did their best to kill me. At first they were beating me tentatively and watching the reaction of the police. They were actually saying, "Is it okay for us to get this guy?" And the cops were saying, "Absolutely."

We were up near the steps of the city hall, and then this huge mob out in the street just started screaming like banshees, just hysterically, "Bring him to us. We'll kill him. Bring him here." So they picked me up bodily and were carrying me out like a tide into the street, and I realized that if I didn't do something I was going to die. Earlier somebody had given me a Bible, so I had been holding this Bible, and I remember thinking, rather ironically, God helps those who help themselves. So I put the Bible down as I passed down the steps of the city hall, and grabbed ahold of the rail with both hands. Now this was resistance. I wasn't fighting back or anything, I was just resisting being carried out to the street, where I thought I would die.

So there began a whole contest about getting me loose from the bannister. They started hitting my fingers with baseball bats and prying them loose. They got ahold of my belt and five or six guys got ahold of my legs, and they'd pull. They ripped practically all my clothes off. One guy started gouging deep into my eyes with his fingers. He pulled my eyeball out onto my cheek and tried to get it between his finger and his thumb, to pull my eye out. Because I was holding on to the rail, I couldn't protect my eye very well.

My brain was functioning extremely well the whole time. Along with moving my hands to keep the baseball bats from crushing them, I was moving my head in such a way that just as he would get a grip on my eye, my eye would pop back into my head. I remember it would just *thunk* right back into my eye socket. And I also remember being amazed at the hardness and toughness of my eyeball. I never had understood what eye gouging meant, but that's what it means, reaching into your head and getting ahold of your eyeball and pulling it out. This was raw, downright raw violence.

Anyway, I worked my way up to the top of this rail, and then they all just clambered on top of me and pressed me down, and I fell loose from the rail. The last thing I remember was somebody kicking me in the head repeatedly with a big boot.

Students march to downtown Atlanta. Winter 1963.
(Photograph by Danny Lyon)

Then I woke up inside the city hall, and the police chief was saying, "I ought to let 'em have you. I ought to let 'em have you." I immediately said, "I want to make a telephone call," and he laughed, and everybody else laughed. The mob was inside city hall by this time, so he just said, "You're free to go." I said, "I don't choose to go. I want to remain here and make a telephone call." He said, "You got no choice," and he pushed me out, and the mob just took me away. Loaded up in cars and away we went.

They said they were taking me to the county seat, which was Magnolia, about ten miles away or so. But at the edge of town the sign said Magnolia to the left, and they continued straight. We went out into the woods, and they threatened me with a lynching. They had a rope and everything, and I really thought that I was going to die.

At this point, the men started arguing among themselves. They said everybody saw them leave town with me, and then they were saying, "Well, we'll turn him over to those guys down at Liberty, and they'll do it." So then I started accusing them of being cowards. By this time I was so convinced that they were going to kill me, I just wanted them to remember me as a brave person.

Anyway, they lost courage or lost interest, and eventually they did take me to Magnolia and turned me over to the police. That was the first time I was ever in jail. I remember when that jail door finally slammed closed, it was the sweetest sound that I've ever heard.

Then the FBI came. Three or four guys in nice suits and ties. I remember them being clean and crisp. They took me outside the jail and started taking pictures of my eye and all. I must have been a wreck. My clothes were all ripped up, and my face was all bashed. And I remember one of them sort of sidling up, and he said, "It was really rough out there on the city hall steps, wasn't it?" And I said, "Yeah, it was nip and tuck there for a while." He said, "Well, we didn't want you to think you were alone. We were out there, and we wrote it all down. We've got it all down." This was my first experience with the FBI, and I realized they were a bunch of gutless automatons. I never had any illusions about the FBI from that point on. This guy thought that it would *comfort* me to let me know that he was out there recording my death.

Anyway, that was my first demonstration. After that, I thought everything else was *lagniappe*. That's a French word popular in New Orleans. It means "extra." Everything else was extra. That was the baptism of fire. And I never worried about anything else that I had to do, because nothing was ever as terrifying or as close to death as that was for me.

That was news all over the South, especially since I was a Southerner. My parents supported me, but it was very alarming to my mother. She was always pleading with me to be careful. Once, when we took up a freedom march, my mother sent me a telegram, and she said, "Bob, in the unlikely event that you're allowed to march through Alabama, please, for God's sake, drop out of the march if it goes through Birmingham, because your grandfather and uncle have threatened to kill you." I took that rather seriously; they were members of the Ku Klux Klan. But, in any case, we weren't allowed to even get near Birmingham. We were arrested when we reached the Alabama line.

In those days, people were giants. Ordinary people did heroic things—people who were totally unknown and totally unsung. There was a little-known but very bloody campaign in Danville, Virginia, in the summer of '63. There were sit-ins at segregated restaurants, theaters, and so forth, mass meetings and marches, demands for more hiring of black workers in stores and in the mills.

One of the most brutal attacks on any march that I ever saw occurred there—a demonstration by 120 people, 99 percent of whom were hospitalized. It was a march from the church to the jail to demand the release of some civil rights people. The marchers were trapped in an alley by fire trucks, and then the white sanitation workers—the garbage men—armed with table legs from a furniture factory, went in and beat the goddamn hell out of everybody. Dorothy Miller, whom I married later that summer, was one of the people who was beaten and washed under a car with a fire hose.

I was staying out of the march, because at this time they were arresting me for whatever I did. I was with the press, with my camera, taking pictures, when the fire trucks came. I realized what was happening because I saw the garbage men behind the fire trucks with these big clubs. They were opening up with the fire hoses, and these garbage men were converging, and nobody was moving, nobody was taking a picture. I said to the press, "You've got to take pictures of this. This is the only protection anybody's got." And they said, "No, they said we can't. They're going to kill us if we do. They'll bust all our equipment and everything."

So I stepped right up with my camera, and I said, "This is the way you do it. You aim your camera, and you say, 'snap,' like that." I had a flash and everything. The chief of police spun around, grabbed my camera, swung it down, and beat it on the pavement. He looked back at the rest of them and he said, "Anybody else takes a goddamn picture of this, they get the same treatment." Then the police rushed me and bundled me into jail, under arrest. I said, "What for?" And he said, "For assault on the police chief."

They arrested the minister who was leading the march, and then they had me out of the way and the minister out of the way. Then they started beating the people. We were under arrest, but they deliberately set us right inside the door, where we had to watch this carnage that was going on. Two cops stood right in front of us with their guns on their hips, and one of them said, "Your girlfriend's out there, isn't she? They're washing her under a car right now and beating her in the head. Don't you want to go help her?" That was the kind of taunting that you got. They were offering to kill you if you moved.

It went on for ten or fifteen minutes. They literally hospitalized practically everybody in the demonstration. There were split noses, skull fractures, many, many broken limbs, women with their breasts lacerated—absolute mayhem. And who knows about Danville, Virginia, 1963?

I don't know how in the hell I ever survived that summer. They must have shot at me on at least a half-dozen occasions. One night we were having a party. We didn't do this very often, but we just sort of let our guard down a little bit, and we had a party out behind somebody's house in the black community—there was a little record player, and we had some beer and some wine. We felt safe right in the middle of the black community. Everybody was dancing and just having a totally wonderful time relaxing.

Well, in the middle of all this, the cops surrounded the place and just out of the blue started shooting at this party. I mean fire erupted from everywhere. I don't know how in the world there weren't tremendous casualties. Everybody scattered, and I ran into the house next door, along with a couple of black guys.

I tried to hide in a closet, but the woman of the house said, "Oh, my God, you gotta get out of here. If they find you in here, I'm done for." I had run in the back door, and I said, "Well, they're after me. If I go out there, I'm afraid they're going to kill me." She said, "Well, I'm sorry, but you have to go. I'll put you out the front door." So she took me to the front door, and out I went.

The minute I got outside, a big spotlight hit me, and they said, "There he is!" And shooting just erupted. The fire was spitting out of the guns, leveled at me, and the wood was splattering all around the house. I couldn't believe they weren't getting me. I turned and ran down the porch and jumped off the end. It was on a big hill, probably ten feet in the air, and I remember just jumping and wondering where in the hell the ground was. Eventually I hit the ground, and I rolled over two or three times, but it gave me enough time. The house was between me and where the cops were, and I ran to the back. And as I ran, the cops rounded the corner and were shooting at me again.

You know, the sound of a bullet that's next to your head is the most horrendous sound in the world, because eventually there's going to be one you don't hear, which is the one that's going to kill you. But in these situations something takes over, and you just think extremely clearly. At least I always did.

There was an outbuilding behind this house, and behind the building was a huge pile of brambles and brush, and I said, There's my one chance. I knew that behind this house was a lot of woods. So I said, Okay, if I can make it around this building before they hit me, I've got a chance. So I zipped around that building and leaped just as high and as far as I could into that bunch of brambles, and as I did, I just turned a flip on my back. I didn't even know what was in there. I didn't know whether there were wrecked cars or nails or glass or anything, but it looked solid enough for it to sort of hold me. I remember crashing down through this stuff not knowing what I was going to land on, but it sort of cushioned my fall, and I just totally relaxed when I hit the bottom.

The bushes and everything kept crackling, and I said, Oh, my God, they're going to know I'm in here. But they were shouting so much and shooting when they rounded the corner of that outbuilding that they didn't hear all this going on. They literally ran by about four or five feet away, convinced that I had gone into the woods. And they searched.

I heard them going all through the woods. I just stayed there like a possum, and pretty soon I couldn't hear anything, but I stayed there for what seemed like hours. I said, Well, I'm safe here. I'm not going to move.

Pretty soon I heard a little voice saying, "Bob, Bob," and I realized that it was a friendly voice. I said, "Yeah." He said, "I know you're in there. I saw you jump in there. They're all gone. Come on, I'll show you how to get out of here." So this little black kid, about ten or twelve years old, pulled me out of the brambles and walked me through the woods.

T hen there was the beginning of the whole Black Power movement. A lot of that came out of the summer of '64 and the huge influx of white volunteers who came down to Mississippi. One of the things that happened was that young white students had skills—typing, mimeographing, and all that stuff—and a lot of the local young black people were still learning the skills. Everybody would say, "Well, of course, let Mary do it. She types 68 words a minute, and you can barely get a thing done all day." So there were a lot of hard feelings.

There were exceptions made in my case. The blacks would say, "Bob's not like that. Bob is a Southerner. He's just one of the niggers." But eventually it was decided that white people wouldn't be on the SNCC staff. I thought it was a mistake. It was playing into the hands of the enemy to have a formal policy of exclusion of whites from SNCC. I didn't think it was necessary. SNCC was always a black-controlled, black-led organization. Whites never seriously threatened the leadership.

They didn't want to say outright, "Bob Zellner, you can't be on the SNCC staff anymore." I was a charter member of the staff, and I had paid my dues, as they say. That was very important in the Movement. If you had paid your dues, you were one of the band of brothers and sisters, part of the circle of trust. To say that that no longer existed was a tremendous thing to say. So they wanted to compromise.

It was sort of like a union negotiating: I was in one room, and the ruling body of SNCC was in another part, and people were shuttling back and forth. They said, "You can remain on the staff, but you can't come to meetings as a staff person, and you can't vote." And I said, "I won't accept that. SNCC has never required second-class citizenship of anyone yet, and now is not a good time to start, so I won't do that." Then later they came back: "Well, you can come to meetings, but you can't vote." And I said, "I can't accept that either, unless everybody can't vote. I'm not going to accept any special conditions. I'm either going to be on the SNCC staff as a full staffer, with all the rights and privileges and responsibilities of anybody else, or not at all." And the final vote was that white people would no longer be on the staff of SNCC.

I have a lot of difficulty talking about that. . . . It hurt. SNCC was the most important thing in my life. But I decided a long time ago, after the first year or two in the Movement, that it was going to be a long-term commitment, that I was not going to burn out. I was not going to get bitter.

. . . Anyway, those were heady days to me, to have the effect we had. I mean, we made a difference in history. The civil rights movement destroyed segregation in the South. I go down now to visit my family and friends, and I think about it a lot. When I see the waiting room at the bus station in Mobile, Alabama, I say, "I integrated this bus station." When I see blacks and whites bowling together and going to movies and not thinking a thing about it, I say, "You know, I had something to do with this. I integrated this theater. I integrated this bowling alley."

■■■■■■■■■■■

Voices in the Plaza: Berkeley in the Sixties

Louis Simpson

Life is the best commentary, and no satire could be as cutting as a recent article about Jerry Rubin in the *New York Times*. It seems that Mr. Rubin, one of the leading student activists of the Sixties, has discovered the joy of making money, and nowadays this is what he does. The rebel has become the yuppie, and anyone who didn't see it coming was a bit of a fool.

I certainly was. People of my generation that had lived through World War II, and settled down to a job and raising a family, thought the next generation would be braver than ours. "Don't trust anyone over thirty," Jack Weinberg said. To hear them, they would live on air and never do anything wrong.

I have never enjoyed politics—it's like going to the bathroom, something you have to do but not to be lingered over. In August 1964, however, I became involved. The President, Lyndon Johnson, seemed hell-bent on getting the United States into a shooting war. I was invited to sign an ad that appeared in the *San Francisco Chronicle*. It showed a Vietnamese man holding in his arms a child that had been burned by napalm, and it was headed, "The American people will bluntly and plainly call it murder . . ." The ad listed statements by congressmen who opposed the war, and called on the United Nations to reconvene the 1954 Geneva Conference in order to negotiate a settlement.

Some who had signed the ad were invited to appear on television and explain their reasons. One of the questions we were asked was: "Don't you think the President is better informed than you?" I said, "But he doesn't know how I feel." That evening I received a long-distance telephone call—Los Angeles? The John Birch Society? The caller said, "We're going to get you." I told him I wasn't the pacifist he seemed to think I was—it was this war I objected to—and I owned a rifle. The next day I told a friend about the call and he said I should call the police. A Berkeley policeman, intelligent and conscientious, came to my house and took notes. I wouldn't be bothered anymore, he assured me—those people only tried to frighten you.

My dislike of the war made me sympathetic to the Free Speech Movement at Berkeley. This, the forerunner of student uprisings all over the country, began in the fall of '64. A Dean of Students announced that no tables, fund-raising, membership recruitment, or speeches would be permitted on the sidewalk at Bancroft and Telegraph. The heads of off-campus organizations formed a "united front" to protest the new ruling and requested the Dean's office to restore "free speech" and remove the various restrictions on free expression.

While we held our classes the voices of the student leaders could be heard in Sproul Plaza excoriating the Administration. Every few days brought a new crisis. On October 1, the police arrested Jack Weinberg and put him in a police car. The car was surrounded by a crowd so that it could not move; Mario Savio took off his shoes and climbed on top, and addressed the crowd while Weinberg sat inside looking out, being fed with milk and sandwiches as Elijah by the ravens.

On December 2, to the singing of Joan Baez seven hundred students marched into Sproul Hall and refused to leave. The next day the police carried them out, put them in wagons, and took them to jail. Bail was raised by voluntary contributions but the students would have to appear in court to answer charges. This was where I came in, with other members of the faculty: we formed a committee to provide legal assistance for the arrested students, that is, to hire lawyers and raise the money to pay their fees. While we discussed the wording of an appeal for contributions we could hear the voices of Mario Savio, Art Goldberg, Jackie Goldberg, and Bettina Aptheker, sounding in the Plaza. A professor on the other side of the table was speaking of revolutionary theory in Vienna forty years ago. He spoke tediously and long. "Bliss was it in that dawn to be alive / But to be young was very heaven." Hardly . . . but to be young certainly helped. The speakers in the Plaza were having all the fun.

One day I happened to be passing through New York, and a man I knew at the *Times* invited me to meet some important people, editors, managers, and trustees. They wanted to know what was happening at Berkeley. I told them . . . they listened politely, then talked of more important matters. People who lived in the Bay Area said it was the greatest place in the world, and we at the university thought our words had world-shaking consequences. But in the view of the *Times*, they were not shaking so much as glasses on a sideboard.

B ut protests against the war did have an effect. They were like pebbles cast in a pool, sending out wider and wider ripples. A handful of people on a platform speaking against the war would show hundreds of others that it was possible to speak out—and some would resist the draft. At the same time, media coverage of the war brought it home to the people... the picture of a South Vietnamese officer shooting a prisoner in the head, the picture of a marine setting fire to a village with his cigarette lighter. Finally the average American got the point: Vietnam was the wrong place for Americans to be, and this was a war they could not win—unless they were willing to start World War III.

One day I spoke in the Plaza against the war. That evening there was to be a peace march to Oakland, with lighted candles, and I thought I could not urge others to act without acting myself, so I went on the march. I found the way they marched annoying... all out of step, in jerks and halts. The young woman beside me lost a contact lens and I had to dissuade her from getting down on hands and knees to look for it. As the candles moved into Oakland, people came out of their houses to see. "You people," a resident said, shaking his head, "don't know what you have in this country." Yes, I thought, but did not say—we had been warned not to provoke anger—we know, and that's why we're marching, in order to keep what we have.

Up ahead the Hell's Angels charged the line with their motorcycles. It was said that the Oakland police looked on while the Angels were breaking arms and legs. Did this really happen? I don't know... maybe it did. The Oakland police were not like the police in Berkeley—they were your average hippie-hating cops.

At a poetry reading against the war at Longshoreman's Hall in San Francisco we anticipated some further violence by the Hell's Angels, but Allen Ginsberg went and talked to them, and came back to report that they were a bunch of "sweet guys." And in fact they didn't appear again to molest peace-marchers. There was some talk, reported in a San Francisco underground newspaper, *The Oracle*, of mollifying the police too by raising their consciousness. They might be "equipped with the words and mystique of an ancient mantra still used in India to disperse crowds and multitudes." The hippies were already wearing buttons that said, "LOVE A COP" and "TEACH A COP TO FUCK."

But nothing came of these attempts to love their enemies and teach their enemies to love them — the police continued to disperse crowds and multitudes by using clubs, hoses, and paddy wagons.

I took part in several poetry readings against the war. These left me with mixed feelings, for I loved my country and found it hard to listen to those who obviously didn't. I remember one poet at a rally in Philadelphia who, upon mounting the platform, pointed to the flag and said, "Get that rag out of here!" What, I thought, am I doing in the company of such *canaille?*

During these years my tax returns were audited and I was gouged a few thousand extra tax dollars, on one pretext or another. This was Richard Nixon's way of punishing those who protested against his administration. A man came to my house seeking information about a student who had applied for a government job. As his eyes darted here and there I realized it wasn't the student information was wanted about, but me.

I see Richard Nixon these days sitting in the stands at ball games — the TV camera picks out the spoon-nosed, lantern-jawed profile. What is he doing there? Why isn't he in jail?

Yesterday, Allen Ginsberg said, he had seen Mario Savio weeping. Saying he wanted to go out and live in nature.

Beautiful, said Timothy Leary.

So I mean, Ginsberg said, he's basically where we are: stoned.

Activists and flower children had a lot in common. But the activists wanted to change the System, flower children just wanted to be left alone.

IN THE WIND: a 130-acre ranch for use as combination farm, ashram, center for Human Be-Ins, country fairs, dances . . . a cooperative marketplace in the Haight-Ashbury, to distribute farm products, crafts, health foods, etc. . .

Gary Snyder told how he'd dropped out and survived, and this was before there was a "community." It meant "mastering all kinds of techniques of living really cheap." He would get free rice off the docks, spilled from sacks when they were being fork-lifted. He had it worked out with the guards to gather fifteen or twenty-five pounds of rice for him, and also tea. He'd pick this up and take it around and give it to friends.

"We used to go around at one or two in the morning, around the Safeways and Piggly Wigglies in Berkeley, with a shopping bag, and hit the garbage cans out in back. We'd get Chinese cabbage, lots of broccoli and artichokes that were thrown out because they didn't look sellable anymore. So I never bought any vegetables for the three years I was a graduate student at Berkeley. When I ate meat, it was usually horse meat from the pet store."

Activists and flower children came together for a Human Be-In on the Polo Grounds of Golden Gate Park. Let *The Oracle* tell it:

> And with the sun setting, Allen Ginsberg and Gary Snyder chant the night with the Om Sri Maitreya mantrum, turned toward the sun, double disks revolving in the red-gold glare, small groupings arms linked moving gently from side to side. She a beautiful Nubian princess, he a motorcycle wizard and warlock, and I poet and participant, swaying, good people, Om Sri Maitreya. The sun moving down behind the trees, heading for the Pacific . . .

Shall we leave it there with activists and flower children gently moving from side to side, Om Sri Maitreya Om?

Yes, it would be best to leave, before Ginsberg puts on a suit and tie, and Leary is an old man telling stories to lunch clubs, and Jerry Rubin discovers how nice it is to have money.

■ ■ ■ ■ ■ ■ ■ ■ ■ ■ ■

An Inside/Outsider
in Mississippi

Rosellen Brown

ohn Fowles saw the French Lieutenant's Woman standing in
black at the edge of a quay. Joan Didion watched a young
woman in obvious distress stride across the lobby of a Beverly
Hills hotel and make an anxious phone call. The image, real or
imagined, begets the book.

In our case, the indelible impression, a man-begetting image, not a
literary one, is of a gnome—round, bald, smiling, talking to us, although
we were strangers, without let-up—eating a chop decorated, for himself
alone, with a shiny canned peach. His table is covered with the kind of
old-fashioned red checkered oil cloth that people and restaurants search
out these days for its naive "charm." This table, only incidentally
charming, is in the rickety, fluorescent-lit basement of a seedy wooden
building near the center of a college campus in Mississippi. It is June of
the summer of 1964.

There have, by now, been a great many anatomies of "the troubles,"
as a friend calls them with an appropriately broguish lilt. They
have featured black folks, whose movement it was, and white folks,
who were there as midwives but who also felt the ultimate freedom of
their souls at stake. Bob Moses, Fannie Lou Hamer, John Lewis,
Stokely, all of them have been written about, and many of the ancillary
forces as well, private and public. But there are dozens, many dozens of
other players who had their roles in this time of exceptional flux, this
floodtide. Their influence is a subtle force, whose results are hard to
measure. They need voices to *testify* (as they say in the little churches).
Ernst Borinski, the man at ease in his own lively, peculiar and self-
designed domain, wielded a very distinct kind of influence that has

rarely been celebrated because it was *sui generis* and modest and in many ways seemed to run counter to the times. But it was genuinely important as one piece of the whole.

"The-three-civil-rights-workers" — that terrible phrase that came all in one word — had been missing for a week or two when my husband Marv Hoffman and I went to interview for our first jobs, at Tougaloo College, just outside of Jackson. As students we had stood on the safe sidelines of the civil rights struggle long enough, we thought; too cowardly to volunteer for front-line action, we answered the call of the Woodrow Wilson Foundation which was looking for former grad-school Fellows to work in "developing" — i.e., poor, mostly southern, mostly black — colleges. Alternately brave and craven, we asked for a "safe" posting, maybe something in a border state, at the edge of the fray where we could do our little bit, which we saw as intellectually, not overtly, combative: One of us would teach English, the other psychology. They suggested Tougaloo, nicknamed "Cancer College" around Jackson for its place at the raging center. Tougaloo was a private college which had always been integrated — private funding made it independent of the kind of financial sanctions by the state that persistently threatened to sever the lifeline of schools like Jackson State. At Tougaloo you lived on the campus, because off your safety was too difficult to assure. Even inside its gates, houses on the periphery of the campus occasionally took rifle shots through their windows; the sheriff chased you as far as the arch of the front gate. Intrigued, we went to have a look; compelled — the alternate placement in the border state suddenly rendered pale and tame by comparison — we took the jobs.

The June meeting with Ernst Borinski was by way of interview. (Six months later when we reported to work, the civil rights workers were assuredly dead, and a few more besides.) There he sat over his solitary dinner in the back room of what was called the Social Science Lab, although a conventional lab it was not. He had furnished the long, low-ceilinged basement room with a random, catch-as-catch-can assortment of unmatched and scuffed tables and chairs, and an equally motley collection of books — anthropology, sociology, psychology, history. I remember a particularly unused-looking copy of *Bleak House*, possibly, given his relative indifference to literature-as-such, shelved with Urban Studies.

The room in which we confronted Dr. Borinski at his chop — we couldn't bring ourselves to call him "Ernst" until many years later when we were bona-fide adults out of his employ—was partitioned off from the rest for a privacy that was only relative. It was never off-limits to anyone and student assistants roiled through it casually in search of assignments, conversation, life-direction. It was a combination mess-hall, office and boudoir, a space so lived-in and so much a piece with its inhabitant that if there was no bed back there it felt as if there ought to have been. We were surprised when we learned that he actually had an apartment elsewhere on the campus—what else could the man own, or even care about, that he might put into it?

Ernst had an extraordinary accent and allowed himself a flamboyant indulgence of Germanic syntax, all inversion and circumlocution, which we soon understood he was not eager to lose. In Mississippi, where even the inflections of Chicago or Boston sounded foreign, his language made a kind of magical space around him, kept him enigmatic, and forever innocent (no matter how sly), moored, apparently forever, in foreignness. Every time he picked up the conversational ball he raised his eyebrows and said, in a rising tone of anticipation, "Zo-*zo?*" His speech sounded approximately like Sid Caesar doing Freud.

But Ernst played his myths for all they were worth. Once he told us that, spawned by his outrageous speech, rumors had circulated locally that he could understand every extant language. People began to bring him letters in Hungarian, Italian, and Russian to translate; apparently even in the most all-American of neighborhoods exotic needs will surface. Rather than dispel so convenient a reputation—who could guess what power and authority it might engender for later use?—he would put the supplicants off while he shipped their mail to the appropriate consulates with a request for translation.

Still, if he was not quite as extraordinary as he seemed, he was extraordinary enough. By the time he had left Germany, somewhere in Silesia near the Polish border, in 1938, Ernst had already had what would suffice many for an entire career: he was a lawyer and a judge. He must have traveled in prominent circles: Kathe Kollwitz was a friend. The advance of Nazi power was apparently more evident to him that to the rest of his family, who would not budge. Alone, he went to request a visa, was asked if he was planning to return and, where many of his confreres lied and said Yes, assuredly Yes, they only wanted a vacation, and were denied exit, he was straightforward—"I'm never coming back"—and received one. He didn't use the visa for a long time, though, while he worked at persuading his family to flee with him. Lawyer or not, he could not convince them to leave. They stayed behind;

every one of them perished. On the train, leaving finally, he told us, once again he trusted authority where many another would have found it impossible, with a Blakean innocence that had passed through experience, beyond hopelessness and beyond cunning. He gave all his money to the conductor, told him he was going to take a sleeping pill and did not wish to be awakened until they were across the border, did so, and was delivered. So went his story anyway. He landed first in Cuba as did so many refugees; came to the United States just in time to serve in the Army and, long before the English language imposed itself on his consciousness, became a citizen, along with a wildly assorted crowd of recruits in North Africa. (In anticipation of the arrival of the Germans, the U.S. government wanted to protect its German soldiers by annexing them as formally as possible.)

Finally he was able to get down to the business of reconstructing a life: he worked in Rochester for Bausch and Lomb because in Germany they had had an adult education program he had been involved with, and somewhere along the way, probably later, he took a Ph.D. in sociology at the University of Chicago. Somehow he heard about Tougaloo and it too resembled the adult education work he had done in Germany. Suffice it to say that, although he probably did not have a multitude of choices, his arrival was no accident. (When I graduated from high school in 1956, one of my most culturally-attuned and serious friends chose to go to college in North Carolina because she said—and I was far too benighted even to have an opinion about the probabilities—that the next "action" was going to take place in the South and she wanted to be there to take part in it. There are those, apparently, who know at least one of two things, if not both: where there is need, and where there is movement, however potential, however seismic, coming to an underground boil.)

It was the late 40s when Ernst surfaced on the campus of the small black college, founded in the late 19th century by white Methodists. There has always been white faculty at such colleges. The old photographs in the library showed us very sober young black faces—men and women buttoned to the neck, their collars sternly starched—arranged in ranks or else in the random I'll-look-this-way, you-look-that-way fashion of group pictures of a century ago. Behind them, or in the corners, were their white mentors, modestly tucked out of prominence: they were there in the spirit of Christian helpfulness, and one imagines their ministrations—this was not terribly long after the Civil War—were gentle and more than tinged with noblesse oblige. They played a very necessary role in readying these young people, whoever they were, from whatever kind of tenuous, determined pre-middle class, for the worlds of teaching, of the church, and, once in a while, of the professions.

When we arrived in the mid-60s, there were still white professors cut from the same cloth, with theological backgrounds and a cheerful air of service about them. Most were dedicated in the way of missionaries, or at least of ministers, with a slightly strained but rarely shattered patience in the face of intellectual shortfalls, and a set of standards just a little too forgiving to be wholly useful in the "outside" world. (For "outside," of course, read "white.") There were black professors too (Negroes then) whose tolerance, similarly, was often dangerously excessive: much of the work they accepted was barely of high school quality. But they were dealing with the shambles a poor and segregated Mississippi education (separate but nothing like equal) made of most minds, good, bad, indifferent, too often irreversibly, and at least their shared color and common experience gave them a different kind of edge. They could be sharp-tongued, even harsh, and it sounded parental. The old-guard white faculty tended to tiptoe because, stepping down hard they did not sound parental, they sounded *white*, and this was the deep South, and it was all too easy to stimulate connotations, associations, terrors, and watch ears and eyes close up and minds close down. They were sensitive to that, but generally helpless. A good bit of black higher education was felt to be in the hands, however benign, of the enemy.

Ernst, though—what to make of Ernst? He was, by careful design, not so much enemy as stranger. His origins remained in dispute; he was unclassifiable. (One morning in a sociology class, the question arose: How many Jews are there in America? Estimates ranged from 40 to 70 million. "Any here on campus?" "Oh no." "Borinski?" "Nah." "Feldstein? Hoffman?" Certainly not, our students said indignantly: they *liked* us all. Wherever the dangerous horde preyed, it had not yet penetrated the front gate here.) Ernst had a "complete new concept" for where he dwelled in the imagination of Mississippians of all colors. It was more than mildly sociological, as were all his ideas: he called it "inside-outside." "Some vays," he would say, rubbing his pudgy hands together like a man diabolically plotting, "some vays zis vorks to everyone's advantage," implying, I think, that, like drinkers who can excuse their behavior by blaming the bottle, those who might be discovered yielding up their racist behavior or their laziness in the face of difficult head-work—those caught living up to his alien expectations whatever they might be—were merely victims of his beguiling exceptionality, his

45

empowered marginality. So he went about building his empire of
elevating aspirations, his laboratory of worldly enrichment.

The first thing he did when he arrived at Tougaloo set the tone of
daring pseudo-naiveté. Many of his students were recently returned
veterans, hungry for an education, more comfortable in the world-at-
large than their provincial brothers. He gave them an assignment that
must have sounded like the first command of a fairy godfather to a
prince in search of a kingdom: "Go," he ordered them, "und bring back
for me desks, typewriters, tables, bookshelves. Und do not tell me vere
you got them, zis I do not vant to know." Sweet are the uses of ignorance.
So they constructed the charmed domain of the Social Science Lab in a
boarded-up space beneath the building that housed faculty offices.
(Next door the administration ruled in a pillared antebellum mansion
that felt like the domesticated palace of a conquered nation.)

The second use Ernst made of this willful blindness to
"appropriateness" was a wholly unique series of weekly lectures he'd
been staging for years, to which all manner of speakers came, and all
colors of listeners. He invited to speak anyone who would oblige —
journalists, scholars, psychiatrists, activists — the whole assortment of
intellectually qualified passersby who, especially in the inflamed 60s,
were flooding the state. From Ernst's point of view, which could be
irritatingly dispassionate, anyone with a firm perspective, anyone who
represented passion and brought along facts, was welcome; his enemies
were ignorance and stagnation, an inaccessibility to outside voices and
multiple world-views that is hard to reconstruct two decades later.
Somehow he trusted that along the way his listeners would form their
own judgments regarding morality, decency, necessity. He'd have invited
the Klan if they'd have come. (On our first visit to the campus during
that long hot dangerous summer, a black man from the village of
Tougaloo nearly scared us into the bushes screeching up beside us in his
tattered car. "Is this where the rabbi from Arabia speakin' tonight?" he
asked us eagerly. And indeed it was: an Arab diplomat from some
infinitesimal new oil country, passing through on business, was on the
agenda that night, and the man from town was there in his work-
clothes to hear him. So came Indians, Japanese, Harvard professors,
congressional aides.)

But that would not have been enough to justify Ernst's efforts. Very
carefully he planned pre-lecture dinners to include, among students he
thought could benefit, the small contingent of daring whites who would
drive out from Jackson and not mind letting it be known that they were

coming to this place of public contamination. The wife of the head of the Chamber of Commerce was a prize catch; even her husband was sometimes on the guest list. Two brave and significant civil rights figures who, in the 50s, had been students at Millsaps, the white college in town, told us that Ernst's forums, to which they snuck out rashly under cover of darkness, were influential in their "alternative" education. A city like Jackson is unrecognizable today in its openness; no one much cares where you spend your time. You won't lose your job or your house or your life for "fraternizing." But in order to understand how unique were Ernst's efforts at rapprochement — his understanding that "casual" social contact could precede and encourage tolerance — one must re-imagine the truly Gothic atmosphere, the sense of heart-stopping danger, in which his small but always growing cadre of white friends lived, and all they had to overcome to show up in the dazzling light of the Lab on Forum nights.

Working with Ernst was another story, although his scheme fit together better than we could appreciate at the time. We were very young (as was most of the hot-shot faculty — many programs were "plugging in talent" in those years) — and rather more aggressive and impatient about change than our experience warranted. And we were short-termers; Ernst, in for the long haul, had the larger picture and the lighter touch. He did not particularly encourage (though he didn't oppose) the kind of sit-in activism the Tougaloo students favored. He was rarely eager to confront the administration over its frequent and distressing lapses in commitment to the "movement." (The book has yet to be written about the ambivalence of black college leadership toward radical change and toward community, toward attitudes that included respect for the "unwashed" classes just outside the gate that so embarrass it, unless that book is the old standard *The Black Bourgeoisie*.)

In general, the old man (for so we thought him even in the face of our respect for his sharp analytical powers) favored conciliation. It was well for certain populations to petition and demonstrate, for others to raise hell with the powers that ran the college (while they, its leaders, dug in and prepared to wait us out, a mere rainshower of clamorous voices). But his role, he patiently explained while we listened with undisguised impatience, was to hold down the middle: he was the buffer we could shoot across if we chose to. To understand social dynamics we needed to learn to focus — "focoos" was the word — on the balance of forces. Dispassion was not indifference; disinterest was not betrayal. He regarded us more coolly than we regarded him: we were like impatient lovers, and the many crimes he saw us commit, he knew, were crimes of passion. Where would we be without his avuncular temperateness? We viewed his various concilations with bewilderment. Given his background it was difficult to accuse him of fear so we accused him of optimism. We found him guilty of trusting his enemies and smiling when he should have been shouting.

Did he expect things simply to change without antagonists? Shouldn't he "of all people" decry silence in the face of injustice internal to the college or external? Didn't he sometimes put too much emphasis on delivering his students out of this narrow and embattled place—he cultivated every conceivable contact to get them off to distant graduate and professional schools—without considering the impoverished community right down the road? "Ve send away children," Ernst insisted, "und zey vill come back to be leaders. Zo-zo, zis is vere ve fit in: ve uncover ze road for zem. Ve cannot take it for zem." (And many of them, degrees in hand, did follow it back to serve at home: lawyers, a young man I taught as a semi-literate freshman who brought his Princeton Ph.D. back and became chairman of the Tougaloo history department.)

We nattered on, and not always without justification, but in many cases we were the wrong ones to do the nattering, wholly sincere kids with good "eastern" educations, contemptuous of institutions—the black fraternity was one—far stronger than we, with histories we could hardly comprehend. Fashioned by other histories, we were relevant and irrelevant at the same time, resentful at having to give instruction in black pride and the righteousness of anger but patronizing in other ways we couldn't begin to imagine. We were role models chiefly for the sensitive kids who already felt alienated from local ideals, who could respond to our confident egalitarian chumminess. In a place where every hard-won higher degree placed an honorific beside one's name like an immovable stone, we—this was the mid-60s, after all—were the kinds of professors who asked to be called by our first names and had no patience when the homegrown faculty thought we were slumming. (In retrospect, we should have recognized a very familiar insecurity in needing to maintain all those letters: my husband's mother wanted to have his graduate degrees laminated and framed for her living room—he had done something no one else in the family had done.) Ernst understood far better than we where it was worth pitching battle: he was always Dr. Borinski and he in turn addressed every faculty and administration member by title, however absurd he may have looked doing so.

W e left Mississippi in 1968 when we wearied of the mischief "black power" was making for white activists (by then—predictably?—having left the all-too-quiescent Tougaloo to work for the new and urgent poverty program). Ernst had no reason to move on. He had defined himself as a power outside the force-field of daily politics—"Today zis comes, tomorrow it goes. Zo-zo." He sounded like Billy Pilgrim. He was no Marxist, though his style was endlessly dialectical; he was not even a standard-issue determinist, but he would never be out of work—the conciliator's position would always be right there between the poles. Eventually, in the late 70s, he cut back to half-time teaching (full time for most mortals), and he began to visit us every fall where we were living in rural New Hampshire, between trips—he was nearly 80 by now—to Israel, Lebanon, China, the Soviet Union.

He came to us in the fall in a cap with earflaps, wearing the clean white sneakers he had used to walk the Great Wall. ("Zey would not let me in the University Club in zese. Zey vere afraid I would start a new fashion!") Cast in a new role he was a remarkable house guest, having calculated carefully: A man with no family needs his friends. (He was our daughter's self-appointed godfather, and many others' besides.) Thus he called on a regular rotation of us yearly "in Vanderbilt University, in Chicago, in Columbia, here in ze deep country vere you play at Marie Antoinette and le petite Trianon." He insisted on cooking for us ("I must earn my keep, yah?") a series of unrepeatable dishes in the "Polish-Cherman-Chinese" style, heavy on soy sauce, mustard and cabbage; he amiably accompanied everyone to work, sitting with fifth grade rural/blue collar children, a one-man lesson in geographical multiplicity; with pre-schoolers, letting them play with his accent as if it were a toy; with graduate students in administration, about whose work he had abundant multi-purpose sociological theories.

Every Sunday afternoon, as regularly as a dutiful son calling his parents back home, Ernst would phone the president of Tougaloo, ostensibly reporting in and getting the news, in actuality demonstrating a courtly respect, honoring an absolute structure of command we had always observed with difficulty. Children of our time, we demanded "substance," "earned respect"; we easily dispensed with hierarchy which smacked of elitism, class division, "phoniness." But we Holden Caulfields had, since the last time around, grown up some. Now we could appreciate the care and nurturing Ernst gave out of his finely nuanced sociological grasp of the uses of seemliness. Where we had thought him a rank conservative and a sentimentalist, now we saw him for what he was: on the one hand a politician, on the other a good and decent man whom it cost little to bend the knee to ceremony.

The fluidity and playfulness of his mind, the ego that could withstand endless, because temporary, re-definition, all of it was disciplined by his belief that society is made up of groups who will avidly pursue their interests; and in the middle, a stiff-armed referee pushing the forces back a little on both sides, stands the virtuous and disinterested man. How could someone who had seen his family, just about all of it, fall to a madman in pursuit of *his* interests, stay quite so detached? How could an orphan of history restrain a passion for vengeance or for reparations? To what can one attribute the natural buoyancy that keeps some souls afloat in bloody churning waters — keeps them not only afloat but smiling? (We have known a few "boat people" in the last few years who came through such waters literally, not figuratively, and they suggest the same question.)

It would make good but not adequate sense to say that the fury of their reproach to circumstance could be so uncontrollable, so terrifying were it loosed that they have inhibited it, as people inhibit anger in their lives and present themselves safely encapsulated, repressed, undemonstrative in love and work. But Ernst doesn't fit the paradigm, somehow — perhaps his dispassion does and his apparent refusal (inability? unwillingness?) to create his own family. But, true to his own sense of the complexity of all things, he will not lie down and be analyzed. "Zo-zo," he might ask. "Und vut vill you learn if you answer zese qvestions?"

Years after we had left Mississippi, I had the only near-mystical experience of my writing career. I heard a voice — not a hallucination of a voice because I am too constrained by sanity for that, but a sort of echo of a familiar tonality, an accent I knew intimately. I heard this contorted Germanic language as a woman's speech that wouldn't leave me until I wrote inside it. I gave this woman a childhood shattered by anti-Semitism, pre-Holocaust, and I wished on her a daughter without much sense of history, to torment her when "outside" circumstance had finished wreaking its havoc. She became Gerda Stein, a not-very-lovable, and certainly not very buoyant character — I hesitate to say heroine — at the center of my first novel, *The Autobiography of My Mother*. Far from delineating my own mother in even the slightest detail, Gerda, I realized somewhere along the way, represented for me, tranformed, the essential "secret," if I dare make his life into a conundrum, of Ernst's unmotivated serenity. Having been hounded into exile by historical catastrophe, both of them, real and imagined, had abandoned certain psychic comforts such as the concept of home and biological family, and had taken refuge in that persistent "optimism" we had so deplored when we worked with him, that refusal to take a belligerent or rash or even hortatory stand on urgent issues. This was a paradoxical trust born of a pessimism whose roots were buried too deep, I suspect, for tears; an almost absurdist refusal to worry, let alone mourn. It placed an outrageously, demonstrably unjustifiable faith in the institutions of law, self-regulation, constitutional guarantees. Yeats's old men's eyes are gay in "Lapis Lazuli," having stared at "the tragic scene" long enough to have witnessed everything, and so were Ernst's, the darkest possibilities already having overtaken them. "Ya, zo-zo, some vays it vill all vork out," he would say, who had escaped by a shirttail the ultimate working out of the Final Solution. I don't think there was anyone in whom he had confided intimacies—intellectual formulations and analytic sang-froid stood in their place—and I wonder if anyone, since his arrival here, had seen him personally fearful, or even vulnerable. That he chose to be useful and to stay energetic and undepressed was a gift of temperament, but it was a gift wrung forever from its opposite, a hopelessness, a cynicism about outcomes, too dire to be borne. Thus were "the troubles" of one era connected by a slender thread to "the troubles" of another.

Ernst has been buried since 1984 in the little cemetery on the Tougaloo campus, a quintessentially southern graveyard inside a low gate under trees hung with Spanish moss. It is the kind of place that seems made for drowsy summer days, too antique to be threatening, too charming to depress a visitor. He is not the only white buried there, if memory serves, but surely he is the only one who was destined for the anonymous ash-heap of Europe; whose stubborn survival, even if he was never quite at ease, ultimately empowered him to be vividly present everywhere. It was a better use of exile than most people make of the safety of home.

■■■■■■■■■■■

Bob Dylan

Jim Miller

Bob Dylan's eyes darted restlessly. Unshaven and puffy, his face poured sweat. Flanked on stage by Keith Richard and Ron Wood, fellow pop aristocrats from the Rolling Stones, he stumbled through a heartless version of his most famous song, "Blowin' in the Wind." The audience, responding to the nostalgia of the moment and the predictability of the gesture, cheered, as if on cue, as the scene was beamed live via satellite around the world. It was the climax of the 1985 Live-Aid concert. At 46, Dylan was rock's unofficial poet laureate. He looked like a waxen effigy.

Twenty years earlier, on another stage, at the Newport Folk Festival, the scene had been entirely different—Dylan had nearly caused a riot. He had done this by deliberately defying the expectations of his audience. His most famous song he ignored. Rather than accompany himself, as usual, with an acoustic guitar, he had launched into a loud new blues called "Maggie's Farm" with the help of an amplified band. In 1965, the crowd had jeered: "Play folk music! . . . Sell out!" Dylan, as was his wont in those days, had kept his own counsel. After singing two more songs, he abruptly left the stage, as did his band. He returned alone for an abbreviated encore, performing acoustic versions of two more songs, "Mr. Tambourine Man" and "It's All Over Now, Baby Blue." Superficially, both were gentle ballads. But their lyrics were filled with obscure and delirious images as remote from the conventions of folk music as the amplified roar of his band. Whether the crowd fully realized it or not, Bob Dylan had just fired another salvo in his one-man cultural revolution. In the months to come, he would become a self-styled rock and roll Zarathustra, dramatizing a different way to live.

How could the existential daredevil of 1965 have turned into the lifeless pop icon of the Eighties? How could the man once widely acclaimed as the greatest composer of his generation have become the cadaver of Live-Aid? These are among the greatest mysteries of Bob Dylan's strange career.

Some great rock stars—Paul McCartney springs to mind—live, breathe, and eat music. They take pleasure not simply in fame and money—these things most of them have in excess—but also in composing melodies, writing lyrics, trying to craft a pleasing song. Their audience may abandon them, their creative skills may atrophy— yet their natural and unfeigned joy in making music allows them to grow old with a certain gracefulness and dignity.

Other great rock stars—David Bowie, for example—are essentially manipulators of cultural signs. Their genius is less a matter of musical talent than of giving form to passing fashions, epitomizing a certain life style, defining a cutting edge for their audience. Once they lose their knack for defining that edge—perhaps because they become bored, perhaps because their perceptions of the broader culture become dulled by fame and wealth—such rock stars produce a kind of cultural static. They release new records, tour as living legends, and even command the continuing attention of the mass media—they are bona fide celebrities, after all. But the *music* they produce—and they are, of course, still in the business of pop *music*—is more often than not an empty shell, an inadvertent self-parody. Out of touch with their times, they have become *irrelevant*.

Ever since his heyday in the mid-Sixties, it has been assumed that Bob Dylan was and is a great musician. Yet the mummy on stage at Live-Aid makes that claim seem absurd. Could it be that Dylan, like Bowie, matters less as a musician than as a manipulator of cultural signs?

The appearance on compact disc of classic Dylan albums like "Blonde on Blonde," coming on the heels of the anthology "Biograph" and Robert Shelton's unreadable but highly revealing biography, *No Direction Home*, encourages a fresh examination of such questions. The digital reissues vividly capture Dylan in his prime—and so, in its way, does Shelton's clumsy book. Shelton, formerly the pop music critic for the *New York Times*, was the first important writer to review Dylan, in 1961. Perhaps because his frequently expressed enthusiasm gave a boost to Dylan's career at several crucial junctures, the singer agreed to help Shelton when he first began his book, more than twenty years ago. Although the text is a mess, it is full of new information gleaned from a host of previously unpublished conversations and interviews, many of them remarkably candid. To piece together Dylan's early life from these fragments and to listen again to his first seven albums is to rediscover a major cultural figure — and a major puzzle.

H e was born on May 24, 1941, in Duluth, Minnesota, the oldest son of Abraham and Beatty Zimmerman, both second-generation American Jews of Russian ancestry. After the war, the family moved to Hibbing, a Minnesota mining town where the Zimmermans ran a furniture and appliance store. "Hibbing was a vacuum," the singer told Shelton many years later. "I just wanted to get away." At first, imagination was the readiest means of escape: his father recalls that the boy loved the tall tales surrounding Paul Bunyan. And his high school sweetheart says that "he was always making up little fantasies and telling little fibs." She remembers Bob calling her on the phone one night and playing her "something he had recorded" — it turned out to be Bobby Freeman's hit recording of "Do You Want To Dance."

The Zimmerman boy developed a passion for music early. He began singing at the age of five, got his first guitar in junior high, formed his first band in 1955. During a visit with Bob's parents, Shelton heard some of the group's practice tapes— "Rock and Roll is Here to Stay" was part of their repertoire. Shelton also examined the record collection that Bob had left behind: a pile of 45s and LPs that included singles by black rhythm and blues stars like Johnny Ace and the Clovers, American Bandstand pop idols like Pat Boone, country-western artists like Webb Pierce and Hank Williams, rockabilly singers like Gene Vincent and Buddy Holly—and a stack of hits by Elvis Presley. In the 1959 Hibbing High School yearbook, Bob declared his ambition "to join the band of Little Richard."

Besides playing and listening to pop music, the Zimmerman's oldest son was an avid reader—John Steinbeck's *Grapes of Wrath* was a high school favorite. He started writing poetry at the age of ten. He was also a great fan of Matt Dillon, the sheriff of the television series "Gunsmoke." In 1958, he confided to his high school sweetheart that he planned to devote his life to music, adding that "I know what I'm going to call myself. I've got this great name — Bob Dillon." That was how he told new friends to spell his (assumed) last name. He also told them that Dillon was his mother's maiden name (it wasn't), and that Dillon was a town in Oklahoma (it isn't).

The turning point in Bob Dillon's life came in the summer of 1959. Shortly after graduation from high school, he discovered — and became enthralled by—the music of the legendary bluesman Leadbelly. An imposing singer with a voice of granite, Leadbelly accompanied himself with a barrelling 12-string guitar, shouting out songs like "Rock Island Line" with savage authority. His music was tough, jagged, commanding. A friend remembers Dillon playing a Leadbelly record and exclaiming "This is the thing, this is the thing"—he had never heard anything like it. After a brief, ill-fated stint playing piano for Bobby Vee (at that time, a Buddy Holly imitator based in Fargo, North Dakota), Dillon decided to try his hand at becoming a solo artist like Leadbelly. After hearing from a friend that Denver had a thriving club scene, he hitchhiked West. So began his informal education in folk music.

A lthough Dillon didn't know it at the time, "folk music" as a pop genre was scarcely twenty years old. It had been virtually invented in the late 1930s by a handful of musicians, many of them urban, college-educated and socialists—a number were members of the Communist Party. These musicians, Pete Seeger most prominent among them, were students of indigenous American musical traditions. They were also critics of capitalism: one of Seeger's first important ventures was to help form the Almanac Singers, who adapted new lyrics celebrating the trade union movement to traditional ballads and hymns. Seeger and his associates also sought out living representatives of older musical styles, bringing artists like Leadbelly and Woody Guthrie to New York City. As sociologist Richard Flacks has recently put it, such artists gave "proof that an unschooled and uncommercialized creativity thrived at the grass roots and could create an alternative culture," unspoiled by the vices of the bourgeoisie.

Still, the relationship of folk singers like Seeger to the commercial culture they criticized was complex and contradictory. In the late 1940s, Seeger himself deliberately aimed his music at a larger, mass audience. His vehicle was a vocal quartet called the Weavers, whose repertoire consisted of traditional songs sung with full orchestral accompaniment. In 1950, their Decca recording of Leadbelly's "Goodnight Irene" sold over two million copies, becoming the biggest hit single of that year. In the months that followed, the Weavers scored a total of four top ten singles, in the process establishing "folk music" as a commercially viable genre of pop. Their string of hits might have continued but for McCarthyism. Seeger and the Weavers were blacklisted; popular interest in folk music waned.

In cities like New York, Boston and San Francisco, a folk music scene nevertheless survived. And by 1959, that scene was in the throes of a major revival, thanks to the Kingston Trio. This Bay Area group strummed guitars, sang in soothing harmony, and recorded a number of original songs written around innocuous Western themes—"Tom Dooley," their number one hit in the fall of 1958, nicely captured the atmosphere of "Gunsmoke." Sparked by the continuing success of the Kingston Trio, folk clubs began to sprout up in almost every college town across America, creating a nationwide circuit for oldtimers and aspiring young amateurs.

During the summer that Bob Dillon spent in Denver, cutting his teeth on the folk scene, the new local sensation was a singer named Judy Collins. But the young visitor was even more struck by Jesse Fuller, a 63-year-old blues and ragtime singer who played in Denver that summer. Fuller was a freewheeling one-man band, cut from the same larger-than-life mold as Leadbelly; he hollered out lyrics, hammered out chords on his 12-string guitar, and pounded home the beat on a pedal-operated drum, punctuating songs with wheezing roughhouse harmonica solos in a style that Dillon would closely copy.

By the end of the summer, when he arrived in Minneapolis to attend the University of Minnesota, Dillon was a confirmed folk fan, hungry to learn more. The scene he discovered in Minneapolis was in many ways typical of what was happening at other large Midwestern universities in the late 1950s. Thanks to their rapid expansion in the previous decade, these institutions were attracting an increasingly diverse population of students, including a large number of East Coast Jews from Old Left families traveling west of the Catskills for the first time. By definition outcasts in the Midwest's predominantly Protestant mainstream culture, these young urban migrants often found themselves frequenting the few bookstores, coffee houses and folk societies that welcomed alienated eggheads and local beatniks. At the University of Minnesota, the folk music society, as one oldtimer told Shelton, was "eighty percent Jewish, mostly university people" and "very much underground. The older people came from the Old Left."

Dillon fit right in. He quickly became a fixture in "Dinkytown," as the city's off-campus bohemian district was called. "The whole scene was an unforgettable one," Dylan recalled in a 1985 interview. "It was outside, there was no formula, never was 'mainstream' or 'the thing to do' in any sense. America was still very 'straight,' 'post-war' and sort of into a gray-flannel suit thing, McCarthy, commies, puritanical, very claustrophobic and whatever was happening of any real value was happening away from that and sort of hidden from view and it would be years before the media would be able to recognize it and choke-hold it and reduce it to silliness. Anyway, I got in at the tail-end of that and it was magic."

In Dinkytown, Dillon met other young fans of folk music like "Spider John" Koerner and began to tap their knowledge, poring over their record collections. He discovered the jazz of Monk and Coltrane. He began to read the poetry of Pound and Eliot, Ferlinghetti and Ginsberg; the novels of Jack Kerouac, John Rechy and William Burroughs; and the works of Dylan Thomas, rebaptizing himself as Bob "Dylan." It was here, above all, that Dylan first discovered the music of Woody Guthrie.

I n the recollection of the Minneapolis people whom Shelton interviewed, what drove Dylan East was his passion for Guthrie. "Bob almost fell in love with Woody Guthrie," one old friend told Shelton. "When he learned Guthrie was in a hospital in New Jersey, he decided he had to go out and see him." For the next two years, Dylan almost obsessively identified with Guthrie. He would listen to Guthrie's famous dust-bowl ballads endlessly, mastering his Oklahoma twang, mimicking his vocal style, admitting to one Minneapolis friend that "he was building a character."

In the 1940s, Guthrie had been the archetypal "working class minstrel," an Okie who seemed drawn straight from the pages of Steinbeck's *Grapes of Wrath*, a hobo and migrant laborer who embodied the romance of the road, of the West, of the uncorrupted proletarian. When Mike Quin, a writer for a West Coast Communist newspaper, first heard Guthrie sing, he alerted friends. In 1939, Guthrie traveled East; he recorded for the Library of Congress and then joined Pete Seeger's Almanac Singers, briefly living with the other members in a commune in Greenwich Village. A singer of artless simplicity, he was the real McCoy, an honest, almost ingenuous craftsman with a vast repertoire of mythic lore, tall tales and traditional melodies. He wrote and sang of hard times with humor and hope. But his own career proved short. He suffered from Huntington's chorea, a crippling degenerative disease; by the early Fifties, he was no longer able to play music.

In 1960, in quest of Guthrie, Dylan dropped out of school and began to work his way East, making stopovers in university towns like Madison. He arrived in New York City in December. At first, he tells Shelton, he supported himself by hustling in Times Square: "Cats would pick us up and chicks would pick us up. And we would do anything you wanted, as long as it paid money." In February, he appeared on the Greenwich Village folk scene. Finally he made the pilgrimage to meet Guthrie face-to-face.

Although his health continued to deteriorate, Guthrie still received visitors on Sundays, at a house near the hospital in New Jersey where he was staying. These Sunday afternoon visits became one of Dylan's entrees into the New York folk scene. Among other people, he got to know "Ramblin' Jack" Elliott, a folk singer who, like Dylan, ardently admired Guthrie. More than a decade earlier, Elliott had invented a new alter-ego for himself by donning a cowboy hat, affecting a Western drawl, and mastering Guthrie's musical style. In fact, Elliott was a native of Brooklyn and the son of a Jewish doctor. His "Ramblin' Jack" character belies the myth that folk music is somehow more honest than pop. At the same time, to an understudy like Dylan, "Ramblin' Jack" offered living proof that fictive masks and folk music could perfectly well coexist.

Dylan was an eager student, devouring every bit of wisdom he could glean from older friends like Elliott and Dave Van Ronk, another Brooklyn-born folk enthusiast whose specialty was blues. As an outsider new to town, Dylan could freely reinvent the character he was working on. He told people he had come from Gallup, New Mexico. He claimed to have traveled with blues singer Mance Lipscomb. He reported that he had learned songs during some time he had spent on the Brazos River in Texas. He kept on polishing his Oklahoma twang and assumed the seedy look of a heartlands hobo, picking as his trademark a black corduroy cap. "His concern about image started then," recalls one New York acquaintance. "He would ask if he looked right, jiggling with his dungarees."

I t had become a very compelling act. Shelton, for one, was bowled over the first time he reviewed Dylan on stage, in the fall of 1961. "Mr. Dylan's voice is anything but pretty," he explained in the *New York Times*. "He is consciously trying to recapture the rude beauty of a Southern field hand musing in melody on his back porch." When Shelton interviewed him afterwards, Dylan cheerfully retailed an elaborate series of lies and half-truths, climaxed by the claim that he had played guitar with Gene Vincent.

When he wasn't on stage or in the streets, Dylan spent endless hours listening to records: Ewan McCall, Blind Willie McTell and—above all—the three boxed volumes of the Folkways *Anthology of American*

Folk Music. First released in 1952, this anthology is an extraordinary collection of 84 vintage recordings; as the critic Greil Marcus has pointed out, it is also an important clue to Dylan's sensibility. Most of the material dates from the late 1920s, when the commercial labels, spurred on by the fantastic sales enjoyed by country star Jimmy Rodgers and blues singer Bessie Smith, had feverishly recorded a host of black and Appalachian singers, often on location in the South. The most striking thing about the Folkways anthology is the air of utter *strangeness* that saturates almost every cut. Listen, for example, to "James Alley Blues," recorded by Victor in New Orleans in 1927 by the black singer Richard "Rabbit" Brown, whose sandpapery singing is full of disturbing, unfathomable mannerisms. Or listen to the equally weird "I Wish I Was a Mole in the Ground," recorded by Brunswick in North Carolina in 1928 by "The Minstrel of the Appalachians," Bascom Lamar Lunsford, an Ashville folklorist (and lawyer). The song describes a topsy-turvy world where the insignificant are mighty. "I wish I was a mole in the ground," drones Lunsford. "Like a mole in the ground I would root that mountain down." In a 1965 interview, Dylan suggested that the putative "authenticity" of such music fascinated him far less than its ineffable peculiarity: "Folk music," he said, "is the only music where it *isn't* simple. It's weird, man, full of legend, myth, Bible and ghosts . . . chaos, watermelons, clocks, everything . . . "

It was this sense of strangeness and out-of-time otherness that Dylan now began to reach for in his music. On *Bob Dylan*, his debut album, released in March 1962, most of the material is secondhand. The album contains several boisterous imitations of Guthrie. But what jumped out at the time, and stands out today, are several songs about death. The music is compelling because Dylan's *voice* is compelling—here is the key to his musical greatness. Consider "In My Time of Dyin'," a song that the black blues singer Josh White frequently sang. White's version of the song on the album *Josh at Midnight* is urbane, atmospheric, reserved—perfect café society fare. Dylan, by contrast, lashes into the song with a crudely played bottleneck guitar. His voice is raw, histrionic, utterly unnatural and perfectly unsettling. He actually *sounds* like he's just about to meet Jesus in the middle of the air so that he can "die easy." You hear the lyrics for the first time—they feel real. And then you look at Dylan's picture on the cover, and blink: he's a baby-faced kid of 21.

I n retrospect, it seems clear that Dylan knew perfectly well what he was after. "I hate to say this," he told Shelton in 1966, "because I don't want it to be taken the wrong way, but I latched on when I got to New York because I saw a huge audience was there." By all reports, he pursued this audience with single-minded diligence. He stalked the streets of the village with a spiral notebook in his hand, jotting down ideas and observations about everything from the poetry he was reading to animals in the street or a newspaper headline, beginning to work up new songs of his own. At the same time, he became actively involved in a new little mimeographed magazine called *Broadside*, which Pete Seeger and some friends, inspired by the resurgent student left and civil rights movement, had started up to publish new (left-wing) topical songs.

The folk music craze had by now become a phenomenon certified by the mass media. In the spring of 1963, ABC television began to broadcast its "Hootenanny" show, an upbeat musical jamboree that enforced the old blacklist against Seeger, was scrupulously boycotted by artists like Dylan—and nevertheless exposed the music to an audience of millions. At the same time, the civil rights movement was entering an exuberant new phase of protest. Accurately reading these cultural trends, Dylan sensed that a "huge audience was there"—and that topical songs were one way to reach it.

He had begun work on his second album in the fall of 1962. It was planned to showcase the topical songs that he had been publishing in *Broadside*: "Masters of War," "A Hard Rain's a-Gonna Fall," and, of course, "Blowin' in the Wind." Meanwhile, Albert Grossman, his new manager, was peddling Dylan's new songs to other artists, including the Chad Mitchell Trio, and Peter, Paul and Mary, two of the more frankly commercial folk acts that had sprung up in the wake of the Kingston Trio. At one point, Grossman even coaxed Peter, Paul and Mary into investing in Dylan; they then recorded a pretty version of Dylan's "Blowin' in the Wind." When it was released as a single in the summer of 1963, the record took off, selling over one million copies. Shortly afterwards, when *The Freewheeling Bob Dylan*, his second album, was belatedly released, it, too, soared into the upper reaches of the album charts. In late August, Dylan joined Peter, Paul and Mary at the great civil rights March on Washington led by Dr. Martin Luther King, Jr. By then, "Blowin' in the Wind" had joined "We Shall Overcome" as the political anthem of the hour.

But what different kinds of anthems! "We Shall Overcome" is a song of resolute faith, imbued with confidence in the certainty of final victory. Cast in the mold of an old Afro-American hymn, "I Will

Overcome," the song had originally been given new lyrics in the 1940s to serve as a union song, "We Will Overcome." Pete Seeger and some friends then rewrote the lyrics again, this time to create a civil rights anthem, teaching the new song to civil rights militants at the 1960 founding convention of the Student Non-Violent Coordinating Committee (SNCC). Passed along orally—and inconspicuously—in this political context, "We Shall Overcome" insensibly acquired the aura of a "real" folk song. Even today, most people are unaware that it was almost as much of a self-conscious creation as "Blowin' in the Wind."

Dylan's anthem, by contrast, was identified from the start with Dylan himself. Grossman shrewdly marketed it using time-tested Tin Pan Alley techniques. Most people first heard the song on the radio, as a hit single. And what they heard, if they were listening to the lyrics and not lulled to sleep by the bland melody, was no uplifting affirmation of faith, but a series of questions, with no answers offered.

The song's rhetoric of restless searching faithfully echoed the sentiments of the fledgling New Left, an affinity that Dylan himself recognized, and went out of his way to underline. In December, 1963, he put in a brief appearance at a national meeting of the Students for a Democratic Society, where (as one witness later recalled it) he mumbled a vague benediction: "Ah don' know what yew all are talkin' about, but it sounds like yew want somethin' to happen, and if that's what *yew* want, that's what *Ah* want." A few weeks later, Dylan performed in Mississippi at the invitation of SDS leader Tom Hayden and Bob Moses of SNCC. When *The Times They Are a-Changin'*, Dylan's third album, was released in February 1964, young activists were elated—it was Dylan's most topical recording to date, and it reflected the temper and tone of their own politics with almost uncanny accuracy. (This is not entirely surprising: they were members of Dylan's generation, and many of them had first developed a passion for politics and folk music in the same kind of off-campus bohemian environment that Dylan had discovered in Dinkytown.)

Throughout 1963, Dylan consolidated his reputation as the most promising young folk singer in America. He embarked on a series of concert appearances with Joan Baez, then at the peak of her popularity. He had won the esteem of the first audience he cared about, the folk musicians, beat poets, and young radicals of the burgeoning avant-garde college-student youth culture. But friends recall that he was already itching to move on to something else. "He is a complicated, problematic, difficult person," Baez told Shelton in 1966, "more fragile than the average person" — and, she added, far more ambitious than the average folk singer. "At one point in our little scene," she says, "although I was enjoying these concerts, I froze up and said to him: 'Bobby, you'd be doing it as a rock'n'roll king, but I'd be doing it as peace queen.'" Later, Dylan himself agreed: "This is what made me different. I played all the folk songs with a rock'n'roll attitude."

That attitude came across in Dylan's cockiness, in his tacit ambition to touch as large an audience as possible, and in the chip-on-the-shoulder sullenness conveyed by his stock photographic pose. But it also was conveyed in subtler ways. As early as 1962, Dylan had expressed a desire to start writing more songs about himself, and fewer songs about other people. Some of his most touching early songs in fact were not topical at all. Singing ballads like "Girl from the North Country" and "One Too Many Mornings," he evoked a bleak yearning at odds with the hardboiled worldliness he normally affected — and strangely redolent of the keening adolescent ballads that rock singers like Ricky Nelson had made popular in the late Fifties. (Nelson later recorded a number of Dylan's songs — and on his 1986 tour, Dylan in turn sang Nelson's 1958 hit, "Lonesome Town.") Here was one lost and desolate — and very young — soul, his voice on these ballads seemed to say; and this, too, was part of his "rock'n'roll attitude."

In February 1964, Dylan set off from New York on a cross-country car trip with three buddies, heading for Mardi Gras in New Orleans, the Rockies, the San Francisco Bay — the heart and soul of America, approached in the spirit of Guthrie and Kerouac. But as the car rolled West, America's airwaves were filled with foreign sounds. The "British Invasion" had just begun — and suddenly, with the music of the Beatles everywhere, rock'n'roll, and not folk music or politics or beat poetry, was the most exciting and fashionable thing happening on the cutting edge of pop culture.

Within a matter of months, Dylan had begun to turn his own music inside out. In June 1964, shortly after returning from a tour of England, Dylan recorded a number of new songs in a marathon session that would be his last as a solo artist. Love songs like "It Ain't Me Babe" were vitriolic and barbed; political songs like "Chimes of Freedom" were a whorl of fantastic imagery; none of the songs was narrowly topical. On the back cover of *Another Side of Bob Dylan*, he underlined the change. "You tell me about politics," he wrote, "an' i tell you there are no politics . . . i know no answers an' no truth / for absolutely no soul alive / i will listen t'no one / who tells me morals / there are no morals / an' i dream a lot."

The style was clumsy, the sentiments an almost embarrassing melange of modernist cliches and pulp existentialism. But once the sentiments, set to a howling beat, were groomed for the top ten, the clumsiness of the style scarcely seemed to matter. Dylan had reinvented himself first as a hobo minstrel, then as a troubadour of dissent. Reaching out to a wider audience still, he was about to become a rock'n'roll Rimbaud.

W hen it came, the metamorphosis was abrupt, surrounded by controversy, and greeted in some quarters as a shameful artistic scandal. In April 1965, Dylan released a raucously bluesy rock single called "Subterranean Homesick Blues," which became his first top 40 hit. In the 15 months that followed, Dylan released three albums with electric band accompaniment (*Bringing it all Back Home* in May 1965, *Highway 61 Revisited* in October, and *Blonde on Blonde* in July 1966). He also released six singles, three of them top ten hits, starting with "Like a Rolling Stone" in July 1965. In these months, as he barnstormed across America and England, Dylan became one of the most storied figures in rock history, completely transforming the music and its expressive possibilities in the minds of those who played it, and of those who listened to it.

Dylan's demeanor in these days had just as much impact as his music. A tangled aureole of hair crowned a pale and wraith-like figure. Dylan's face seemed frozen in a scowl. The growing unpredictability of his performances—and his glazed, impassive gaze—fueled speculation about drugs. At the time, Dylan did nothing to dispel the speculation. "Being a musician," he said, "means getting to the depths of where you are at. And most any musician would try anything to get to those depths." Try *anything*—that was the message. And once again, a huge audience was waiting, ready to listen.

What they heard was, in many ways, singularly odd. Dylan, it should be obvious by now, was no musical virtuoso. Technically, he has always been a singer of severely limited range, with a voice that verges on a whine. His concerts have often been sloppy. Even on recordings like *Highway 61 Revisited*, instruments are out of tune, arrangements a clutter. And some of his most memorable songs and lyrics seem helter-skelter. "'Like a Rolling Stone' was really vomitific in its structure," Dylan tells Shelton at one point. "It seemed like it was twenty pages, but it was really six. . . . You know how you get sometimes." The voluble lyrics to a song like "Rolling Stone" lie dead on the printed page. What matters, as always, is Dylan's *voice*: the poetry of the song depends on the incendiary energy of his singing. Consider, for example, the way he pounces on a phrase like "How does it *FEEEL?*," —turning the question into an insult. The song cannot be separated from the performance—in that sense, "Like a Rolling Stone" is rock'n'roll through and through, closer in spirit to "Tutti Frutti" than to "We Shall Overcome."

By now, Dylan's distinctive approach was fully formed. Many lyrics he shouted out helplessly, like a sailor at the helm of a storm-pitched ship. His performances often had an exalted, almost ecstatic quality, as if Dylan's songs were singing him. A Long Island reporter who saw Dylan perform in early 1966 described "a sad marionette . . . he looked half asleep or half dead." An Australian journalist a couple of months later was reminded of "Harpo Marx . . . walking like a marionette." The critic Langdon Winner, who saw him in California that year, remembers "a puppet with most of his strings missing—he wobbled onstage like he was *unstrung.*" An unnatural apparition giving voice to pell-mell rhymes, Dylan could seem eerily like the medium for somebody else's messages. "I am just a voice speaking," Dylan tells Shelton in 1966. "And anytime I'm singing about people and if the songs are dreamed, it's like my voice is coming out of their dream."

When they weren't simply filled with tumult, Dylan concerts came to resemble a kind of seance. This was something radically new in the world of pop music. In the past people had gone to rock concerts to see somebody famous, to hear a familiar hit, perhaps to dance or to jump up and down and scream—that is what happened when the Beatles and the Rolling Stones first toured the United States, because that is what rock concerts were all about. Folk music concerts of course were different—reverent students thoughtfully hung on every word. What Dylan in 1965 and 1966 managed to do was to blast himself free from the insular complacency of the folk scene while daring the pop crowd to *listen.* His music was full of surprise—and the disembodied, sometimes vehement way in which it was sung made it seem like a revelation.

The best evidence of Dylan's peculiar gifts in this period is *Live at Royal Albert Hall*, a bootleg album recorded in the spring of 1966 during a tour of the British Isles with the Hawks, the group later known simply as "The Band." As the group's guitarist, Robbie Robertson, has recalled in an interview, "That tour was a very strange process. You can hear the violence, and the dynamics in the music." Indeed. From start to finish, the music on the bootleg surges with reckless power, threatening to fly apart at the seams, held together by the relentlessness of the beat, driven furiously forward by Robertson's guitar solos—anything but flashy, they are rough and hard and spiked with rhythmic tension. Dylan's singing is demonic. He barrels through "Tell Me, Mama" and "I Don't Believe You" and "Baby, Let Me Follow You Down" and "Just Like Tom Thumb's Blues," his voice rising and falling, almost without pitch, before homing in on a note with a dive-bomb drone. On the climactic "Like a Rolling Stone," he taunts. He yells. Words come hurling out. The atmosphere is thick. Anything could happen, you think—even listening twenty years later.

Of course, Dylan once more was acting out a role—but this time, the role was also devouring him. He sounded on edge because he *was* on edge: the unpredictability and volatility in his voice was real—more real, because far less controlled, than the Woody Guthrie imitations and protest songs of his previous incarnations. Dylan throughout this period was a key cultural bellwether, but he was also, for these few months in 1965 and 1966, something more, and something far more disturbing: an artist flirting with death.

The most revealing pages in Shelton's book describe an interview that he conducted with Dylan on an overnight flight from Lincoln, Nebraska, to Denver, Colorado, in March 1966. For several months, Dylan had been on the road with the Hawks. He had become adept at putting on—and fending off—the press with non-sequiturs, sarcasm, and humiliating jokes. On this occasion, though, talking through the night with his would-be Boswell, he simply flew, riffing on ideas and images, breathlessly leaping from topic to topic.

On his music: "My thing is with colors. It's not black and white. It's always been with colors, whether with clothes or anything. Color. Now, with something like that driving you, sometimes it gets very fiery red, you understand? And at times, it gets very jet black."

On Woody Guthrie: "What drew me to him was that hearing his voice I could tell he was very lonesome, very alone, and very lost out in his time. That's why I dug him."

On folk music: "Folk music was such a shuck. I never recorded a folk song. My idea of a folk song is Jeanie Robertson or Dock Boggs. Call it historical-traditional music."

On drugs: "It takes a lot of medicine to keep up this pace. . . . I got very strung out for a while. I mean, really, very strung out. . . . I can do anything, knowing in front that it's not going to catch me and pull me . . . 'cause I've been through it once already. A lot of times you get strung out with people. They are just like junk. . . . The same thing, no more, no less. They kill you the same way."

On death: "I have a death thing, I know. I have a suicidal thing, I know. . . . I was actually afraid of death in those first years around New York. When I started writing all those songs and everyone started calling me a genius . . . I knew it was bull, because I still hadn't written what I wanted to. . . . I've really got a sickness, man. I don't write when I'm feeling groovy, you understand. I play when I'm feeling groovy, I write when I'm sick. . . . Man, nobody knows what is the matter with me, and I'm not going to tell anybody. . . . I can't decay. I would not let myself decay. I'm against decay. That's nature's will—decay. I am against nature. . . . I think nature is very unnatural. I think the only truly natural things are in dreams, which nature can't touch with decay. . . . I don't want to see myself die. . . . All this talk about equality. The only thing people really have in common is that they are all going to die."

On July 29, 1966, while joyriding on his motorcycle, Dylan was thrown from the bike, suffering a concussion and several broken vertebrae in his neck. For more than a year, he disappeared from public view.

It was the seedtime of Dylan's myth. In his absence, "Don't Look Back," D.A. Pennebaker's documentary film about Dylan's British tour of 1965, made the rounds of college campuses, offering a behind-closed-doors glimpse of Dylan's cruel and deliberately mystifying manner. Meanwhile, fans played Dylan's old albums over and over and over again, giving the music fresh weight and more importance than it had ever had before.

For some, the music largely served as a backdrop—mood music for acid trips and antiwar rallies. For others, the lyrics acquired a mysterious new resonance: keys to experience were waiting to be discovered in the epic dreamscapes of "Desolation Row" and "Sad-Eyed Lady of the Lowlands." And as the country's political culture progressively unravelled in 1967 and 1968, the barely contained chaos and violence of Dylan's rock came to seem more and more *right*, inevitable, a prophetic mirror of the disorder and uncertainty of the times.

In one of his earliest essays, the rock critic Greil Marcus described how, after watching the police riot at the Chicago Democratic convention of 1968, he put on *Blonde on Blonde* and let the record track through "Memphis Blues Again." "I've heard that song hundreds of times before," Marcus wrote, "but this time it was different. It became a journey, a rite of passage, a struggling effort to pass out of an inexplicable contradiction, only to find another, with no escape, only a change to a new chord, a new movement of the guitar or organ, intensifying the desire that it all be over . . ." For Marcus, and for many others, Dylan's music became a paradigm of what pop culture can mean: a song like "Memphis Blues Again" was not a stereotyped entertainment but a work of phantasmagorical creativity, something that could seduce a listener, capture the imagination, challenge the understanding, move a person to *think*.

The period of Dylan's greatest popularity was still to come. In the 1970s, he enjoyed three number one albums, sang to sell-out crowds in cavernous arenas, even belatedly made the cover of *Newsweek* magazine. But in the 20 years since his motorcycle accident, the palaver of many critics to the contrary, Dylan has never come close—even remotely—to making music of the power and freedom and apocalyptic intensity of *Blonde on Blonde* or the *Live at Royal Albert Hall* bootleg.

Perhaps that is because Dylan's greatest music was, just as he told Shelton in 1966, in part the product of "sickness"—a suicidal will to live, an unnatural and chemically sustained state of feverish free-association. It was also the product of a fleeting moment—the tumultuous few months in which Dylan furiously fed off of the hostility and adulation of the pop music process at its most frenzied and least predictable. For a time, he seemed a spectral whirling dervish, a musical magician smashing and recombining images with manic energy and blinding brilliance.

After the crash, this all changed. "Until the accident," he told Shelton in 1971, "I was living music twenty-four hours a day"—but now, he confided, writing songs had become a labor. In pastoral retreat in Woodstock, isolated from his audience, glad to be healthy and apparently wary of the vertiginous nihilism and wild cultural myths hatched in his own delirious imagination, Dylan cut himself off from the wellsprings of his greatest work.

You could hear the change in his voice: after 1966, he never again sang with the same authority and abandon. Instead, he sounded like a chastened and sadly weary pilgrim (perhaps his most appealing post-accident voice, heard on *The Basement Tapes* and *John Wesley Harding*), or like a trumped-up smoothie (as on *Nashville Skyline*), or like a mean-spirited caricature of his former self (as on his widely hailed 1985 "comeback" album, *Empire Burlesque*).

Since many members of his audience by the end of the Sixties felt chastened and weary, too, an album like *John Wesley Harding* had a real resonance—for one last time, Dylan was giving voice to the feelings of a broad audience. But with the old spark gone, and his personal demons in retreat, Dylan after 1968 had painfully little left to say. Even worse, what he did have honestly to say—for example, about the need for faith in God—most of his fans didn't want to hear. Out of touch with his times, he had become irrelevant—a once brilliant manipulator of cultural signs, fated to produce cultural static.

It is of course possible to sift through Dylan's later career and pick out bright spots; but it hardly seems worth the effort. For better or worse, his claim to greatness rests on the music of his early years—the soundtrack of his singular quest to reinvent himself as something irreducibly *other* than the Robert Zimmerman who grew up in Hibbing, Minnesota, listening to "Hound Dog," watching "Gunsmoke" and wishing he were Elvis, or Matt Dillon, or Leadbelly, or almost *anybody* else. In pursuing this quest with relentless energy and a vaulting ambition to touch the heart of a mass audience just like Elvis, and Matt Dillon, and Leadbelly, had touched him, Dylan helped to make the modernist themes of exuberant negation and romantic reaffirmation into the shared obsessions of a generation. In his day, he was a genius at such cultural alchemy. At the same time, he was a great and unusual singer, passionate in his disembodied mannerisms and able to convey, in the chaotic ecstasy of his most memorable performances, an unsettling and unforgettable sense of death-haunted yearning. Just listen, again, to his first seven albums. The music is protean, but with each passing album, the voice rings truer. It is the sound of someone "very lonesome, very alone, and very lost out in his time." Which is one reason why that voice, more than twenty years later, still defines that time.

■■■■■■■■■■

A Poet of the Sixties

Peter Stine

"Back in those days, we were all encouraging ourselves to drop out. That was the really big thing. By doing so you were disengaging yourself from what we all perceived as the evils of American society . . . " An amused and distant smile forms on the lips of Richard Tillinghast. "But dropping out is easy. It's getting back in that's really hard." And he laughs in full recognition of reality.

The forty-nine-year-old poet and new member of the English Department at the University of Michigan is conversing on his porch on Granger Street in Ann Arbor. "I feel as if we've done it now," he continues. "But it's kind of a funny feeling to sit in what still seems like an expensive house, with a good job, with four kids . . . " The smile returns. "And I do regard the whole thing as a kind of odyssey. An oddity and an odyssey both at the same time."

Again his laughter, a sense of mindslip and memory play, the psychic life as vaudeville, all the signs of a veteran of the Sixties. One is reminded of the opening lines of "Today in the Café Trieste," a poem Tillinghast wrote in San Francisco twelve years ago.

> A face in the mirror:
>   someone else's for an instant
>   as I order coffee.
> A smile-line cuts the flesh on the left side
>   like a scar
>   in an otherwise balanced face,
> as though everything I've smiled at
>   in thirty-seven years,
>   or accepted with irony,
> pulled me toward one side of the universe.

69

T he odyssey of Richard Tillinghast began in Memphis, Tennessee, where he passed an artistically precocious childhood. His father was an engineer, his mother an English teacher with a talent for storytelling. Pursuing an ambition to be a painter, he studied at the Memphis Academy of Arts. He also played the drums in local bands and drew political cartoons for local newspapers. At the University of the South, a small episcopal college in Sewanee, Tennessee, Tillinghast settled into writing. Here he came under the tutelage of novelist Andrew Lydell. His college poems reveal a romance with literature, matched by a fugitive desire "To leave home, / Books, everything. / I hear truck tires / Alone empty highways droning their siren song / Of ultimate longs and fars."

The late Fifties offered few distractions from his aesthetic pursuits which, ironically, prepared Tillinghast for the next decade. "My interest in the exotic deepened when I went to Europe in my junior year," he recalls. "There is a tradition here from Baudelaire on that goes with altered mental states. Exotic things are metaphors for that. It became part of our generation. The Symbolist poets used drugs. Appollinaire was into intoxication. People like to fall in love because it's a form of intoxication. . . . Drugs offered moments of self-understanding for me, an occasion for going back to the origins of childhood. Smith's Cactus Farm in Texas sent peyote through the mail to Sewanee in 1961."

Tillinghast kept his bearings and graduated from Sewanee, then advanced immediately to Harvard graduate school where he specialized in Renaissance literature. Here his breakthrough was not psychic, but literary. He had the good fortune to encounter a man of literary genius. "Robert Lowell had just started teaching writing there," he recalls, "and I took classes from him. I remember Lowell saying a poem 'must be tinkered with and recast until one's eyes pop out of one's head.' That was my real apprenticeship, learning how to be tough-minded about my own work—learning how to revise."

During the summers of this graduate school period, Tillinghast slaked his wanderlust by traveling in Europe as editor of *The Harvard Student Guide to Europe*. In 1967, he lived in London, Paris and Rome on a Harvard travel grant, and that year he wrote the major part of his first volume of poems. A year later he earned his Ph.D. in English.

P ublished in 1969, *Sleep Watch* is the debut of a romantic poet with a wonderful mastery of words. The title refers to the characteristic mental state in these poems and the burgeoning youth culture at large:

consciousness as it trails off into dreams. But the chronic drowsiness of the poet is balanced by an exquisite self-consciousness, an exact grasp of the natural world, and a brilliant eye for metaphor.

"A lot of this is apprentice stuff," Tillinghast says now. "I'm glad they're preserved, but there are very few that I ever read at poetry readings. There are lines and phrases that would make me wince . . . " Still the poems are interesting in a technical sense because they show him going from a precocious use of verse forms through a conversion to free verse. Of course, *Sleep Watch* is also interesting as a record of Tillinghast's spiritual odyssey.

"The Old Mill" is a long hallucinogenic descent into the psyche, reviewing the memories and ambivalent securities and chains of affection of his Tennessee boyhood. At poetry readings he still returns to "Come Home and Be Happy." Approached obliquely enough, the blood tie and one's native ground are everything. But most of this volume was written in Europe and under the influence of Robert Lowell, the father of confessional poetry. "Most of those poems are about the disintegration of my first marriage," Tillinghast says. "They embarrass me a little bit now. They're about relationships, adolescent infatuations."

As sleep walker, the poet can halt the dazzling tour of his psyche short of any real self-disclosure. There is no guilt of confession here. Instead there is escape into reverie, projected departures, a phantasmagoria of exotic cityscapes. But any dream of dramatic action remains just that. What is real is the poet's spiritual apprehension of the physical universe. Rising from a political nightmare of execution by soldiers in "Ascension Day: Waking on the Train," he is soon engulfed by dislocated dialogues of hopeless marital strife. But this moment lies between:

> But after the commuters
> cigars   windows being jerked open
> your body begins to know it hasn't slept
> It thinks of all the parts of itself
> that would touch a bed   all the ways
> It knows
> a riverbank nodding with wild bluebells
> Cattle low on the pasture path
> Sunlight at the edges of leaves
> is a golden blur   like the buttered toast
> in pictures of healthy children

Generally the poet is too infatuated, and too lacking in experience to deeply reflect Tillinghast's later mature themes: love and politics. But he does confess to ennui and doubt about his chosen career: "Favorite theory of mine / I am in love with my own thinking . . . What has happened / to turn my mind to trivialities?" Bluntly put, the poet was sick of graduate school—not an insignificant matter in grasping the Sixties. Ultimately, the fragile mental equilibrium in these poems is welcome:

> Is everything sliding?
> Nothing
> to worry about—
> Getting lost means sliding in all directions.

It seems providential that Tillinghast drew his first teaching assignment the next fall at the University of California at Berkeley. Since the Free Speech Movement four years before, that campus had been the beachhead of a national radical student movement, part of a larger generational war that was now as wildly romantic and irrational as the Vietnam war that fueled it.

Tillinghast found in the Bay Area what he was probably looking for: "The vintage years in Berkeley started in 1964, but 1968 and after were good years too," he says. "I think of California as being devoid of any kind of literary or intellectual life. . . . For me it was People's Park."

This was the name given a pitched and bloody confrontation that spring of 1969 between UC students and police over possession of a neglected and vacant acre of land off Telegraph Avenue just south of the campus. The university planned to transform the land into a mall, while street people went ahead with its conversion into a community park. There were seventeen straight days of street fighting, resulting in countless arrests, beatings, and acts of vandalism. Eventually about 150 demonstrators were shot and wounded, one blinded, and one killed by police gunfire.

"Those were heady times," Tillinghast says. "It really did look as though the walls were about to come down. My enthusiasm was genuine, as was my naiveté."

Both were revealed that spring when Robert Lowell was offered a visiting professorship in the English Department. Tillinghast wrote his mentor and friend a glowing description of the political struggle at Berkeley and of the overall atmosphere of the place. By poetic license, his words appear as the opening lines of Lowell's poem, "The Revolution":

> We're in a prerevolutionary situation
> at Berkeley, an incredible, refreshing relief
> from your rather hot-house, good prep-school Harvard riots.
> The main thing is our exposure to politics.

(Lowell wrote back at the time that this was like him inviting Tillinghast to his place in Maine because "we seem likely to have a tidal wave and you should see the morale of a village in danger. I have so little faith in any of the sides, though some in some things." In graduate school at Berkeley then, I did not cross paths with Tillinghast, but a friend of mine did, and remembers him barebacked on the barricades at People's Park—and also "into rugs" on the side because, if the revolution came, they would be "easy to tote.")

So what did it all mean?

"It meant you got up in the morning," Tillinghast says, "and you went down to the riot. It was fun. So in retrospect you could say it was just a lot of nothing." But beyond the theater of revolution was a deeper satisfaction that was closer to learning. "Any writer's lucky to be able to participate with a lot of other people in a significant larger human drama," he says. "I've always envied those who fought in World War II and survived. It's exhilarating to be even arrested or part of a mob or tear-gassed with a lot of people. . . . Those were good years."

For instance, there was Tillinghast's first California poetry reading in 1969, an extravaganza at California Hall on Polk Street in San Francisco, a benefit for Berkeley's embattled People's Park. "There were nothing but good vibes at that reading," he recalls. "A gathering of the tribes. Brothers and sisters. I remember Tom Parkinson, professor-poet, Dutch uncle to the Beat Generation, calling Michael McClure and Gary Snyder onstage to lead the crowd of two thousand in the choral part of his 'Litany for the American People.'

"Parkinson would reel off something like:

> We will dam up all the rivers so that no one of them reaches the
> sea and we will use the power to make people buy more and
> more and more television sets and deep freezes and we will

destroy the powerful salmon and sluggish bass and wily
steelhead.
"Or:
We will pave over Viet Nam with cement and paint it for
parking strips so that it will be exactly like Los Angeles.

"Then Snyder and McClure would exhort the audience to shout
back: 'COUNT ME OUT, COUNT ME OUT, COUNT ME OUT!'
"After my own reading, as I came offstage, Gary Snyder greeted me
with the extended-palm gesture employed by Indians in movies when
they say 'How!' Backstage Richard Brautigan and Jim Morrison were
smoking a joint and polishing off a bottle of champagne. Right in the
middle of somebody's reading, a man dressed as a giant penis, the
People's Prick, climbed onstage and seized the microphone to read his
own poems. It seemed that everyone was a poet in those days, even this
man who was dressed as a sexual organ. His poetry sucked. . . . But
those were heady days for everyone in the communication business."

But none of this advanced his career. Not only was Tillinghast not
writing much, but his zeal for experimental teaching was suspect
among some colleagues. Maybe his most imprudent move, however,
was voicing his opinion in the faculty meetings that were rife with
heated debate over student activism. "I never even thought about it," he
says. "In retrospect I can see that for a non-tenured faculty member to
confront the tenured faculty on ideological grounds is nothing short of
academic suicide."

But there were dividends. By doing everything wrong for tenure,
Tillinghast wasted no time. The odyssey broadened. In the summer of
1971 he camped out in the French Alps, attending the International
School of Meditation, then, with a year's leave of absence from
Berkeley, traveled overland by bus to visit spiritual teachers in India.

On the way were political lessons.

"I saw Iran before the Ayatollah," he recalls. "Soldiers were
everywhere. It was during the Shah's expensive 1000th anniversary
celebration, which is funny because his father's coup had installed him.
There was no legitimate tradition so he had a celebration cooked up."
The Shah's sham frustrated one of Tillinghast's quests. "I had an
interest in the dervishes of Kurdistan. They get into a mystical trance
and then run swords through their cheeks or walk on fire. But they
weren't being allowed to do their thing. The police didn't want
foreigners to see something this primitive and fanatical going on during

the celebration. They wanted *control*."

Tillinghast reached his destination in time for the Pakistan/India border war, and has memories of being inside the Y in Lahore with yelling armed crowds in the streets, or a wild night drive around Delhi during a blackout in a scooter-rickshaw with no lights. But the main reason for going to India was to get on the ashram circuit. Tillinghast went on a retreat with a Buddhist meditation teacher, lived in a Muslim spiritual community, a Hindu ashram, met the Dalai Lama and Tibetan meditation teachers. "I covered all the bases," he says, smiling. There was a trek through Nepal and Tillinghast saw Afghanistan before the Russian invasion. "They're a really tough and independent people," he recalls, "goofy, fun to be around."

He admits this year of wandering was not a major contribution to his academic career. But the serious work was getting done. "If you're in the academic track," he says, "it's hard to do these things. And it's important for a writer to see other cultures. It's like being an anthropologist so you can get a comparative hit on your own culture."

Now a wiser student of that culture, Tillinghast could not have been surprised that he landed on the curb two years later: tenure denied.

O nce again he was probably where he wanted to be. Now the odyssey changed. With money saved up, Tillinghast became a dropout in Marin County, not working for three years, writing songs, not much poetry, and playing the drums again with such regularity that he partially deafened one ear.

Two things straightened him out in 1976.

First Tillinghast started teaching at San Quentin and continued for three years. "Prison is such a hopeless place," he says. "I went in very idealistic and came out very disillusioned. The association of the criminal and the artist that you get out of Genet doesn't have much basis in reality that I could see. We romanticize convicts a lot, but would a lot less if we spent more time around them. Your ordinary criminal is quite often somebody of low intelligence who can only figure out the only way to get money is to knock over a liquor store. Something decent in us wouldn't let us hit an old lady upside the head with a gun or shoot a grocery-store keeper. Criminals don't seem to have any trouble hurting other people. They don't think twice about it."

Such a steady exposure to this side of human nature must have engendered a new realism. And if violence was real, what could he make of figures like Black Panthers Huey Newton and Eldridge Cleaver, two ex-convicts lionized as revolutionary heroes in the late Sixties? (Newton's Black Panther Party, regarded by supporters as a persecuted "vanguard of the revolution," soon unraveled into criminal violence, including extortion, drug trafficking and alleged murder. A sardonic harlequin, Cleaver espoused a principle of "insurrectionary rape" in *Soul on Ice*— and once challenged Ronald Reagan, then governor of California, to a duel, saying he could beat him to death with a marshmallow.)

The second thing that straightened Tillinghast out was his wife Mary's delivery of their first child. "That was a tremendous impetus to get my act together," he recalls. "I realized I had to stop living this very casual and disorganized life." Essentially this meant "rediscovering" poetry after an interruption of eight years. The gap of silence admits of many reasons, but Tillinghast sees as one an excessively complete empathy with the Sixties.

"We all look back at that as an important time," he says. "But it also represented a rejection of a lot of important values. The revolution failed because its leaders came to hate America. It wasn't populist enough. We all knew who 'the people' were, and they didn't include all the middle-aged middle-class squares who were also living in California. It was profoundly anti-intellectual and it was very tough on anybody who does something that might be regarded as elitist like writing poetry." The odyssey swung back to rescue a former self. The effect was exhilarating. "I realized that poetry was something that I know how to do, and do well," he recalls. "And my training was extraordinary. You only have one lifetime. This was what I should be doing."

The poems that Tillinghast started to compose would be twice-written, the Sixties first lived and then recollected in detached wonder. "I had a lot of half-written poems around," he remembers. "We were living in San Raphael. I had a writing room above the garage, just a table there. I could only stand in the middle of the roof. I started working on these poems, writing during the day and teaching in prison at night. I'd thumbtack poems to the walls. I could walk around and look at them and change things . . ."

P ublished in 1980, *The Knife and Other Poems* is a requiem for what is already a vanished era. The poet is haunted by "ghosts": visions of lost love, images of himself along the trail of the previous decade, the presence of the Symbolist poets who nourished him. Refrains of the counterculture—Janis Joplin, Dylan—drift in the air, elegiac and inaccessible. News of the end of the Vietnam War reaches the poet in the Rockies, and "From halfway down the valley / bamboo flute notes rise, beat / flutter and shatter / against the Great Divide."

The recurring image of return is now ironically a reversion to the present: In "The Return," the poet drives a truck of mythically ripe fruit down the northern California coast, only to have this epiphany in San Francisco:

> I find your house by feel.
>   How many years are gone?
> Your name is gone from the mailbox.
> The tropical birds and palm trees and Hawaiian sunset
>   you painted with a small brush
>   are peeling off the beveled glass door.
>
> Forever must be over.

In "Today in the Café Trieste," the poet meditates at length on the "revolution" at Berkeley, exposing the origin of all those high ideals and expectations that came to nothing.

> From a poem by Mao:
> *I remember how vivid they were*
> *as they gazed upon rivers and mountains:*
> *The Chinese earth gave strength to their words —*
> *and the ancient feudal lords*
> *were something they scraped off their boots.*
>
> I look around the café at faces,
>   knowing so many.
> Ferlinghetti comes in after work,
>   smiles and frowns at the same time
>   as if to say:
>   "Where did we meet?"
> A student drinks hot chocolate and reads *Dubliners*.
>
> Ten years ago
> we fought all day and ran,
>   and watched ourselves on network news at night.
> The Revolution seemed no farther away
>   than squadcar blue-lights whipping

>   hypnotically through fuchsias
>   in the Berkeley hills—
>   fear and love in a crowd,
>   a nose full of tear gas,
>   plate glass heavily smashed.
>
>   People say "*Our* Revolution
>   had its effect."
>   I yawn, and nod in agreement.
>   But what I see is
>   "urban guerrillas" cleaning houses,
>   pumping gas,
>   cooking eggs at six in the morning
>   for someone else,
>   collecting food stamps,
>   teaching grammar to convicts,
>   —revolutionized into poverty—
>   or invisible in some good job.
>   "The best minds of *my* generation" too,
>   self-exiled from America,
>   strangers to power,
>   a wasted generation.

As an epitaph the final line may be premature: the mistake was one of youth. "The Chinese Revolution was a great romance," Tillinghast says. "We saw it as Berkeley writ large back then. Now we know more about what really went on. In reality eight million people were liquidated. You start killing people and you get hardened, corrupted. You stop being a human being."

After such self-deception, any longing is futile: you can't go back here again. There is even imagined retribution from a more primal home in "Lost Cove & the Rose of San Antone," where the poet, sipping his bourbon in California, dreams up a man drinking in Lost Cove, Tennessee in 1938, and the poet must lock his door as his creation, now armed, stalks him.

Yet *The Knife* is curiously without remorse, passionate, its gloom relieved by lucidity, the language ripe and gleaming. There is still the escape into nature, whether the poet is shooting ducks in Louisiana or driving "out over the Golden Gate / and the spirit of all the dead . . . into the redwoods and foothills, into the open darkness."

There is also the next generation:

> *Children are all that matters*, you said
> last night, and I agreed.
> The children's play-song — repetitive, inane —
> keeps sounding in my head.
> I get up — last night's spirits alive
>   this morning in my blood —
> and write these perishing words down
> in the voice of summer rain.

And far more reviving, there are the possibilities of poetic transcendence. "Nature has a spiritual as well as physical life," Tillinghast says. "I really believe that there's the spirit of a stream or tree, and that it's easy to get out of touch with it. But these are the origins of religion, the moral component to nature. Symbols are not something laid over reality. They are windows into another dimension." As in the title poem, when the knife the poet "almost lost" 20 years before in the "depths of Spring River" is miraculously recovered by his brother:

> Now I call to him
>   and now I see
> David burst into the upper air
> gasping as he brings to the surface our grandfather's knife
>   shaped now, for as long as these words last
>   like all things saved from time.
>
>   I see in its steel
>   the worn gold on my father's hand
>   the light in those trees
>   the look on my son's face   a moment old
>
>   like the river   old like rain
>   older than anything that dies can be.

Now Tillinghast grew more realistic and interested in getting back into teaching. "Since 1979 I've made a serious effort to get my career back on track and provide financial security for my family," he says. "And I've largely succeeded. I'm still very interested in the ideas of the Sixties and the notion you can do something about your mental state through meditation—but I've had to shelve those interests in the name of the mortgage."

First he went back to Sewanee to teach a year, and then was appointed Briggs-Copeland Lecturer in poetry at Harvard, a 3-year non-tenure track position that allowed him to mind his own literary business. Then in 1984, with the publication of *Our Flag Was Still There*, he joined the English Department (with tenure) at the University of Michigan.

Tillinghast recognizes his good fortune, at the same time that he holds a vigil of curiosity for those comrades who didn't make it back on the bus. "Sometimes the lives of these people are tragic," he says. "Some burnout druggie who might have been one of your friends in 1970 might be just one of the bums who's picking soda-pop cans out of the garbage now."

His own feat of self-rescue has enabled him to come to a more sober assessment of the political enthusiasms of the Sixties. "The inequalities we were all worked up about still exist in society," he says, "and I'm still very interested in the idea of changing society. Our goals to provide for a better society and alleviate poverty were serious. And we did some good things. We stopped the Vietnam War. My disillusionment is with what actually happens in countries where revolution takes place, like in the Soviet Union or eastern Europe. The main result has been to put the military in charge. The ideas are good ones, but they founder when you actually try to make it happen."

At present Tillinghast has shed all political labels and seems recommitted as never before to the importance of poetry and his cultural legacy from the Fifties. "One thing that interests me in education now," he says, "is the assertion of the value of poetry and the humanities. People will very often imply there is something wrong with poetry because it is not read by more people. I think the real question is: What is wrong in a culture where most people don't read anything but those books that you buy in airports or *People* magazine? I think the fault lies with the mass media. The worship of celebrity is so powerful it scares me. Other industrial countries (in Europe and elsewhere) have a strong literary culture. In America we're turning into a homogeneous dish of jello. We're going to have a price to pay for the effects of TV on American values."

P ublished in 1984, *Our Flag Was Still There* is a kind of journey back to native ground. Here are six thematic poems on the

American experience. The Sixties a dead space, the poet now celebrates two earlier spots of historical time when people "stood shoulder to shoulder in a good cause" — the Forties generation that fought World War II and the history of the University of the South after its devastation by Union troops in the Civil War. "That things you love disappear is a totally unacceptable idea," Tillinghast says. "Anyone who concerns himself with the past is motivated by outrage that things come to an end. Writers are servants of what has disappeared with the passage of time."

"Sewanee in Ruins" is a poem of epic proportions that traces the history of that community after 1865, "when everything burned / but the brick chimneys and a way of talking." Relying heavily on versified letters, journals and local history from the late 1800s, and in flashbacks of his own experiences as both student and faculty member, the poet memorializes a lost way of life:

> As in any
> human utopia,
> the soul was free to follow its own bent or warp,
> to be eccentric, kind, queer, ornery, plain, or even good.
> There were miles of room for wit,
> even for artful malice and scandal.

The inclusion of an 1871 lynching, the troubling legacy of slavery, saves the poem from becoming a nostalgic evocation of the Old South. A generosity of spirit and fine intelligence guide us through the raw material of history. "Why do I let these ghosts talk?" the poet asks at the end. Is it because the "present is a perpetual Never" and the past "demands to be articulated"? No totally convincing answer is given, but Tillinghast seems to offer one now. "I don't know if I would make any big claims for 'Sewanee' as poetry," he says. "Yet I think I performed a service for my college. The people of that community lost everything, and it's nothing short of heroic the way they came back."

In "Fossils, Metal, and the Blue Limit," the poet discloses with unconscious irony what has become of those earlier romantic trips up the California coast. His 1966 VW Microbus, now a "decrepit old wreck," breaks down, leaving him stranded with a companion and his two irreverent sons — whereupon a "thirtyish drunkish ex-biker" emerges from "blue-collar suburbia" to help make repairs. What follows — literary associations of the oil and smoke with the Ayatollah and

Marxist "pollution-stacks," and a meditation on the machine in America sparked by his "disconnected engine" brooding "like a fifth element, / like an alien life-form from a slower planet" — suggests by the end a genial and resigned debunking of the poet's former prophetic self:

> Stained with the bodies of half-billion-year-old plants,
> releasing my breath upward,
> I stare upward uncomprehendingly
> at the blue, cloud-woven limit of the sky.

Actually, the title poem seems offered in expiation — an ironic reflection on the World War II generation and after. The elders either fought or "labored to make aluminum fly / and set afloat fleets of destroyers / and submarines radaring to the kill." It was their sacrifices that made possible the political deviations of the Sixties. Now the poet's own generation looks effete, the forgetful offspring of a "stern taboo-ridden tribe," delayed progeny who

> . . . in twenty-five years
> stood baffled on the 4th of July among uncles,
> drove good German cars,
> floated in tubs of hot, red-wood scented water with friends
> and greeted each other with the word, "Peace."

Lest one concludes that Tillinghast has succumbed to a mindless patriotism, be aware of how he came upon the title for this volume. "I was watching basketball on TV one night," he recalls, "and they played the National Anthem. When they got to 'our flag was still there,' there was loud applause. It was because the game was about to begin, but any foreign observer might figure a great outburst of patriotic enthusiasm had just occurred. . . . That was it. I had my title."

Given the number of Big Wheels and wagons parked on Tillinghast's porch, it looks like his kids are taking most of the adventurous trips these days. But he does get on the road for regular poetry readings.

"The opportunities came after *The Knife*," he says, "and now it's become a pattern in my life. At least once a month I go to the airport and fly off to some place like Omaha, or Tulsa, or San Diego or New York." The experience has been mixed. "As in the theater, there are 'live' and 'dead' houses. Hearing a well-written poem read expressively in a responsive room is like watching one of those Japanese paper flowers blossom in a glass of water. A tuned-out crowd makes you feel as though you've been buried up to your neck in sand, honey poured over your head, and been left waiting for the ants. The question period that follows can be compared to being pecked to death by a duck."

Fortunately things improve in many ways when Tillinghast swings west on his circuit. "For me this annual return to the Golden State is a trip back in time, a good excuse to regress. And traveling up and down the state—from Claremont to L.A., from Arcata to San Francisco to Santa Barbara, giving eight readings in six days, crashing on unfamiliar couches, relying on the kindness of strangers—is not that different from life as an itinerant hippie. Only now I'm not hitchhiking, and every few days I mail home a few checks."

But time is no illusion and things aren't like the old days. Still Tillinghast is happy to be back in the fold at U of M. Last year he administered the MFA program in the English Department.

"I don't find the writing time that I'd like to find," he says. "Frost wrote out of 'idleness,' Keats out of 'indolence,' and I feel that way too. I need long periods of time when I have absolutely nothing to do. (Laughter.) That's kind of a problem for me."

Yet he has cornered enough periods with absolutely nothing to do to nearly complete a detective novel and finish several lyric poems for his next book. This is good news. His odyssey is doubling back again. Perhaps Lowell offered the most serious reservation about *Our Flag Was Still There* when he said that a poem "is an event, not a record of an event." As the Buddhist masters teach us, the present is not a perpetual Never, but rather All There Is.

It was in this frame of mind that Richard Tillinghast wrote *The Knife and Other Poems*, a lyrical illumination of the Sixties, preserving that era with an uncommon lucidity and at the same time capturing its visionary gleam.

■ ■ ■ ■ ■ ■ ■ ■ ■ ■ ■

Existential Politics

Lawrence Wright

F rom the day Lyndon Johnson took office I had been grooming my accent to rid it of the Texas twang, that dead giveaway. The first time I heard myself on a tape recording was in language lab, and I felt a shock of dismay. To a Texan there was as much difference between my nasalized North Texas drawl and LBJ's Hill Country brogue as there was, to a Southerner, between the pinched vowels of the Tidewater and the diphthongs of Alabama. When Lyndon Johnson said "wire" it came out "war," as in a "bob-war fence." When I said "wire" it made a noise like a Civil Defense siren in my nose. But when I heard myself saying *"hablo muy bien el español,"* I sounded like Lyndon ordering a platter of tamales.

I could not help feeling a grudging kinship with Johnson. We were stained by the same brush. The same hatred directed at him—from the East, the liberals, the Ivy Leaguers, especially from the Kennedys themselves—reflected on me as well. It was a class hatred. When Johnson complained to Hugh Sidey of *Life*, "I don't believe that I'll ever get credit for anything I do in foreign affairs, no matter how successful, because I didn't go to Harvard," I knew what he meant. Harvard was a chord often sounded in the new world, which saw the country being controlled by academics in Cambridge and New Haven, and by New York newspaper barons and network executives ("the malevolent press of the Eastern Seaboard," Johnson bitterly labeled them), and by old-money lawyers and bankers in the Boston-to-Washington corridor. These people held the reins on the lobbyists and elevated bureaucrats who were themselves moneyed, privileged, and conditioned to represent the interests of their class. They were the Eastern Establishment. Outside their circle the rest of us stood about like orphans peering into shop windows. It was the classic and predictable confrontation of new money versus old, of a raw new breed trying to wrench respectability out of the hands of the effete old families, who were bound to deride our nose-picking manners and our undisguised ambitions. We were playing out the comic drama America itself had played for the amusement of Europe during the last two centuries. We were the new New World, and Lyndon Johnson was our innocent abroad.

Everything about Lyndon—his size, his earthy way of speaking, his legendary gaucherie—was a caricature of Texas qualities. He never seemed like a real person to me; he was not only larger than life, he was a sort of mythic Texas freak, like those jackelope postcards tourists bought when they drove through the state. His touch was more than common, it was coarse. He didn't pet his dog, he picked him up by the ears. His idea of entertaining foreign leaders was to take them to the ranch and speed about in his open Lincoln with a six-pack of beer. When he went around the world in 1966, he took along a planeload of plastic busts of himself, which an aide dispensed from a shopping cart—he even gave one to the pope. The Kennedy entourage detested him, largely because of the clash of styles between their elegant champion and his indomitably tacky successor. Their attitude toward him was sealed in Dallas, when Johnson abruptly took control. "We didn't like Johnson taking over *Air Force One* when his own vice-presidential plane, with identical facilities, was available," Kennedy aide Larry O'Brien remembered. "We didn't like his delaying takeoff. We resented his calling Jackie 'honey.'" Bobby Kennedy never forgave Johnson's demand to be sworn in immediately; it was unseemly and constitutionally unnecessary. Despite Jackie's state of shock and the panic of the Kennedy aides to get the hell out of Dallas, Johnson held the plane on the ground until Judge Hughes arrived to administer the oath—not on a Bible, as Johnson believed, but on Kennedy's Catholic missal. In the sharp-eyed view of the Kennedy men, it was typical of Johnson to get even this historic moment just wrong.

Jackie wouldn't leave the White House. Of course Johnson wouldn't hurry her. She said she had "nowhere else to go." In Texas we felt that her reluctance to leave was a personal slight—against us. We felt her grief, but we also felt her resentment. She didn't want to relinquish her husband's bedroom to Lyndon, the archetypal Texan. She was in pain,

85

but so were we, so were the Johnsons. Liz Carpenter, Mrs. Johnson's press secretary, expressed the sentiment of many guilty Texans when they faced the coincidence of Kennedy's murder in their state and his succession by Lyndon Johnson: "It's a terrible thing to say," Carpenter told Lady Bird, as they rode together to The Elms, where the new President resided, "but the salvation of the State of Texas is that the Governor was hit." And Mrs. Johnson replied, "I only wish it could have been me."

This was the bloody transfer of power between the new world and the old—a by-product of madness, an incidental coup. The new world was bound to come to power someday; the census was on our side; but the fact that it came too soon and that it came through murder made our accession illegitimate. Johnson believed that Bobby Kennedy actually considered preventing his presidency. "I thought that was on his mind every time I saw him the first few days, after I had already taken the oath. I think he was seriously calculating what steps to take. For several days he really kept me out of the president's office. I operated from the Executive Office Building because it was not made available to me."

Johnson understood that his presidency was premature, that he was acting as a regent for Kennedy's ghost. Kennedy had drawn around him a Cabinet of pedigreed intellectuals, exactly the sort of men who were most likely to add luster to Kennedy's own polish, but they would make his successor appear ignorant and crass, a Texas yokel. In their presence Johnson became intensely conscious of his background. He used to joke uncomfortably about how many men serving him were Rhodes scholars, how many had gone to Harvard, how many to Yale, but there was only one man in the room who had gone to Southwest Texas State Teachers College in San Marcos, Texas. He seriously considered not running for his own term in 1964, he told *New York Times* columnist James Reston, because the country was "not far enough from Appomattox" to accept a president from his part of the country. "I was not thinking just of the derisive articles about my style, my clothes, my manner, my accent, and my family," Johnson recalled in his memoirs. "I was also thinking of a more deep-seated and far-reaching attitude—a disdain for the South that seems to be woven into the fabric of Northern experience."

But the choice that year was not between the new world and the old, it was between Johnson and Goldwater, the one running under the banner of the Kennedy legacy and the other sounding the trumpet of new world insurgency. Johnson's historic mandate in that contest was a repudiation of his own region and origins, and in a subtle way a slap at himself. If he had been running against Rockefeller, he might have understood more clearly how the nation was shaped, for him or against him.

I have wondered since then how much of the antiwar movement was actually an Eastern Establishment reaction to President Johnson. The same Establishment had drawn Kennedy into Vietnam in the first place and had steadily pulled Johnson in after him, until suddenly the Establishment changed its mind. Johnson watched them desert him and questioned what his critics would have said if Kennedy were alive and running the war. What would the students say, who loved Kennedy so? Johnson believed that if he had backed out of Vietnam, Robert Kennedy would be leading the pack against him, crying out at the betrayal of his dead brother's policies.

In fact, Robert Kennedy did that anyway. I watched, with complicated feelings of guilt, obligation, and suspicion, as Bobby entered the primaries in 1968. He had a tie on my loyalties that went back to the School Book Depository, and yet I had always distrusted him. I didn't understand how, exactly, a man who had worked for Joe McCarthy during the worst days of the anti-Communist witch-hunts, who had been a hawk all during the early days of our Vietnam involvement, could present himself as a liberal peace candidate. His appeal actually had little to do with the war. From the beginning his supporters were evenly divided between those who approved of the war and those who opposed it. He was a Kennedy—that was what mattered—and the hysteria that surrounded his campaign had more to do with celebrity than politics, more to do with myth than reality.

When John Kennedy was alive, we understood him as a political man. In death, however, he was wrapped in the myth of Camelot, a myth invented by an anxious widow as a way of forestalling the judgment of history. After the assassination Jacqueline Kennedy summoned Theodore White to Hyannis Port, and as *Life* magazine held the presses she sold him on her own version of John Kennedy, the creature of destiny. "All I keep thinking of is this line from a musical comedy, it's been an obsession with me," Mrs. Kennedy said, according to White's notes of the interview. "At night before we'd go to sleep . . . Jack liked to play some records . . . I'd get out of bed at night and play it for him . . . on a Victrola ten years old—and the song he loved most came at the very end of this record, the last side of *Camelot*, sad *Camelot*: . . . 'Don't let it be forgot, that once there was a spot, for one brief shining moment that was known as Camelot.'"

White dictated this story to his editor forty-five minutes later, with Jacqueline Kennedy standing over his shoulder, and the result of this collaboration was the most powerful myth of modern American politics. It ruined Johnson's presidency. Even after he received the greatest majority vote in history, Johnson was overshadowed by the vastly romanticized re-creation of his predecessor's brief term. Part of the message of Camelot was that the Kennedys were America's royal family, and the White House rightfully belonged to them, especially to Bobby. Columnist Murray Kempton compared the Kennedys to the Bonapartes: "They identify with the deprived, being the radical foes of all authority when they are out of power."

This is what the crowds were screaming about when Bobby's campaign wheeled through America five years after his brother's death. They were responding to the ideal of a golden age, an era of charm and sexiness that had been celebrated on television and in the fan magazines and then cut short by murder. Added to this nostalgic brew was a kind of spiritualism that saw Bobby as our link to his dead brother, and in a way to a dead America. And yet Bobby was not Jack. He was not elegant, he was not handsome; he was toothy, and his voice sometimes sounded as if it were floating on helium. In place of Jack's charm, Bobby offered a grim drive for power. He was "ruthless"—that tag placed on him by Jimmy Hoffa, the corrupt Teamsters Union boss whom Kennedy hounded during his years as attorney general. He was also an opportunist. He had won election as senator from New York on the barest excuse of residency. And in 1968 he was late coming into the primaries to challenge LBJ; he had waited for Eugene McCarthy to show it could be done.

Nineteen sixty-eight was the year the Baby Boom arrived at the voting booth. Before the general election I would turn twenty-one, which was still the legal age required to vote, and for the first time I heard the candidates speaking to me, a fully vested citizen. The voice that most appealed was dry, witty, haughtily intellectual, and politically alienated; it was the voice of Eugene McCarthy. Norman Mailer characterized him as looking and feeling "like the dean of the finest English department in the land"—no wonder students accepted his authority. What we admired was his intelligence and his courage. Everybody knew that it was impossible to topple Johnson, especially from within his own party. But McCarthy ignored conventional wisdom. He refused to kiss babies or flatter campaign contributors, and he always said what he thought with eloquence, though without drama. He was pointedly anticharismatic. To the frustration of the press,

McCarthy never permitted himself the hollow gesture, the hypocritical statement, or the trumped-up pseudoevent, which had become the mainstays of the evening news. He refused, as the *New Republic* noted, "to respond in kind to ersatz seriousness and spurious conscientiousness." His genuineness was turned against him.

McCarthy came within 410 votes of beating Lyndon Johnson in the New Hampshire primary. His main appeal, beyond his pledge to end the war, was the fact that he wasn't supposed to run. Even my father admired him for that. McCarthy gathered support from unlikely quarters, including Republicans and the Wallacites. (George Wallace was nominated in Dallas as the presidential candidate of the American Independent party.) Three-fifths of the people who voted for McCarthy in New Hampshire actually supported American involvement in Vietnam and thought that Johnson wasn't pressing the war aggressively enough. McCarthy was bucking the system, that was what mattered. Although he arrogantly advertised himself as the most qualified man ever to have run for the presidency, he was actually an interloper, and it is easy to perceive in him the same outsider appeal that became the basis for the more successful candidacies of Jimmy Carter and Ronald Reagan.

On March 31, 1968, I stood in the lobby of my dormitory and watched Johnson declare a halt to the bombing of North Vietnam. As always with Johnson on television, there was a languid, underwater quality to his speech and movements, as if he were hypnotized by the TelePrompTer. I could never square that awkward figure on the tube with the legendary muscleman of the Senate cloakroom. Whenever he came on TV my instinct was to leave the room, in the same way that I might steer clear of some pathetic relative at a family reunion. "I call upon President Ho Chi Minh to respond positively and favorably to this new step of peace," Johnson said—a statement that was quietly and, I think, cynically received by the students around me. Then Johnson hesitated. He glanced away from the camera (he was looking at his wife) and continued: "There is division in the American house now. There is divisiveness among us all tonight. And holding the trust that is mine, as President of all the people, I cannot disregard the peril to the progress of the American people and the hope and prospect of peace for all people. . . . I do not believe that I should devote an hour or a day of my time to any personal partisan causes. . . . Accordingly, I shall not seek, and will not accept, the nomination of my party for another term as your President." There was an instant of shocked silence before the room erupted in cheers. "We did it!" someone cried, and I knew what he meant. We—the American student body—had brought down the President of the United States.

We had booed him off the stage, that miserable creature with his compulsive fibs and grotesque piety. But there was another part of me that felt repudiated—as a Texan once again—and that made my hatred of Johnson seem cheap and traitorous. In some non-political, purely human region of my soul I felt ashamed of what had been done to Johnson. No president had ever known the hounding mob that followed Johnson wherever he went, and finally kept him a prisoner inside the White House gates. What a relentless, formidable enemy we had become. In a way our persecution was a kind of assassination; at least Johnson thought so. "The only difference between the Kennedy assassination and mine," he later said, "is that I am alive and it has been more torturous."

Now that he was beaten I allowed myself to recognize him as a great man, in his own failed fashion. He had been trapped in the war, which he had no stomach for—although the war was the one issue that might have saved him. Until the Tet offensive that spring no more than 20 percent of the electorate favored withdrawal. When Johnson decided to bomb North Vietnam, his popularity rating immediately jumped 14 percent. If he had prosecuted the war more vigorously, he would very likely have been reelected, or else, if he had declared the war unwinnable and pulled out our troops, he would at least have been seen as a decisive leader. But Johnson was equally afraid of winning and losing. Finally the people who mattered to him, the liberals and the Eastern Establishment, turned against him and sent him off to the Siberia of permanent disgrace. He came home to Texas and let his hair grow down to his shoulders.

"It's narrowed down to Bobby and me," Eugene McCarthy said the day after his victory in the Wisconsin primary. At the time, neither Vice President Hubert Humphrey nor Richard Nixon appeared to be serious candidates. George Romney and Ronald Reagan were not giving Nixon much of a challenge in the Republican primaries, but Nixon had a reputation as a chronic loser; he was still trying to live down his tantrum before the press in 1962 when he was drubbed in the California governor's race. McCarthy ridiculed the Republicans for their characteristic blandness: "They're somewhat like the lowest forms of plant and animal life. Even at their highest point of vitality there is not much life in them; on the other hand, they don't die." As for Humphrey, he had lost his standing with the liberals during his hawkish years on

Vietnam, and the moderates saw him as a hypocrite. He was trying to paint himself as a peace candidate, although he had advocated American troops in Vietnam as far back as the Eisenhower administration, and as Johnson's vice president he called the war "a great adventure, and a wonderful one it is." In the Senate, Humphrey had been a hero of the left because of his impassioned support for civil rights, but by 1968 he had become a buffoon, a tool of the Establishment. He launched his campaign bubbling about "the politics of happiness, the politics of purpose, the politics of joy." He never approached Kennedy or McCarthy in the polls, so he stood back from the primaries and let the party bosses quietly assure him of the nomination through secret pledges and old debts now called in. He might not have campaigned at all, but he raced around the country nonetheless, unloading an unmatchable torrent of verbal energy. "I don't know what kind of president Hubert would make," marveled Groucho Marx. "He'd make a hell of a wife."

McCarthy believed that Kennedy was his real opposition, and once he adjusted to Bobby's entry into the race, he affected a certain relish for the idea of running against Kennedy. "So far he's run *with* the ghost of his brother. Now we're going to make him run *against* it. It's purely Greek: he either had to kill him or be killed by him. We'll make him run against Jack." Then McCarthy added enigmatically, "And I'm Jack."

When Johnson withdrew, however, it took the war out of the campaign, and without the war McCarthy was lost. He was not Jack after all. I continued to support him, although perhaps, as Abbie Hoffman noted, it was easy to cheer for McCarthy now, knowing he would never win; it was like cheering for the Mets. It was different with Bobby.

More than anyone, Bobby Kennedy knew the dangers of public life. He saw the nearly hysterical adulation he excited, which left his hands bleeding and his clothing in shreds. His supporters, such as journalist Jack Newfield, spoke of his "existential dimension," acknowledging in that term the possibility of death that accompanied his candidacy. It was just such a possibility that sent the crowds into frenzies. Politics had become a blood sport for the Kennedys, and in that sense Bobby was playing a different game from that of the other candidates, and we were bound to notice him above the rest. "One of his possibilities was that he was always doomed," the poet Robert Lowell remembered. "It's very strange when you sort of anticipate something; then, when it happens, you're almost *more* astonished than if you hadn't anticipated it." Kennedy himself acknowledged, "I play Russian roulette every time I get up in the morning. I just don't care. There's nothing I can do about it anyway." That wasn't true; he could have protected himself better than he did, but he made a show of thrusting himself into crowds and disdaining security. He refused the assistance of local police everywhere he went. When Jimmy Breslin asked aloud, "Do you think this guy has the stuff to go all the way?" John J. Lindsay of *Newsweek* replied, "Of course he's got the stuff to go all the way, but he's not going to go all the way. The reason is that somebody is going to shoot him. I know it and you know it, just as sure as we are sitting here—somebody is going to shoot him. He's out there now waiting for him."

In fact Kennedy probably could not have gone all the way. McCarthy had the momentum in the primaries, and Humphrey had the party bosses in his pocket. Even if Kennedy had secured the nomination there was a scandal lurking that could have destroyed his candidacy, having to do with Marilyn Monroe. Rumor said that Bobby had been with her the night she died, trying to persuade her not to give a press conference detailing her relationship with him and with Jack. His brother-in-law, Peter Lawford, had spirited him out of town after Marilyn killed herself. This was all gossip; on the other hand, Bobby's nemesis, Jimmy Hoffa, had hired private detectives to bug Lawford's seaside villa and Marilyn Monroe's Hollywood bungalow. Hoffa supposedly had tapes of trysts between Marilyn and the Kennedy brothers, which he planned to distribute to newspapers.

Kennedy was in Indiana when news came of Martin Luther King's death. That afternoon Kennedy spoke to a shocked crowd in the Indianapolis ghetto. It was the finest moment of his career. More than any other politician, perhaps more than any other white person in America, Bobby Kennedy had an authority to speak on the subject of political violence to the black community, which would so soon explode. "In this difficult day, in this difficult time for the United States, it is perhaps well to ask what kind of a nation we are and what direction we want to move in. For those of you who are black—considering what evidence there evidently is that there were white people who were responsible—you can be filled with bitterness, with hatred, and a desire for revenge. We can move in that direction as a country, in great polarization—black people amongst black, white people amongst white, filled with hatred toward one another.

"Or we can make an effort, as Martin Luther King did, to understand and to comprehend, and to replace that violence, that stain of bloodshed that has spread across our land, with an effort to understand with compassion and love."

Privately he acknowledged the absurdity of events. He had lost patience with meaning. Perhaps that was his most existential quality. He told speechwriter Jeff Greenfield that King's death was not the worst thing that ever happened. Then he remarked, "You know that fellow Harvey Lee Oswald, whatever his name is, set something loose in this country." He knew that what was loose in the country was looking for him, and would find him, and when he was dead it would all have been pointless, for naught. "I am pretty sure there'll be an attempt on my life sooner or later," he admitted to French novelist Romain Gary. "Not so much for political reasons. . . . Plain nuttiness, that's all." As he walked in Martin Luther King's funeral, with his coat slung over his shoulder, he observed how few white faces were in the crowd. Jimmy Breslin said that you'd think a few would come out to look, even for curiosity. Kennedy agreed. "Then maybe this won't change anything at all?" Breslin asked. "Oh, I don't think this will mean anything," said Kennedy, and then he turned to Charles Evers, brother of another murdered civil rights leader, Medgar Evers, who was walking beside him. "Do you think this will change anything?" Kennedy asked. "Nothing," said Evers. "Didn't mean nothing when my brother was killed."

"I know," said Robert Kennedy.

In life, Martin Luther King had become a sad figure out of control of his movement, derided by the young as an Uncle Tom, but in death it was possible to believe he was a saint. He was not a perfect man, as the FBI wiretaps would prove. He was an egotist and an adulterer and something of a peacock. No doubt the minister of my own church in Dallas had a higher set of personal morals. Furthermore there was the problem of the Great Man—who is he to presume on history? Why should I follow him? Isn't he flawed after all? Toward the end of King's life people were turning away from him everywhere; even his disciples were talking about his naiveté and his irrelevance. King insisted on remaining nonviolent as the power passed into the hands of the Black Panthers and the hard-faced kids of SNCC (Student Non-Violent Coordinating Committee). Black Power and the upraised fist were the appropriate responses now. The gospel of revolution was not the New Testament but Fanon and Camus. The passive resistance of Christianity was pushed aside by the existentialist doctrine of "necessary violence," which supposes that justice is more important than life. King was written off by the white liberal intelligentsia as being middle class and out of date. "Conventional commentators these days like to speak of King's 'nobility' and the purity of his humanism, and they sigh that the world is not ready for him. But it is more accurate to say that King is not ready for the world," wrote Andrew Kopkind in an infamous issue of *The New York Times Review of Books,* which had a diagram of a Molotov cocktail on the cover. Kopkind also wrote: "Morality, like politics, starts at the barrel of a gun." The younger black leaders, such as Stokely Carmichael, believed that King deserved part of the blame for the riots in the summer of 1967, in Harlem, Chicago, Cleveland, and elsewhere, which indicated the impatience of the black community for change. "Those of us who advocate Black Power," Carmichael wrote, "are quite clear in our own minds that a 'non-violent' approach to civil rights is an approach black people cannot afford and a luxury white people do not deserve."

Of course it was ironic that the reaction to King's death was massive violence, but perhaps it was only the weight of his spiritual authority that had kept the ghettos unburned until then. In the final months of his life, King himself realized that the nonviolent tactics that had succeeded in the South were failing as the movement traveled North. One of his last marches in Memphis had turned into a riot over which he had no control. Now that he was safely martyred, the country just cracked in two, the black part and the white part. Everything King lived for seemed to be undone by his death, which sparked the worst eruption of civil disorders in the history of the nation. That night there were 711 cases of arson and ten people killed in Washington, D.C., alone. In Baltimore over the next four days there were more than a thousand fires, and it required 12,000 troops to subdue the riots. Before the convulsion subsided, more than 150 other cities in the country were in flames, more than 21,000 people were arrested, and 45 were killed, all but five of them black.

I had not loved John Kennedy until he was dead; then I fell guiltily in love with his legend, his promise—with Camelot, in short. With Martin Luther King my feelings were more confused. I thought I had moved beyond him. In 1968 *Soul on Ice* appeared, and I read it excitedly, because Eldridge Cleaver connected the black movement with the student movement and both with liberation movements throughout the world. The same connections had been made before—notably, by Martin Luther King—but they had not been made by a black rapist in a California prison, who was for me an American Camus. What appealed to me so strongly about *Soul on Ice* was the mood—romantic, existential, violent. I think those three adjectives described me and my generation as well. Reading Cleaver had persuaded me that Martin Luther King was beside the point. And yet if John Kennedy's death in Dallas had marked the end of my age of innocence—and perhaps the nation's as well—then Martin Luther King's death began another period for me, having to do with my role as a man and my place in the world. The question for me was violence.

The greatest hypocrisy of my childhood was the notion of Christian love—that is, the pacific brotherly love that Jesus preached. "Turn the other cheek" was a failed doctrine in Dallas. I grew up celebrating violence. It was not just the ritualized violence of sports, which have always been important in Texas. It was a matter of history. Hadn't my father's heroic violence contributed to the end of the war? What might have happened if America had stayed out of the fight, allowing the Axis to overrun the globe? What if Hitler ruled the world? You would never hear a word against the military from the pulpits of Big D. As an American boy I subscribed to the proposition that might makes right; after all, America had never lost a war, and hadn't we always been on the side of truth and justice?

My ideal American then was John Wayne. He was always setting people straight, with his fists or his gun, and he was invariably right. You could never imagine John Wayne turning the other cheek, but he did live by a code. Never back away from a fight, but don't go looking for trouble. Never draw first, but when you do, shoot to kill. In his humbler moments, when he was lying in his bedroll under a billion stars, John Wayne might gaze upward and realize what a small figure he was in the universal scheme of things, but that was a passing thought and he found no solace in it. The night was filled with bandits and Indians, so John Wayne never slept. In the morning the sun lit up the existential landscape and you knew there was no God, there was only John Wayne.

That was my image of America's role in the world. We lived by the code. In the real world the only certainty of justice came from our power, our willingness to use violence appropriately. It seemed to me then that strength and truth were welded together and that if one exercised power, justice would naturally follow.

Moreover, I *liked* violence. I liked the aesthetics of it—the beauty of the gunfight and the glory of the battlefield—it was noble action. My father brought home several weapons from the wars, including a samurai sword from the Occupation of Japan. When I drew it partly out of the black lacquered scabbard and tested the blade, it sliced my finger. I went light-headed at the sight of my blood running down the brilliant blade. Death, I thought, and I am its messenger.

In the Sixties my faith in violence was shaken, first by the Freedom Riders and then by the assassinations. In Dallas we didn't know what to make of the Freedom Riders. On the one hand, the Supreme Court said black people had the right to use public accommodations involved in interstate commerce, the right to use public rest rooms, to eat in restaurants, to ride on buses, and in Dallas we were great respecters of the law. We desegregated our own public facilities—except for the schools—without a fight. On the other hand, there was custom to consider. Texas was never a part of the Deep South, but it had been a member of the Confederacy, and we were southern in our prejudices. When the first busload of Freedom Riders approached Anniston, Alabama, in 1961, a mob punctured the bus's tires and set it on fire. The next bus made it to Birmingham, where the police stood aside and let the white mob beat the riders nearly to death. The news reports never made it clear to me that the race riots we kept hearing about were actually white riots, often police riots. I didn't clearly understand that the Freedom Fighters were not fighting back. Nonviolence was such a foreign idea to me that I assumed the blacks and several whites on the buses had provoked the mob and got what was coming to them. I didn't grasp the philosophy of nonresistance—but then nothing in my years of churchgoing had prepared me to understand the power of suffering, or redemptive love. The buses kept coming, and then the marches began, into the wall of fire hoses and mounted patrolmen and billy clubs and police dogs. I was surprised by the violence at first, but I gradually began to realize that these marchers and these Freedom Riders, who were always singing, expected to be hurt. They had come for two reasons: to be hurt, and for me to see it. They would not defend themselves. They would keep coming. How would John Wayne handle this? Which side of the line would he be on? You couldn't see him charging his horse into the line of hot and frightened Negroes, clubbing a teenaged girl who was crying "Freedom!" Still, you wouldn't expect him to hold hands with her and march unarmed into the face of the mob, or to stand still when some redneck spit in his face. Not to fight back was cowardice—wasn't it? But in my heart I knew the limits of my courage. I was brave enough to fight, but I didn't think I would ever be brave enough not to.

It was unsettling to hear Martin Luther King, in those early days, talking about Jesus. "I am still convinced Jesus was right," he said in 1960 at the lunch-counter sit-ins in Durham, North Carolina. "I can hear Him saying, 'He who lives by the sword will perish by the sword.' I can hear him crying out, 'Love thy enemies.'" These were injunctions I also heard nearly every Sunday, but didn't we, as a nation, live by the sword? I never heard a sermon preached on God's commandment Thou shalt not kill. And you couldn't say in Dallas that we loved our enemies.

I remember the hypothetical game we used to play in Sunday school: What would happen if Jesus came back? How would we treat him? Would we recognize him? Would we acknowledge the divinity of his message? Or would we ignore him, harass him, and ultimately kill him again? The lesson of this game was that saints are intolerable to society. We were supposed to be steeling ourselves for the return of the Redeemer, following that time when brother would rise against brother, and children against their parents. Yes, we were soldiers of the Lord. Our doctrine was brotherly love. And yet no one ever proposed that Jesus might return as a Negro.

Perhaps if President Kennedy had not been assassinated the civil rights movement would have remained nonviolent. It was strange, because Kennedy never had the emotional commitment to civil rights that Lyndon Johnson did—certainly Kennedy never intended anything like the Great Society—but his murder shattered the idealists. After that, nonviolence seemed ineffectual and naive. With three shots Lee Harvey Oswald did more to change history than Martin Luther King, with all his talk about the beloved community, had done in a decade. After that, good no longer seemed certain to triumph over evil.

It may sound absurd to say that Oswald murdered my faith in God. Indeed I was never more pious than the year after Kennedy's death. Religion became a sanctuary for me, and I put my questioning aside. But it happened, slowly, that my faith was dissolving inside this shell of piety, and although the shell remained a while longer, the animal inside was dead. Martin Luther King had helped me see the hypocrisy of the religion I grew up in, but before I might have made the step across to join the ferocious Christians of the civil rights movement, Kennedy was dead, my faith was dying, and the movement was about to turn existential and begin its violent feast.

However, there were certain vestiges—religious ideals—that clung to me; it was all myth to me now, but even myth is a way of seeing things. In this sense I would always be a Christian. Once I had broken free of the church and declared myself agnostic, I found I had an unaccountable weakness for Jesus, or the idea of Jesus. I suspect this longing for Jesus may have been a part of the subconscious of my generation; suddenly there were quite a number of young men who looked like our idea of Jesus, with long hair and beards, preaching peace and brotherhood and stuffing flowers into the rifle barrels of the federal troops. They were trying to rescue Jesus from Christianity. I saw the beauty of their actions. I listened to the lyrics of the songs that called on us to *smile on your brother, to come together, to reach out, to love one another right now,* and I approved these sentiments just as I had in Sunday school. But I could never surrender entirely to the hippie mentality. There was too much anger inside me, too much turbulence and confusion. Also, the nonviolence of hippies seemed harmless and playful and passive; it could not be compared with the death-defying nonviolence of the Freedom Riders.

My attitude toward violence had not changed, except to this extent: In a godless world, you had to fight for justice—even if it meant fighting John Wayne, the arrogant vigilante, the unloving reactionary, the swaggering bully of white America.

In the period between John Kennedy's death and his own, Martin Luther King tried to rebuild faith in nonviolence. He realized that he could not advocate nonviolence at home and continue to support a war abroad. One year to the day before his death, King spoke out against the Vietnam War at Riverside Church in New York City. I didn't hear the speech; it wasn't until after his death that I grew haunted by his words and his example and began to look to him for clues about how to conduct my life. King spoke about how Vietnam was a symptom of a deeper malady of the American spirit, and about the need to turn away from the militarism and violence inside ourselves. "This call," he said, "for a world-wide fellowship that lifts neighborly concern beyond one's tribe, race, class, and nation is in reality a call for an all-embracing and unconditional love of all men. This oft-misunderstood and misinterpreted concept so readily dismissed by the Nietzsches of the world as a weak and cowardly force—has now become an absolute necessity for the survival of man. When I speak of love I am not speaking of some sentimental and weak response. I am speaking of that force which all of the great religions have seen as the supreme unifying principle of life. Love is somehow the key that unlocks the door that leads to ultimate reality."

During King's first march in Memphis to support the garbage collectors' strike, a group of teenaged boys broke off from the march and went on a small rampage of brick throwing and window breaking. The *Memphis Commercial Appeal* described it as a "full-scale riot," although most of the violence was on the part of the police, who fired into the crowd and fatally wounded a sixteen-year-old boy. There were 120 arrests and 50 people injured. King and his colleague, the Reverend Ralph Abernathy, escaped by jumping into the backseat of a passing car. Nearly 4,000 national guardsmen were rushed into town to impose a dusk-to-dawn curfew. That night King could not sleep. He wondered aloud, according to Abernathy, "if those of us who advocated nonviolence should not step back and let the violent forces run their course." He was suddenly quite desperate to get home.

None of his friends had ever seen him so pensive and depressed as he was in the following week. He knew he would have to go back to Memphis, but he put if off several days. When he finally did return, he closeted himself in the Lorraine Motel and sent Abernathy to speak in his place at the rally. The weather was awful—there were tornado warnings out—so the crowd in the auditorium was only a thousand people, but they were so enthusiastic that Abernathy called the motel and summoned Dr. King. He drove through a rainstorm to deliver his final speech.

Did he know he was about to die? As a casual scholar of assassination, I've wondered about the premonitions of men about to be murdered. Lincoln's personal aide, Ward Hill Lamon, recounted a dream the President had a few days before his death. In the dream the President heard a sobbing sound downstairs in the White House, and he arose and went searching for the source of the grieving. He entered the East Room. "There I met with a sickening surprise," he told Lamon. "Before me was a catafalque, on which rested a corpse wrapped in funeral vestments. Around it were stationed soldiers who were acting as guards; and there was a throng of people, some gazing mournfully upon the corpse, whose face was covered, others weeping pitifully. 'Who is dead in the White House?' I demanded of one of the soldiers. 'The President,' was his answer; 'he was killed by an assassin!'" Lincoln, of course, was notoriously melancholy; the thought of death was never far from his mind. Because of threats, he had to be smuggled into Washington for his first inauguration, and during his presidency he was several times the object of assassination attempts. Twice his stovepipe hat was shot off his head. However, that dream suggests to me that Lincoln knew his fate was at hand. John Kennedy also brooded about assassination. The day before his death he told an assistant, "Anyone perched above the crowd with a rifle could do it." Then, on the very morning he went to Dallas, he said to his wife, "You know, last night would have been a hell of a night to assassinate a president . . ." He pointed his finger like a gun and fired twice.

In the last days of Martin Luther King's life, according to Andrew Young, one of his lieutenants, King developed a habit of looking about as if he might see an assassin stalking him. Like Lincoln, King had a preoccupation with death. He had twice attempted suicide as a child, by jumping out of windows, and in 1957 a crazed black domestic stuck an eight-inch letter opener into his chest while he was autographing copies of his book, *Stride Toward Freedom,* at a Harlem department store. After the Kennedy assassination he told his wife, "This is what is going to happen to me also." Moreover, given the depression he had fallen into after the Memphis riot, he may have felt doomed and helpless, so that thoughts of death, which were never far away, rushed upon him. And yet his speech that last evening of his life still seems to me a work of prophecy, in which he saw not only his own imminent death but the future of the movement as well. He compared himself with Moses, who had led his people to the Promised Land but would not be permitted to enter there himself. He talked about the threats of death that followed him. That very morning the flight from Atlanta had been delayed so that the luggage could be searched for bombs. "Well, I don't know what will happen now," King said. "But it really doesn't matter with me now. . . . Like anybody, I would like to live a long life. Longevity has its place. But I'm not concerned about that now. I just want to do God's will. And He's allowed me to go up to the mountain. And I've looked over, and I've seen the Promised Land." As he spoke, with that curiously impassive face of his, which was always like a mask of resignation, the congregation began to moan and cry out, and King's lieutenants looked at each other in alarm. Andy Young thought the speech was macabre. "I may not get there with you," King continued, "but I want you to know tonight that we as a people will get to the Promised Land. So I'm happy tonight. I'm not worried about anything. I'm not fearing any man. Mine eyes have seen the glory of the coming of the Lord."

I had grown up in a world that hated Bobby far more than it had hated Jack. Bobby had shown us the arrogance of power; he had a way of rubbing it in. He was always smarter, tougher, braver, meaner than everyone else. He had none of the easy glamour that made his brother attractive even to his opponents. In Texas he had almost no organized support at all. Partly, of course, this was because of the well-advertised loathing Kennedy had for Lyndon Johnson. One of the few old party men in the state to declare for Kennedy was Judge Woodrow Wilson Bean in El Paso, who said he was doing it "because if he's elected, anyone from Texas will need a pass to get to Washington, and I'm going to be the man handing out passes." But there was more to our fear of Bobby than that. The dread of change and revolt that had run through the new world in 1960 seemed far more palpable now. Bobby was drawing power from the disinvested, the underclass. What frightened people in Texas—and I think this apprehension was widespread around the country—was the subconscious intimation that Bobby was Samson and that he would bring the status quo crashing down in his vastly public death.

Of course, this may have been a miscalculation. Bobby Kennedy had been a liberal senator, but his politics were historically conservative, and in the end he was once again confounding traditional liberals by attacking the welfare system and proposing himself as the law-and-order candidate. "I get the feeling I've been writing some of his speeches," Governor Reagan said in California, and Richard Nixon pointed out, "Bobby and I have been sounding pretty much alike."

To be the existential hero, according to Jack Newfield, Kennedy's friend and biographer, was to define and create oneself through action, to learn everything from experience. The last several months of Kennedy's life are a legend of discovery and change. His candidacy was an extraordinary personal journey through the streets of the northern ghettos, the rural roads of the impoverished South, the oppressive world of migrant labor in California, the boiling campuses everywhere. No doubt he was deeply affected by the needs of the Indians and farmworkers and sharecroppers who became his special constituencies. And yet, as British journalist Henry Fairlie points out, "no constituencies can be bought more cheaply than the poor and the young." Kennedy was a powerful magnet, but his rivals already had nailed down the more significant Democratic franchises. McCarthy had the suburbs and the heart of the peace movement; Humphrey had the labor bosses, the civil rights leaders, and the party mechanics. What remained were the alienated and the dispossessed—people like Sirhan Sirhan.

Sirhan was born in Jerusalem in 1944. He had been traumatized early in life by Zionist terrorism, which left him with a lifelong hatred of Israel and its defenders. His family immigrated to Southern

California when he was twelve.

Not long after that, bitterly unhappy in his adopted country, Sirhan may have heard the first soundings of his own destiny. In high school he underlined passages in two history books about assassination: one concerned the murder of Archduke Ferdinand, the event that precipitated World War I, the other was the death of President McKinley. One of the sentences in the history books read: "After a week of patient suffering the President died, the third victim of an assassin's bullet since the Civil War." Sirhan noted in the margin, "Many more will come."

He was already an assassin in spirit; what remained was to select his victim. Sirhan became a Rosicrucian. He wrote out his objectives in a notebook, a form of mind control practiced by that group. Robert Kennedy's name first appears in the notebook on January 31, 1968, shortly after the senator from New York proposed that the United States sell 50 Phantom jets to Israel to replace aircraft lost in the Six-Day War. "RFK must die," Sirhan wrote. At that time Kennedy was not a presidential candidate, and the chances that he would cross Sirhan's path in California must have seemed remote. "Robert F. Kennedy must be sacrificed for the cause of poor exploited people," Sirhan noted. He also wrote, "I believe that the U.S. is ready to start declining, not that it hasn't—it began in Nov. 23, 63."

Just after midnight on the morning of June 5, 1968, Robert Kennedy stood on the podium in the Embassy Room in the Ambassador Hotel in Los Angeles to acknowledge his victories in both the California and the South Dakota primaries. "Here is the most urban state (California) of any of the states of our Union, South Dakota the most rural of any of the states of our Union. We were able to win them both. I think that we can end the divisions within the United States." He made a pitch for McCarthy to capitulate. "What I think is quite clear is that we can work together in the last analysis, and that what has been going on within the United States over a period of the last three years—the division, the violence, the disenchantment with our society; the divisions, whether it's between blacks and whites, between the poor and the more affluent, or between age groups or on the war in Vietnam—is that we can start to work together. We are a great country, an unselfish country, and a compassionate country. I intend to make that the basis for running."

Sirhan shot Kennedy as the candidate walked through the food service corridor to escape the crowd. "Kennedy, you son of a bitch," Sirhan said as he fired a .22-caliber revolver an inch away from the senator's head. The hollow-point bullet exploded in the right hemisphere of Kennedy's brain. Sirhan fired seven more times, hitting Kennedy twice in the right armpit as he fell to the floor, and wounding five other persons.

Kennedy lay for a while on the floor, as confusion swarmed around him. He fingered rosary beads and asked people to stand back and give him air. The next day newspapers would carry a photograph of him splayed out there, among the shoes, with the puzzled look of a man falling through space. As they lifted Kennedy onto a stretcher, "The last thing I heard him say," recalled Charles Quinn, a television correspondent, "was 'No, no, no, no, no,' like that, in the voice of a rabbit at the end of his life."

Later Eugene McCarthy came to the hospital where Kennedy lay dead, and said to Ted Kennedy that he had heard the name "Sirhan Sirhan" on the radio, and he remarked how odd it was, and mysterious, and coincidental, that he had the same first and last names, like the hero in Camus's *The Stranger*. A man comes out of nowhere and kills.

This was the year of my political education. Nineteen sixty-eight.

Ken Kesey (top) and
Richard Brautigan (below).
(Oil sketches by Peter Najarian)

104

■■■■■■■■■■■

The Big Game

Peter Najarian

I didn't know I was the supreme reality. I thought I was a young man with a passport and a destination. When my friend, Bob Hass, tells this story he likes to make me into a budding intellectual who had just come from London wearing a foreign correspondent raincoat with a copy of Sartre in my pocket. The truth is I actually did have one of those long coats with the big flaps and all those buttons, though Bob thought he was making it up. It was a very old one that my other friend, Bill Belli, gave me and that he got from his friend, James Jones, who used to wear it all the time in Paris until he finally bought a new one. I loved *From Here To Eternity* in those days and so I would wear that old relic as if it were my big brother's, but then it got stolen and I didn't really have it when I got back to the States. Nevertheless it was true that I was still carrying a lot of baggage from the Old World.

I had been gone three very important years. I remember sitting in Jimmy's, a cheap Greek restaurant in Soho where I often had supper, and waiting for my usual stew and *fasulyah* I would read the *Evening Standard* which was covering a new cultural revolution in California. It seemed to have started with the Free Speech Movement in the autumn of 1964, or just after I had left, and by the time I was reading about it the streets of Berkeley and San Francisco seemed covered with flowers. I wanted to go back, I felt I was missing out on something. Then one day I got a letter from my friend, Robert Pinsky, who was in his last year at Stanford, and he suggested I apply for a grant called a Stegner Fellowship. He had something similar and he'd put in a good word for me.

He was gone when I arrived but he gave me some names to look up in case I felt disoriented. Ed McClanahan was one and I liked him right away. He was also a friend of Ken Kesey and I told him how much I liked Kesey's second novel, *Sometimes a Great Notion. Cuckoo's Nest* was okay, I said, but *Notion* was really special. He must have remembered because a few days later he woke me up and said Kesey just got out of the joint and was crashing at his place for a few days. He needed a ride to his probation officer in Redwood City that morning, and Ed had to teach a class. Maybe I could take him? Sure, I said, and since I had to rush I couldn't have had more than a slice of toast, if I remember right, because my empty stomach was going to play a big part in the rest of the day.

Kesey was only in his early thirties at the time, but I was even younger and I looked up to him a bit. He was by then quite famous, which is why he got busted for grass and had to spend six months in a work farm near Soledad. He was a very good young man, wise for his years, and his big handshake was gentle and confident. He had a very strong presence and yet he looked rather odd. He had good posture and was planted solid and straight, and yet wearing those old free-box clothes that were too small and tight for his chunky limbs he looked like an enormous child, especially with his shiny bald head and his curly blond hair around his ears. Later I would learn that innocence was indeed his best quality and he was the kind of person who could trust you immediately because why shouldn't he trust you? Was there something bad about you that he should beware of? Getting ready to go I took a closer look at one of his front teeth and noticed it had a patch of blue and some red stripes. His dentist did that for him, he said. He lost his cap in the joint and his hip dentist made a new one dyed like the U.S. flag.

We got in my bug with the sunroof down and he introduced me to his wife, Fay, a quiet and attractive young woman with a solidness not unlike his own, and she asked where I was from. West Hoboken, New Jersey, I said, and they both chuckled. Why were they chuckling? Oh nothing, they said, it was just that McClanahan hurried the message and not getting it straight they thought they were going with someone who was either a Nigerian from Armenia or an Armenian from Nigeria.

We chatted along the way, Kesey about the joint and I about social work in Harlem before I went abroad. They were invaluable experiences and through them we got a closer look at the underside of our America and the forces of the straight world. We were kinfolk in a way, at least I like to think we were. All sentient beings are kin of course, but we are so limited in our separate shells that, especially when we're young, we look for others who share our way of life. Kesey was one of the family; he was not only an artist but a seeker with a free-box wardrobe and I felt at home with him. Many of us had grown up feeling so alone in an alienating society that it was a tremendous boost to find others like ourselves and to roam our continent sharing pads and simple meals. We all need each other but very often our separate paths become narrow and nuclear, as we used to say, and should something go wrong with them we find ourselves in deep water. Many of us, then as now, had come from deep water and were looking for a shore where we could be at home again.

Back at McClanahan's everyone was at work or school, and after Fay took off to meet someone Kesey and I hung out in the rec room which was a cozy little space with a warm rug and batik spreads. One of the walls was covered with a huge blow-up of the Marx brothers fooling around and Harpo smoking a hookah. He was popping his trademark eyeballs and his curly hair looked a little like Kesey's. Kesey was no Harpo but he would've liked to have been, I think. There was a heaviness about him that he wanted to lighten and his shoulders curved under whatever that burden was that he carried so silently. We each have a burden and I felt his in the quietness and gentleness of his powerful body that could hurt someone if he ever let go. I haven't seen him in twenty years, and I'm mostly imagining now for I never got to know him well, but in person, at least with me, he was very different from the unleashed and abandoned voice I heard in his prose.

We lounged around the rug and he opened a book and started reading from it. He discovered it in the joint, he said, and he wanted to share it with me. It was called the *I Ching*. I had never heard of it before; I was reading *Being and Nothingness* in those days, and when he asked me to throw coins on the rug I began to feel a little uncomfortable. But then the phone rang and when he returned he said the Doctor just called and would be over in a few minutes. Expecting a real doctor I was naturally a bit surprised to see a guy wearing denims and looking like an exquisite hood who had just stolen a tank of gas. He wasn't, of course, he was just a sweet young man like your favorite cousin or the familiar delivery boy who brings your goodies each week. What the tank was for I had no idea but Harpo Marx and the *I Ching* and the beautiful weather were all in progress and I was not about to stop it. I was ignorant in many ways but I had been around, I was familiar with hemp and poppies and even ate a few moldy cactus buds way back when I lived in the Village. And yet I had never tasted what may have been the subject of that familiar line I had heard so many times but never thought of before: "It's a gas, man."

They put it in the middle of the rug, inhaled their fill and then let me have some. It was great stuff, to say the least. You can get a mild taste of it from your local dentist if he's hip. It's not paradise, but even with fingers in your mouth and your gums bleeding it can be a moment of bliss, as William James might say, and it wasn't long before we were rolling around the rug and hugging each other, the *I Ching* open to an auspicious page and Harpo raising his eyebrows. It was then that Kesey turned to me and said softly:

—Cosmo, that's your name. The Armenian Cosmo.

It sounded good. I liked it. It had a nice full sound to it. *Cosmo.* Sure, why not?

The tank was not full when we started and we finished it much too soon. Once you start sucking you don't want to stop, and Kesey, to keep the high going I guess, passed around some uppers. I never liked them but I was careless and took one as a gesture of friendliness. Fay happened to return around then and said so and so were waiting in a car for the ride up to San Francisco. I thought it was a private trip and was about to say so-long when Kesey asked me if I wanted to come. Sure, why not, I'd leave my car by McClanahan's and return when I'd return. I was young, I was strong, I could go and do whatever I wanted, right?

We arrived around dusk, which in mid-November must have been just after five o'clock, and we parked by a little church. Why were we going to a little church? Because, Kesey said, his friend and lawyer, an Armenian if I'm not mistaken, had bought this old church and renovated it into a high-class pad. It may have been, Kesey said, an Armenian church.

I was jittery by then. The high from the gas was over and with an empty stomach I couldn't have relaxed even without the dexedrine. There were a bunch of people inside and I was told that some of them were from a new rock group called the Grateful Dead. It felt like an ominous name and seemed to float above the new faces like the tobacco smoke purling in the nacred light of the huge space, everyone hanging around quietly and waiting for the chicken that was frying in the kitchen way back there behind where the altar used to be. Kesey, wanting me to feel at home, touched my shoulder and said he wanted me to meet someone. He said her name was Black Maria and he introduced me as Cosmo. Yes, he took on the role of a paterfamilias, but he sincerely liked people and wished them well. He left me alone with her and mingled with the others.

She must have been in her early twenties then, just a child. But with her long wild hair and her silence she really did seem like a Black Maria and not the young and innocent Jane Doe from an ordinary suburb she had just recently fled. We didn't say much and then the chicken came out, but my stomach was shriveled by now and all I wanted was something to drink. I saw some guys in the corner passing around a big cup and though I figured it was more than tea, what did it matter? I joined the circle and when the cup came to me I finished it, thinking there'd be more. The others looked at me and in my dim memory it seems that one of them may have even said, "Groovy, man."

Meanwhile someone said the Doors were playing in Winterland, neither of which I had ever heard of, and Kesey was calling a Bill Graham to ask if we could all get in. Yes, we could, and so we all piled into the back of a big truck and we were there in a matter of minutes.

As we walked in I asked the Doctor if I could get a ride back to Palo Alto with him later and he said sure, just meet him by this door in the lobby. We walked through the door and Kesey said let's go nearer the stage, but I was starting to feel a little whoozy so I just sat in the last row of seats by the door where I was to meet the Doctor. I'd just sit there, I thought, and observe everything. I was the observer type and this was my first rock concert. The Doors, eh? Why were they called the Doors?

Then I noticed the whoozy feeling was something in particular. What was it? Oh yes, the tea, there was something in the tea. There was something in the tea like those putrid cactus buds way back in the Village. I recognized the same uncoiling flow inside my navel. It reminded me of the slow and mesmeric swirl of tiny bubbles inside those amoebas and cells of grass we once studied in freshman biology. The cactus trip had been mild and thinking it would happen again I decided to just sit back and flow with it. I could handle it, I thought, I could handle anything. I'd just sit there and wait for the Doctor who was going to meet me by the door.

Black Maria came instead. "C'mon," she said. "Let's go join the others." "Oh no," I said very seriously, "I can't." "Why can't you?" she asked, smiling. "Because," I said, and it was then I noticed my hands gripping the seat as if I were on a plane that had suddenly lost a wing, "because . . . because if I leave this seat I'll never get back to Palo Alto." "Oh sure you will," she said. "Why shouldn't you?" "Oh no," I said, and I was gripping with not just my hands but every muscle I could find as if I would unravel into bubbles should I ever let go. "No . . . no, the Doctor said he was going to meet me by this door and take me back to

Palo Alto. I have to get back to Palo Alto." My car, my passport, my typewriter, everything that glued me together was in Palo Alto and if I left that seat I would lose them forever. "Oh, you'll get back to Palo Alto," she said, her voice more and more like a siren's. "Come with me and I'll show you the way." "You will?" I whimpered, and suddenly I was three years old and lost in a sea of alien faces and she might be the great Maria who could lead me home. "Sure I will," she said, and letting go of the seat that was my raft I grabbed her skirt as if it were a lifeline through the maelstrom of the crowd. "Are you sure?" I pleaded. "Are you sure you will show me the way?" "Sure," she said, and looking over her shoulder with a Mona Lisa smile that could have been lethal, her wild hair flowing in the strobes and her eyes like jewels, she said again but now languidly, "Sure, I'll show you the way, and . . .," her voice suddenly selfish and lascivious, "you'll show *me* the way." Oh no, I moaned, she also drank that tea, and I let go of her and fell to the floor with Jim Morrison bellowing in a voice that seemed to echo through the prehistoric mews of an endless labyrinth, "*Show me the way . . .*" yes, yes, show me the way, please show me the way "*to the next whiskey bar . . .*" Oh no, I cried, I would never get back, I would never get back, and it was there on the floor of a former ice rink and now a phantom carnival that this *I* who is typing these words first encountered what could never be expressed in words and is that part of us where we can't hold on any longer nor have any reason to hold on. Yes, there was something in that tea much stronger than a few cactus buds from Smith's Cactus Ranch, something very pure, which was still around in those days, and which, with an empty stomach and some dexedrine, was more than enough to float me through the door and lead me not to Palo Alto but to you know what and if you don't you should. We should all know that place inside us where there is no outside and we're all together in the flesh and blood, yes, this very flesh and blood. Why we ever left it is the great mystery.

But don't misunderstand me, I don't refer the same travel agent. There are different trips and you should have a guide or at least a friend who can stand by so you don't get trampled. Once you're there you're there, but you don't stay there forever, you get up from the floor and if you're three years old again you want to be in a familiar garden, otherwise you're on a bummer, as we used to say.

After the deep crying and the waves of ecstasy *et cetera*, I got up from the floor and had I not resisted losing "my life" I suppose I might have continued through the gates of illumination a while longer. But

I was freaked out, as we say, and the more I resisted the further I went through the other gates where everyone was not only a freak but a possible threat. I knew I drank something but I didn't know if knowing could be trusted. As far as I knew I was not me anymore and I might never be again, I was gone forever and yet I kept struggling to get back, and I mean this physically, with every muscle in my vital centers all struggling to hold myself together lest I dissolve into the overwhelming chaos and the Doors singing, *Light My Fire*. Were you ever lost when you were very small? Do you remember how it felt to panic on an alien planet? Or did you ever go swimming and feel an undertow pull you out where you thrash as hard as you can and yet get no closer to shore? I stood up and searched desperately for some way out or in or back or wherever and suddenly someone like a ghost was saying hello to me. "What are you doing here?" she asked.

It was Marjorie Katcher. Marjorie Katcher was Bill Belli's old girlfriend. In fact I introduced them when she was at Douglass and I was at Rutgers and so forth and so on like buried and hermetic heiroglyphs on a Dead Sea scroll. Bill and I had lost touch with her and now with a face more elastic than flesh she was staring at me and saying, "This is really not the Marjorie you once knew." "It's not?" I asked, taking her more literally than she could have known. "Oh no," she said, "the Marjorie you knew is dead." "She is?" I said, not at all with doubt. "Yes," she said, "I'm reborn now." "Oh," I said, "that's good, that's very good. How did you do it?" "I'm a mother now," she said. "I have a baby daughter." "Oh," I said in despair, "I don't think I can do that." "No," she said, "you can't." "No, I can't," I said, and unable to talk with any logic I wandered off and left her with her daughter on the other side of the universe.

How I got back to the door I don't know and though useless by now it was the only bearing I had. Yet when I walked to the lobby who was suddenly coming in and wearing a Captain Marvel suit?

"Hey, man!" he said. "Good to see you here." It was Ed McClanahan. But not really. The Ed McClanahan I once knew, the one person who was my link back to a face in a mirror, was a jeans-and-flannel young writer with a wife and kids and a warm solid home, not a flashing Captain Marvel suit in a lobby full of beads. Oh no, I moaned, I would never get back, I would never get back.

"What's the matter?" he asked. "Are you all right?" No, I said, I was not all right, and I wandered outside like a street person who's mentally disturbed, as they say, and I would have kept going had he not rescued me. Where would I have gone had he not rescued me? Where was there to go without the ground always tilting? The police? The hospital? Or perhaps a diner or a laundromat? Did you ever see what a city looks like when you have no eyelids? I got a glimpse before he grabbed my arm and led me back.

He understood what was happening. I told him I drank some tea and he knew what was in it. The police didn't know, the hospital didn't know, most of what we called our society didn't know, but there was a growing number who would learn and he was among them, dear Ed McClanahan, who gave up his good time with the gang so he could sit with a lost soul the rest of the night. Where is he now? I just called the English department at Stanford but they didn't know. I haven't seen him in twenty years but I'm still grateful for his kindness. He's out there somewhere, I hope. Someone told me one of his novels was published a while back. I must try and find it.

"Are you sure you're Ed McClanahan?" I kept asking him. Yes, he said, or at least he was the one I needed him to be. Then who was Captain Marvel? Captain Marvel was a little crippled boy who said the magic word and became a god. The magic word. Ah yes, the magic word.

We had come back to Palo Alto but it was not the same of course. We were back with Harpo and the *I Ching* and now I knew what they were trying to say. Now I knew what *far out* meant and *blow your mind*. Now I knew why the Doors were called the *Doors* and why Kesey called me *Cosmo*.

"Are you sure you're Ed McClanahan?" Yes, he was sure and yes, everything would be okay and tomorrow would be the Big Game just like always.

"The Big Game? What Big Game?" The Big Game, I knew what the Big Game was, didn't I? "Sure, I know what the Big Game is. Do you know what the Big Game is?" Yes, he said, but he meant the other one, the Big Game between Stanford and Cal. "Oh, " I said, "they play the Big Game too?"

And so on until dawn, the protoplasmic swirl of galaxies and atoms becoming less and less visible until tables and lamps, Harpos and McClanahans, slowly became solid again, or at least seemed so, and I was back to these fingers that know the alphabet.

The trip was over and I was wiped out, I would never be the same as before. I walked through the door on the porch in the violet glow of dawn and I felt as if . . . no, not *as if*, but that I had actually just returned from a world that is here and now while I am always somewhere else. I felt perhaps a tiny bit of what Helen Keller must have touched when the letters of her first word were spelled on her fingertips. It was the word *water* and it meant life. "I left the well-house eager to learn," she wrote, "and every object which I touched seemed to quiver with life. That was because I saw everything with a strange new sight that had come to me."

A couple weeks later I drove up to Kesey's farm for Thanksgiving. His family just moved in while he was gone. There were other families and friends as well and they were all trying to live together. It was a simple and beautiful scene and not anything like what is in Tom Wolfe's book, which, if I'm not mistaken, was being written at the time. It was quiet and natural and full of earth colors and the odor of wood. They had just built a communal dining hall and it was like a vision to a city boy who had just come from a world of apartments and burglars. The fresh unpainted fir smelled clean and eternal and the long table had just been covered with a kind of resin that preserved inside its amber their photos from the past when they roamed around the country full of youth and hope. Maria was there and she was now just another girl on a farm who wanted to make yoghurt and have kids. I hope she did. Wherever you are, Maria, or whatever your name is now, I wish you well. Everyone wished each other well. We all felt there was so much food and clothing around that all we had to do was share it. Why would anyone want to hoard it? Why would anyone want to live otherwise? I remember asking for the bathroom and I was directed to a room at the side of a barn and walking in I saw a guy on a bowl and a young woman taking a shower. They didn't have such things in London or New York and after I got over the initial surprise I remembered my own childhood where we always left the bathroom door open and when I didn't know I was supposed to close it until I went to someone else's home. It was the tea full of stars that helped us to communal bathrooms, helped to show us that everyone's crap was alike and that no one's was special. I fell in love with that farm up there; it reminded me of a home I had lost and I felt very grateful for sharing all that bread and fresh milk.

Then Neal Cassady came with a few other folk. I didn't know much more about him than that he was Kerouac's pal and I was a little curious. He was in very bad shape and he died not too long afterwards. He was coming down from a lot of speed I was told, and he looked old and decrepit. If he was Kerouac's age he was only about twenty years older than I, or in his forties, my age now. I spent just a few minutes with him but they stuck with me. He was hanging out in the barn and mumbling a bunch of monotony I would have walked away from were he someone else, but I felt a kind of respect and sympathy for where he came from and what he went through. He seemed somehow like one of an Old Guard. He was one of the big guys in that schoolyard that became my hunting ground when I first left my mother's kitchen and wandered into the wilderness of America. He was one of the alumni when I first moved to the Village at the age of nineteen and made friends with other exiles from the wasteland. He was one of those who passed on to us a tradition that went all the way back to young rebels in every age who can't live in America without searching for a way out or in or wherever. And here he was now, mumbling in a boring voice and very close to death. If he ever drank any tea full of stars it didn't seem to lead him to yoga and meditation. It's one thing to see heaven in a flower and another to survive where there are no flowers. Perhaps he died looking for one on a railroad track that kept going.

I drove back to California with a double image of him bobbing nervously by an electric heater and the kids playing outside with a donkey, a sunny landscape all green and sienna and a shivering old soldier who talked to himself. How beautiful the hills were after a rain, how sad and broken he looked.

I stayed in California and took part in that process we call the Sixties, as if it were special and had not been going on forever. And a couple of months later I met Richard Brautigan. I had moved to Bolinas by then.

My new friend, Gatz Hjortsberg, had found me a cheap cabin near his place on the mesa, and his friend, Tom McGuane, lived nearby. But in those days there was hardly anyone else there. You really needed a mate to survive the long rain and grisly fog, and I would drive over the mountain as much as I could. Richard was living in a small apartment in San Francisco and I went to visit him once.

It was a poor writer's apartment, bare and cheap, and though he had girlfriends he lived there alone. "Every once in a while it depresses me," he said, "and then I paint it and it feels like home again." His voice was soft and gentle and his shoulders curved as if he was holding something in his heart that would fall away if he pulled them back. He was about Kesey's age but they were very different. He was very shy and private and yet not at all good at hiding and you could feel his sweetness immediately. Sure, he was sick with selfhood like the rest of us, but he was a very generous and sensitive soul, most good artists are

I think, and with Kesey he is one of the figures who stands tall when I remember twenty years ago and try to sketch how much it meant to me. I didn't know him well either, though years later I would hang out with him some more when he moved to the farmhouse next to Gatz in Montana, but he felt like a brother, and his suicide always hovers in the darkness when I wake at four in the morning and feel so far from home and family.

"You want some lambchop?" he asked me that first time I dropped by. He had just fried some lambchops after writing all day and he was very hungry. I was a meateater in those days and I was very grateful, though he wasn't much of a cook. He wasn't much of anything, I suppose, except a writer. He loved to write, just as Kesey did, though in a very different way. I was very surprised when Gatz told me he never had any acid or even smoked grass. He just tuned in with his own special antennae and was able to transmit that wonderful music which was, beneath the humor, so fresh, delicate, and sincere. He himself was fresh, delicate, and sincere. There were other sides of him, of course, we all have our other sides, but when he was in the spirit of what he loved he was able to gather from the air a certain music that seemed to come through a door from a very special place. And he wanted to share it, freely. Those were the days of the free-box and the Diggers dishing free food in the Panhandle and visions upon visions of everyone living together freely, *from each according to their means, to each according to their needs*, and he stood with his big hat and sloppy mustache and handed out free packets of flower seeds with his poems printed on them and the label: PLANT THIS POEM. Not as a gimmick, not in any way like the stunts performers pull to get attention, but more sincerely and deeply than even he probably realized. He really wanted to believe it was possible; he really wanted his work to plant him in the common earth he felt he had lost.

Then he got famous and that was the beginning of the end. He got famous just about when the flowers got trampled in People's Park and the refugees started pouring in from the murderous suburbs. He was not one who could handle fame and fortune. He never gave interviews, never had anything to do with the media or Hollywood, but America had caught up with him and he could buy as much booze as he wanted. He was drinking hard then. He would get drunk and sit in his kitchen and shoot the clock on his wall. I dropped by one afternoon and when he didn't answer I went to the back and the kitchen door was open. I walked in and the wall and the clock were full of holes like a scene from one of his later books. He wasn't home. He was in his new studio on top of the barn. The valley where he lived was the most beautiful I had ever encountered, and his typewriter was by a wide window that opened to the vast and incredible landscape with the great mountains in the background. He sat there and looked out the window and tried to keep writing but the words didn't come out as they did in that little room on Geary Street that didn't even have a window. I remember talking with him one morning in Gatz's kitchen where he would visit and have a cup of coffee. He had the spread in Montana, a house in Bolinas, a studio in North Beach, but he still kept that bare apartment where he shared his lambchops and his flower seeds. "I don't want to lose touch with it," he said. "It's a part of me I don't want to lose touch with."

He died of "the great American loneliness," someone said after his death, quoting Kerouac or was it Fitzgerald? His father, who had abandoned him at birth, learned of his suicide through the news and remembered he had a son way back in the past. His mother may have disappeared also and he grew up an isolated child, especially during a period when he was very small and got very sick and had to stay in a room by himself.

As I reread *Trout Fishing In America* now, its darkness feels much stronger and therefore its light as well. It is not just an amusing book for the young. The winos, the poor kids, the hermits and the freaks, are not only Richard himself but parts of our America that struggle to survive in the nightmare of our history, and that they do is what makes the book so magical. Like the Kool-Aid wino, it creates its own reality and illuminates itself without sugar because there isn't any sugar to put in it. Richard was no simple-minded naif. He was extremely intelligent and perceptive, perhaps too intelligent and his acute perception too close to paranoia. That he was able to overcome, at least for a while, all those demons I encountered one night in Winterland was a real act of courage and faith. He believed in art so deeply that his belief was able to lead him through the manic crowd and take him back to a Palo Alto where he could survive until dawn. For a while at least. Then came the time, I guess, when there was no Ed McClanahan to rescue him, and he just couldn't do it alone anymore.

Read *Trout Fishing* again now. Read it and think of a little boy locked in a room with no parents around. Read it next to his death. It was written at a time when a flower was able to grow out of all the crap we all had accumulated since childhood, both as a country and as individuals. There were many such flowers, and though they lasted such a very short time they bore many seeds and will grow again someday.

I just came back from a walk in the hills. How beautiful they were just before sundown. Like quiet buffalos tufted with evergreen and glowing around the canyon, their flanks mottled with chaparral and the trail ablaze with lovely college girls jogging in shorts. I climbed to the top and gazed across the bay as the sun sank behind the pylons of the Gate. Then I heard music rising from the stadium below. It was the band practicing their marching songs for the Big Game tomorrow. The sun fell and the clouds took over with their beauty, their copper and ruby all burnished above the Farallons and the Tamalpais range reclining into the bay like a great serpent. Percussion and brass echoed up the redwood grove like atavistic rhythms that would never die, another generation getting ready for the Big Game. The freeway moaned in the distance and the cities spread below like a cancer. I entered my navel through my lungs and imagined how it all might look had I drunk some special kind of tea. They were not really clouds above the horizon and that was not really a bridge. They were the sea breathing and the cable was the smile of Eden, the city of St. Francis a castle across the waves and the island of Alcatraz a prisoner who longed to sail through the Gate. Not as metaphor, not in the mind alone, but in the flesh and blood. Pulsing, streaming, like the metamorphic pods of an eternal amoeba and the tiny bubbles in the cell of a leaf. All those kids driving down to Palo Alto tomorrow and listening to the Doors and the Grateful Dead on their cassettes, a singer bellowing like the ghost of an Indian along the polluted shores of the Peninsula, *Show me the way, oh show me the way.*

■ ■ ■ ■ ■ ■ ■ ■ ■ ■ ■

Two Poems

Terry Adams

WRITING HOME

Much later in basecamp the soldier leans over his letter.
His dogtags let go of his chest,
swing into the air and point down to the words.
                His name,
rank, serial number, and blood type
swing out over the river where he saw the boatman hiding with a rifle
among his family,
in front of the little outboard—
                over this letter which can say nothing
to any woman and child allied with a man
at war—about the enemy
who will shoot,
                who wanted to swing over them on a vine
in a Saturday morning television-jungle,
                on one of those magical arcs allowed by heaven
to the good, the strong, the faithful;
to take them suddenly and politely
away by the waists—
the small pith-helmeted woman and the folded-up child,
before the whole squad saw them.
                The ratcheting
spray of splinters, smoke, and shattered water—
                this letter with the
river running over it
with the words of the river rising
as the squad scrambled down the bank,
to the surface of milky water,
the satiny bubbles of soaked cloth,
suggesting arms, legs.

POINT OF VIEW

They came to me
In a dug-out listening post outside Da Nang,
handed me a green trombone with a rubber eye-piece.
They said Captain from now on
your name is Foxglove, your
social security number is secret.

I pointed the scope into the dark defile,
found three shapes burning amber
beyond the wire. Their hot armpits and crotches winked
as they stepped around the cool vegetation.
Rifles cast infrared
keep-out bars across them.

At ten meters I got them with the muffled
M-16 strapped under the scope.
It sounded like a stifled sneeze.
I looked out again,
one was moving, I fired again—
they were just little, quiet piles of light.

All night as I scanned I saw
the bodies cooling, becoming
smaller, dimmer, the hot head-crowns fading last,
This was the safest

I felt in months. After dawn
I went out there
to tag them. There wasn't a sandal, no
bodies, not a goddamn
fingernail. In my hole

I lit my ration stove, cupped my hands for
warmth, whispered my new name
into the flames which were disappearing
in sunlight.

Group from commune, Ashbury Street, San Francisco, 1968.
(Photograph by Elaine Mayes)

■■■■■■■■■■■
The Counterculture

Jay Stevens

O n October 7, 1966, the day after the California bill criminalizing LSD took effect, a delegation of hippies arrived at San Francisco's City Hall. They carried an offering of morning glory seeds and store-bought mushrooms, which they hoped to use, they told a bemused press corp, to expand the consciousness of Mayor Shelly. They were in the midst of this presentation, which was half loony theatre, half polemic, when a group of antiwar activists, led by Jerry Rubin, arrived to hold their own press conference.

It was a Sixties Rohrschach: on one side of the Hall stood the activists, in work boots and jeans, while across from them were these golden-robed hippies. And in between . . . in between the antagonism was palpable.

T here is no simple way to explain what went on in the Sixties, no easily identifiable event, like the assassination at Sarajevo, which one can point to and say, "there, tensions might have been growing for decades, but that's the spark that touched off the explosion." Indeed, the more thoroughly you study the Sixties, the more comforting becomes a concept like the *zeitgeist*. Strip away the decade's thick impasto of sex, drugs, rebellion, politics, music, and art, and what you find is a restless imperative to change, a "will to change," if you will, and one that could be as explanatory for the latter half of this century as Nietzsche's "will to power" was for the first.

Change jobs, spouses, hairstyles, clothes; change religion, politics, values, even the personality; try everything, experiment constantly, accept nothing as given. It was as though the country as a whole was undergoing a late adolescence, and not just the 20 million Baby Boomers whose leading edge began turning eighteen in 1964. Either that or the Boomers, the largest generation ever, possessed enough mass of their own to alter the normal spin of things.

But alter it in what direction? Somehow the satire of *Mad* magazine and the kinetic electricity of Elvis, the surreal dailyness of Beaver Cleaver and the fear of the Bomb; somehow the awful drabness of Dad in his official corporate uniform, the gray flannel suit, and the awful sameness of the suburbs, those theme parks of the good safe life; somehow all these had combined into a combustible outrage. It was an almost obscene irony, but the kids who had enjoyed the richest, most pampered adolescence in the history of the world had now decided that it was all crap. "We've got so many things we could puke," they said. "We live in the most manipulated society ever created by man."

Since infancy (or so it seemed to the Boomers) their minds had been measured, their psyches sculpted, their emotions straitjacketed, and for what? Why, to preserve the good old Corporate American Way of Life!

The corporations, so omnipotent during the Fifties, were vilified as the source of most of what was wrong with America, whether it was the imperialism that had brought on the Vietnam War or the subtler neurosis that caused people to measure their self-worth in terms of the number and quality of the consumer items they were able to surround themselves with. The same throwaway culture that the parents found convenient and liberating was dismissed by the children as ugly, trashy, and stupid when measured against the ecological cost of living in such a manner.

But the kids also realized that the corporations were only the visible tip of the iceberg, that the real menace was less tangible, although by the late Fifties it already had a number of provocative names: *the military-industrial complex, the power elite, the Garrison Society,* and — the ultimate winner in terms of usage — *the Establishment.*

What these terms attempted to describe was a conspiracy of money and power whose tentacles stretched into every nook and cranny of daily life. Corporations were members of the Establishment. But so were labor unions. Politicians were valued players, of course, but so were teachers, reporters and generals. Republicans and Democrats were merely different frequencies in the Establishment spectrum, while liberalism was nothing more than a clever way of allowing the illusion

122

of change while maintaining the perquisites of power. Uniting these disparate elements was an overt commitment to anti-communism and American hegemony abroad, together with a domestic brand of democracy that sounded more like a well-run corporation than the noble experiment of the Founding Fathers. Instead of "the people," Establishmentarians talked about the managed and the managers, a formula that was not too dissimilar to the one followed in the Establishment's arch-enemy, the USSR.

Reflecting upon this woeful state of affairs, the Baby Boomers decided that not only didn't they want to be managed, but they could do without the occupation of manager as well. Norman Mailer caught their mood exactly when he wrote that "the authority had operated on their brain with commercials, and washed their brain with packaged education, packaged politics. The authority had presented itself as honorable, and it was corrupt, corrupt as payola on television, and scandals concerning the leasing of aviation contracts—the real scandals as everyone was beginning to sense were more intimate and could be found in all the products in all the suburban homes which did not work so well as they should have worked, and broke down too soon for mysterious reasons. The shoddiness was buried deep . . ."

Of course not every Sixties kid accepted this critique. For each one who wanted to seize power, dismantle the Establishment, and redistribute the wealth, there were at least ten others who just wanted to get through school, get laid, get a job, and get out of going to Vietnam; for every kid who grew his hair long, smoked dope, listened to rock music, and proclaimed an urgent longing to make a clean break with American society, there was a corresponding kid who drank beer, worshiped the local football team, and measured his personal worth by the car he drove. The differential between silent majority and noisy minority probably varied little for the kids of the Sixties from that of their parents. But it didn't seem that way, if only because the silent majority is never news. And they are even less so when the *zeitgeist* is changing rapidly.

Compared to the quiescent teens of the Fifties, the Baby Boomers seemed a generation of Jacobins, a rude, unwashed, overeducated mob who, if not precisely endangering the State, certainly threatened one's peace of mind.

One of the difficulties in writing about the Sixties is deciding when the story began. Was it the day President Kennedy was

assassinated in Dallas, a day imprinted on every Baby Boomer the way
Pearl Harbor was for their parents? Kennedy was the Establishment's
best salesman; with programs like the Peace Corp he almost managed
to sell liberalism to the Baby Boomer. But his death left a vacuum that
was soon filled with anger and cynicism.

Or was it during the first freedom marches in Mississippi, when the
kids learned just how loath the Establishment was to extend basic rights
to the Blacks? Reflecting on what had happened to the consciousness of
those kids who went South in the summer of 1964, Michael Novak
later wrote: "Enough young people have been beaten, jailed and even
killed while trying to bring about simple constitutional rights to
American Negroes to have altered the inner life of a generation. The
young do not think of law enforcement as the enforcement of justice;
they have experienced it as the enforcement of injustice."

Or did it begin in the fall of 1964, when a group of Berkeley
students staged a spontaneous sit-in that quickly grew into the Free
Speech Movement?

The seeds of the FSM were sown in early September, when Berkeley
Chancellor Clark Kerr, perhaps acting upon the liberal assumption that
politics in the old sense was dead, banned all politicking outside
Berkeley's main gate on Bancroft Way. For years Bancroft Way had
been an ideological flea market, with groups of every persuasion
soliciting funds and dispersing literature. Although Kerr's decision
drew protests from nearly every student group, from the fledgling
Students for a Democratic Society to Youth for Goldwater, Kerr
refused to relent and in late September suspended eight students for
political activities.

Then, on October 1, a young mathematics graduate student named
Jack Weinberg was arrested for refusing to abandon the table he was
manning for CORE—the Committee on Racial Equality. A campus
squad car was dispatched and when it arrived Weinberg went limp, a
technique he had acquired the previous summer during the freedom
marches in Mississippi. As the security guards dragged him to the car,
an outraged crowd began to form, effectively blocking the exit. For the
next thirty-two hours, speaker after speaker climbed atop the car's
hood, exhorting the students to seize the moment and strike. It was as
though somebody had touched a match to a mood that had been
building for years, not just a few weeks.

I felt "torn open, everything boiling in me," wrote Michael Rossman
in *The Wedding Within The War*, his memoir of the Sixties. A colleague

124

of Weinberg's in the Berkeley mathematics department, and a fellow radical, Rossman described the aftermath of the cop car siege as "the Tearing Loose—the active beginning of the end of my life within the old institutions."

On December 2, 1964, seven hundred members of the Free Speech Movement seized Sproul Hall and held it until they were dragged out singing by hundreds of helmeted riot police. Five days later, an audience of eighteen thousand gathered at Berkeley's Greek Theatre to listen as Clark Kerr poured forth his vision of the true academic community as a "knowledge factory" whose purpose lay in creating socially productive individuals. Now this was the wrong tack to take with students who increasingly resented the factory analogy, but the real mistake came after the speech. As the meeting ended, Mario Savio, a young philosophy major who had become one of the leaders of the FSM, stepped to the rostrum. He intended to invite everyone to a mass rally where Kerr's speech could be debated, but before he could open his mouth to speak he was grabbed by two policemen and wrestled to the floor. A wave of anger swept the crowd. As Godfrey Hodgson later wrote, "one minute Clark Kerr, the champion of liberalism, had been talking about the powers of persuasion against the use of force, and the next moment armed agents of the University were choking his opponent, the symbolic representative of free speech."

The next afternoon the faculty voted 824-115 to accede to the FSM's demands. The Baby Boom had received its first taste of political power.

N ot surprisingly, the facts attending the birth of the FSM were drowned in an ocean of learned speculation, as journalists and political scientists rushed to explain this momentary aberration. Although few of the commentators could see beyond their own ideological categories—Lewis Fuer, a reputed expert in left-wing political phenomena, dismissed the FSM as "intellectual lumpen-proletariats, lumpen beatniks, and lumpen agitators" who espoused a "melange of narcotics, sexual perversion, collegiate Castroism and campus Maoism"— most divined the central theme of the protest, which was a hearty dislike of the liberal ideal of a rationally managed society. It was a revolt against the depersonalization implied by the factory analogy that Kerr was so fond of, which was why the IBM card, with its ubiquitous warning "do not fold, spindle or mutilate," became the symbol of all they despised. Rossman described the target of the FSM as the Big Daddy Complex, which was his name for the species of liberal paternalism that had banished political diversity not only from Bancroft Way, but from the University curriculum as well. The motto of the Big Daddy Complex, he wrote, was the phrase "for your own good," and its "effect is to inhibit autonomous adulthood."

This last was a crucial point: instead of adopting the definition of psychological maturity that the mental health movement had proposed in the Fifties, with its emphasis on conformity and responsibility to the larger ideals of society, the Baby Boomers were moving in the opposite direction. The ability to let go, to explore the depths of one's own psyche, to conform to individual rather than social imperatives—these were the new benchmarks of psychological maturity.

Another element that the commentators completely ignored was the exhilaration that came from collective action. During the fifteen-hour occupation of Sproul Hall, life had been lived in a wholly new key. It was, to bend Maslow's term, a collective peak experience whose import lay not so much in the demands that had brought them together, as in the fact that they *were* together. The protestors had turned Sproul Hall into a carnival, with Chaplin movies on the walls and folksingers in the stairwells. "We ate terrible baloney sandwiches and then established the first Free University, conducting some dozen classes cross-legged atop the Civil Defense disaster drums stored in the basement," remembered Rossman. "People smoked grass in the corners . . . and at least two women had their first full sexual experiences under blankets on the roof, where walkie-talkies were broadcasting news to the outside."

In the months following the seizure of Sproul Hall, the Free Speech Movement evolved into a whole series of Grand Causes, beginning with the Dirty Speech Movement (free speech obviously meant the right to say fuck you) and ending with the first protests against the Vietnam War. Dozens of earnest young politicos flocked to Berkeley to make common cause with the revolution. Typical of the new arrivals was a moustached young Marxist named Jerry Rubin. Although not the first, Rubin was certainly one of the earliest to realize that political organizing—what the establishment always called "outside agitation"—could furnish the basis for an interesting and varied career.

Like Kesey, Jerry Rubin was another of those Fifties teens who had wanted more. "Young kids want to be heroes," he once told *New York Times* reporter Anthony Lukas. "They have an incredible energy and they want to live creative, exciting lives. That's what America tells you to do, you know. The history you learn is hero-oriented: Columbus,

George Washington, Paul Revere, the pioneers, the cowboys. America's promise has been 'Live a heroic life.' But then, when it comes time to make good on its promise, it can't. It turns around and says, 'Oh, you can get good grades, and then get a degree, then get a job in a corporation, and buy a ranch house and be a good consumer.' But kids aren't satisfied with that. They want to be heroes. And if America denies them an opportunity for heroism, they're going to create their own."

Rubin was twenty-six when the FSM provided him with his first taste of heroic action. Having spent the summer in Cuba, Rubin was primed, when the FSM erupted that fall, to see visions of Fidel in Mario Savio. "Like I'd gone to Cuba," he marveled, "and here it was right here." With his fellow organizers, beginning in the spring of 1965 he worked long and hard at building a classic leftist political movement. And by the fall of 1965 their efforts were beginning to pay off. In October they attracted thousands for a proposed march on the Oakland Army Terminal, where an attempt would be made to prevent shipments of war material bound for Vietnam from leaving the port.

But even as it gathered strength, the political protest movement was beginning to fragment. Signs of this appeared at the rallies, where, instead of picket signs and revolutionary slogans, more and more demonstrators carried flowers and balloons, harmonizing on Beatles songs instead of "We Shall Overcome." There was a growing hedonism that didn't jibe with the militant discipline required by previous political vanguards. As Lewis Fuer had observed, there was altogether too much sexual perversion and too many narcotics. To Rossman, it seemed that the energy unleashed at Berkeley was beginning to turn, not right or left, "but into . . . something else, without a name."

An illustration of the forces that were dividing the Baby Boom came during the big October protest. Before setting out for the Oakland harbor, the crowd had been addressed by a number of prominent speakers, Ken Kesey among others. Kesey apparently had been invited on the assumption that the author of *Cuckoo's Nest* had to believe that the Vietnam War was folly. What the organizers of the march hadn't foreseen, however, was that Kesey also thought that marches and speeches about seizing power were equally fallacious.

A few weeks before the march, quite by chance, Kesey had received an insight into the negative side of *Homo gestalt*. It happened during a Beatles concert at San Francisco's Cow Palace. Not only were the Pranksters in attendance, but they were spreading the word that after the concert the Beatles were coming down to La Honda for a "freaking good rout." This wasn't true, of course, but given the Pranksters' record in bending events to their advantage, it wasn't completely untrue either. Who could say whether the psychedelic superheroes could pull the Fab Four into their movie or not; in any case, it was a worthy test of Prankster power.

But then a strange and terrifying thing had occurred. Even before the Beatles appeared on the stage, thousands of teenyboppers had opened their mouths and started to scream, rocking the Cow Palace with a kind of insane animal energy. To Kesey there was nothing mind-expanding about this group mind: in fact the thought that forced its way into his consciousness was cancer! This was *Homo gestalt* about to devour itself. Thoroughly spooked, he had quickly rounded up the Pranksters and had fled back to La Honda.

Standing by the speaker's platform, listening to the yammer of the crowd and the booming oratory of the speakers, Kesey was reminded of his Cow Palace epiphany. When his turn came at the microphone, he bounded onto the stage flanked by a bevy of Day-Glo, guitar-wielding Pranksters. Whipping out a harmonica, he began honking his way through "Home on the Range."

"You're playing their game," he drawled into the microphone. "We've all heard all this and seen all this before, but we keep doing it. . . . I went to see the Beatles last month . . . and I heard twenty thousand girls screaming together at the Beatles . . . and I couldn't hear what they were screaming either. . . . But you don't have to. . . . They're screaming Me! Me! Me! Me! . . . I'm Me! . . . That's the cry of the ego, and that's the cry of this rally! . . . Me! Me! Me! And that's why wars get fought . . . ego . . . because enough people want to scream Pay attention to Me. . . . Yep, you're playing their game."

And then he offered the marchers some advice. "There's only one thing to do," he said between draws on the harmonica. "There's only one thing gonna do any good at all, and that's everybody just look at it, look at the war, and turn your backs and say . . . Fuck it!"

Which is exactly what a lot of kids began doing. And in the process, they also began turning their backs on the political agenda of activists like Rubin and the Students for a Democratic Society (SDS), which was emerging as the most astute and rambunctious of the youth political organizations.

There were quite a few names for these new rebels. They themselves preferred *head* or *freak*, words illustrative of their belief that they represented a new evolutionary branch in the *Homo sapiens* line; Leslie

Fiedler, the literary critic, lobbied for new mutant. But the label that stuck was hippie.

By the end of 1965, the youth protest movement had two symbolic capitals: one was in the Berkeley coffeehouses that lined Telegraph Avenue; the other was across the Bay, in Haight-Ashbury, the birthplace of the hippies.

The word *hippie*, indeed the whole phenomenon of the Haight-Ashbury, first came to light in September 1965, in the course of a *San Francisco Examiner* article about a coffeehouse called the Blue Unicorn.

The Unicorn, which advertised the cheapest food in the city, was a little hole in the wall on Hayes Street, near Golden Gate Park, in the midst of a twenty-five-block district that derived its name from two intersecting streets—Haight Street, which ran in a flat line toward the Pacific Ocean; and Ashbury, a much shorter thoroughfare which climbed up Mt. Sutro and stopped. Like the Unicorn, the Haight-Ashbury was something of a hole-in-the-wall district, full of ornate but shabby Victorian houses dating back to the Teens, when so many politicians had built themselves mansions above Haight Street that the area had been nicknamed "politicians' row."

But in the intervening years the Haight-Ashbury had tumbled so far down the socioeconomic ladder that during World War II it had been considered an appropriate spot for worker housing. After the war refugees from Eastern Europe and a small population of Orientals had tried to resuscitate its former splendor, but when Blacks began moving into the district—encouraged by urban renewal, which was razing their traditional ghetto to the west—these homesteaders had packed up, leaving the Haight in the curious position of offering lavish living for dirt cheap prices. For a few hundred dollars it was possible to rent a whole house, complete with leaded windows and ballroom.

Now it happened that this abandonment coincided with the disintegration of the North Beach Beat scene, due to a combination of rising rents, police harassment, and obnoxious tourists who flocked to see the beatnik in his native habitat. The Haight was an obvious solution, and by the time the *Examiner* tumbled to what was happening, it supported a thriving bohemian community, of which the Unicorn was the heart and soul.

This, then, was the gist of what journalist Michael Fallon had to report to his readers: the Beat movement, far from being dead, was alive and flourishing in what had once been one of San Francisco's tonier neighborhoods. But if the Haight was where the Beat movement had fled to, then something had happened in the passage. Compared to the moody, nihilistic beatniks of old, those clichéd cave creatures in their black turtlenecks, the patrons of the Unicorn were like vivid butterflies in their pink striped pants and Edwardian greatcoats. They were sunny and cheery, and the word *love* punctuated their conversation with alarming frequency: all kinds of love, elevated ethereal love and plain old physical love. And on nights when LEMAR—the acronym for the legalize marijuana movement—wasn't meeting at the Unicorn, the Sexual Freedom League was.

Like any scientist fortunate enough to discover a new class of fauna, Fallon's first instinct was to give it a name, which he did by borrowing Norman Mailer's hipster and contracting it into hippie, a word that caught some of the Unicorn's buoyancy, but one the hippies themselves were never fond of. From their perspective, hippie was just another example of the subtle derogation practiced by the mainstream media whenever it was confronted by something outside its usual ken. Hadn't Fallon's fellow journalist, Herb Caen, done something similar when he tagged Ginsberg & Co. with the diminutive beatnik?

But whether they liked it or not, hippie it was and would be.

Oddly, Fallon's inventiveness later served to obscure the fact that in many respects the hippies were second-generation Beats. This was clearer in the early days, when it was still easy to trace the connection between the old Beat fantasy of creating an alternative culture—the word "counterculture" was still years off—and what was aborning in the Haight. "We have a private revolution going on," wrote Bob Stubbs, the owner of the Unicorn, in one of the policy statements he used to distribute to his customers. "A revolution of individuality and diversity that can only be private. Upon becoming a group movement, such a revolution ends up with imitators rather than participants."

A very private revolution: at the time of Fallon's article, there were probably only a dozen houses scattered throughout the Haight that could have been characterized as hippie. And yet the district pulsed with energy. "Even if you lived elsewhere, your forays to the neighborhood were always important," wrote one frequent visitor. "The Haight-Ashbury had four or five grapevines cooking at all times . . . and the two words that went down the wire most often in those days were *dope* and *revolution*. Our secret formula was grass, LSD, meditation, hot music, consolidation, and a joyous sexuality."

Had you lived in any of those houses in the autumn of 1965, it would have been immediately clear that the key ingredient in that formula, the reason why the Haight was not the North Beach six years later, was LSD. LSD was the Haight's secret weapon, with emphasis on secret. "Taking it was like being in a secret society," remembers one pioneer. "Hardly anything was being said about it publicly . . . [although] not an illegal drug, people acted as if it were. It seemed illegal."

It also seems intensely serious. In the compelling phrase of one hippie, LSD was hard kicks: "hard kicks is a way of looking at your existence, not like mistreating your body or throwing your mind to the crows. It's a way of extending yourself [so that] something spectacular and beautiful can be available to you."

It was axiomatic, in the beginning, that hard kicks were dangerous. They were not a game for the timid or insecure. But insofar as they offered a way out of the white surburban world that so many of the early hippies had been born into, they were worth the risk.

At first the hippies used LSD as a deconditioning agent. This, you may recall, had been William Burroughs's great project, one he had bequeathed to Ginsberg and Kerouac, and one that had become, by the mid-Sixties, part of the Baby Boom's emotional baggage. That American society was manipulative was one of the Haight's basic tenets. LSD put this into perspective, and by doing so (as Leary tirelessly pointed out) it opened up the possibility of reprogramming oneself; using LSD the games could be examined, the defenses leveled, and better strategies adopted.

The word on Haight Street was that a few good acid trips were the equivalent of three years of analysis. But that didn't mean that a few more were the same as six years. You plateaued after a certain number of excursions to the Other World, and at that point the "bad trip" became important. Bad trips, provided they came after an appropriate level of expertise had been obtained, were vital if you were to progress to still higher levels.

According to the hippies, LSD was "one of the best and healthiest tools available" for the examination of consciousness. "Acid opens your door, opens the windows, opens your senses. Opens your beam to the vast possibilities of life, to the glorious indescribable beauty of life." You could "drop down into your unconscious to see the pillars and the roots of the tree which is your personality. . . . You see what your hangups are; you might not ever overcome them but you cope with them, and that's an amazing advance."

The Haight then, in its earliest incarnation, was a kind of sanitarium, an indigenous Baden Baden that offered a therapeutic regime of good vibes and drugs, rather than mountain air and mineral springs.

Which was why the population of the district exploded in early 1966. The catalyst, to the extent that there was just one, was Kesey and the Acid Tests, particularly the Trips Festival, which had been like throwing a switch that sent a surge of energy through the isolated pockets of hipness surrounding the Bay Area. In the course of several impetuous months, Kesey and his Merry Pranksters managed to introduce more people to LSD than all the researchers, the CIA, Sandoz, and Tim Leary combined. Most were college students or ex-students temporarily on the bum until they settled down to a profession. They came to the Trips Festival with their ontological categories intact . . . by the time they left all that remained was a haunting glimpse of the ineffable — the one Leary had given up Harvard to pursue, and Kesey literature. Lacking a Millbrook or a La Honda to flee to, they found their way to the Haight.

By June 1966, an estimated fifteen thousand hippies were living in the Haight, an increase that baffled the hippies about as much as it did everyone else. "God has fingered that little block system between Baker and Stanyon Street," they told the curious. "And we spend all our time, verbally and nonverbally, trying to discover why." Helen Perry, one of the first of the social scientists to arrive on the scene, likened the Haight to "the delta of a river," where all the unrooted sediment of America was washing ashore. But even Perry was unclear as to why the undercurrents of American life should be sweeping so many into this odd backwater. When asked why they had chosen the Haight, the hippies murmured vague things like, "I fell in with some vibrational energies and ended up here."

E ntrepreneurs began refurbishing the abandoned storefronts along Haight Street, opening businesses whose character was apparent in their names: the I-Thou Coffee Shop, the Weed Patch, The Psychedelic Shop. This last, the inspiration of two brothers, Ron and Jay Thelin, was conceived as an information center for the private revolution. The primary focus of the Psychedelic Shop was books — books by Leary and Alpert, by Watts, Huxley, and Hesse, plus a decent selection of Eastern texts. "We went out and asked different friends of ours to compile books that they thought we should have," the Thelins recalled. "It was supposed to be information on dope. It was pro-LSD."

The Thelins, although atypical in that they were natives of San

Francisco, were in most other respects fairly representative of the early hippies: they were children of the middle class, Presbyterians, paperboys, eagle scouts. "I read *Time* magazine when I was in the Army, and I voted for Richard Nixon. I watched TV, and I believed that we were going to legislate equality." For Ron the turning point had come with his discovery of Ginsberg and Kerouac, followed by Thoreau and Alan Watts and, eventually, LSD. For Jay Thelin the transforming event had been a talk by Richard Alpert, during which Alpert had stressed the need for solid information to guide the increasing number of adventurers who were exploring the Other World. After the lecture Jay had persuaded his brother to sell the boat and umbrella business they had been operating in Lake Tahoe, and invest in the Haight.

The Psych Shop had been open only a few days when someone slipped a note under the door: "You're selling out the revolution. You're commercializing it. You're putting it on the market." But the place was an immediate success, socially as well as financially. It rivaled the Unicorn as a hangout and profits were sufficiently high that the Thelins soon expanded, adding a darkened meditation room that became a favorite spot for sexual trysts.

Had you spent a few hours there, eavesdropping upon the conversations, basking in what the sociologists would soon call "the hippie modality," you could have plumbed most of the depths of this odd community. Plumbed them, that is, once you had learned the language.

It is usually forgotten that the psychedelic movement inaugurated one of the great epochs of American slang. Within months a complex argot had developed, most of which had to do with drugs and drug taking, activities for which a private code seemed natural. LSD was acid; a frequent user was an acidhead; a single dose was a hit or a tab. Marijuana was known variously as pot, hemp, hay, grass, reefer, or simply good shit . . . in any case the point was to get high. Getting high at the Fillmore was a groovy (pleasurable) experience, though depending on any number of ancillary factors, it might also turn into a heavy (emotionally fraught) experience, or possibly even a far out one—far out, and its semantic sibling, out of sight, were Edge City words. In those realms things either verged on the cosmic (the very best) or turned into a bummer (the very worst). In any case, it was all Karma (fate) and there was no sense hassling over what was inevitable. That was a game the straights (everyone who wasn't hip) played, all those uptight nine-to-fivers with no appreciation of the Here and Now, so caught up were they in the materialism gig. Ironically, the hippie argot was the one thing the straight world found useful. It wasn't long before Madison Avenue was featuring advertisements for cars and soft drinks with modifiers like "mindblowing" and "far out."

Another thought that would have struck a visitor to the Psych Shop in early 1966 was how esoteric most of the reading was. Among the fiction, Herman Hesse was the obvious best-seller—sales of *A Journey to the East, Steppenwolf,* and *Siddhartha* would make Hesse the largest-selling German author in America by the end of the Sixties, closely followed by the science fiction novels (*Stranger in a Strange Land, Childhood's End,* etc.) that the Pranksters had found so illuminating. Balancing the fiction was a section of technical works on the psychedelic experience, Leary, Huxley, Watts, plus a variety of Eastern and occult texts, ranging from the *Tibetan Book of the Dead* to the *Zohar.*

Aldous Huxley would have been overjoyed at this intermingling of East and West, but he might have been a trifle disturbed at the amount of occult chaff that was getting mixed in with the grains of perennial philosophy. Although Huxley had predicted that LSD would awaken the Baby Boom's slumbering appetite for spiritual meaning, he hadn't anticipated what would happen once this hunger began searching for something to feed upon. In the Haight, the perennial philosophy came heavily spiced with astrology, numerology, alchemy, black magic, voodoo: a crazy quilt of arcane practice and contemporary jargon that affronted the trained Western intellect's need to formalize, to abstract out a workable map from anarchic reality.

Which was entirely appropriate given the hippie's preference for direct experience. Go with the flow, they said, do your own thing. What Neal Cassady had such an abundance of—that ability to be perfectly attuned to the moment—was one of the highest states of grace a hippie could attain. Cassady hadn't written great novels or poems, he wasn't a professor or a scientist; in the normal scheme of things he was a failure; but in the Haight he was respected as a symbol of the balanced man. He was treading the inner path with style and wit, which was all anyone could hope for.

Not that the hippies saw a lot of Cassady; Ginsberg was a much more tangible presence. Rather they absorbed his essential style through the medium of the Pranksters and the Trips Festival. Just as they absorbed Leary and Huxley and Alan Watts, picking up those parts that struck a responsive chord, and dispensing with the rest. When a hippie claimed that "I'm from another race, not black, not white, maybe I'm of a race that's not here yet, a race without a name," what you heard were echoes of Huxley's evolutionary romanticism filtered through the dog-eared science fiction epics that graced every hippie pad. When they talked about life being a series of games and the individual a collection of masks, defenses, and often self-deceptive strategies, the intelligent observer cross-referenced that statement with Tim Leary's transactional psychology—while a descriptive like "hard kicks" was unquestionably a daredevil child of Kesey's can-you-pass-the-Acid-Test perspective.

A diligent dissector could find a bit of all of the above in the hippie habit of replacing baptismal names with newer, psychedelicized handles like Frodo, Chocolate George, the Hun, Coyote. As one hippie explained his own name change: "The Teddybear you see is only a facade. There's another me whose name is Harold. Right now Harold is a very tiny person inside of me, but he's still there. When you come to the Haight, everybody chooses a name and builds a personality to fit it. I built Teddybear, but now I'm starting to lose Teddybear—thank God!—and some day Teddybear will be dead. You come here to change, and I think the ultimate change you come here to find is the 'you' that you imagine and the real 'you' merging into one."

I f, for some reason, the Berkeley activists had chosen one symbol to represent their struggle, they probably would have picked the ubiquitous clenched fist, with its message of angry resistance.

The hippies, on the other hand, dreamed of erecting a statue of St. Francis on the edge of the Haight, an immense figure, carved from a giant redwood, whose outstretched arms would welcome pilgrims to the capital of the New Age.

There was something appropriately medieval about this fantasy—appropriate because to arrive in the Haight-Ashbury during the Summer of Love was not too different from arriving in twelfth-century Paris. There was the same quality of exotic commotion—"That one big street, Haight Street, was just packed with every kind of freak you could imagine . . . guys with mohawk haircuts, people walking around in commodore uniforms"—overlaid by the same overpowering interest in the mystical. "There are at least fifteen hundred saints in the Haight," opined one hippie. "Saints and holymen. I mean they're of all ages and sexes. Some of them are in their seventies and some of them are in their fifteens and some of them are in their cradles." In the local vernacular, these saints were known as "heavy cats."

Daily life in the Haight had a quality of animation that was difficult

Funky Sam, Haight-Ashbury, San Francisco, 1967.
(Photograph by Elaine Mayes)

Krishna group at the beach, San Francisco, 1967.
(Photograph by Elaine Mayes)

to describe, although Leonard Wolf, an English professor at San Francisco State and one of the earliest hippie watchers, came close when he compared it to "an anthill where all the ants are drunk but busy and somehow, when all the tumult has died down, successful." It took a while for the neophyte to understand why the situation was so charged, but eventually it dawned upon them: on any given day roughly half the people in the Haight were either tripping, or had been tripping, or were about to trip.

Everyone, in other words, was living in cosmic time, which was fine if you happened to belong to an ashram or a monastic order. But if you didn't there were certain practical drawbacks to spending several days a week pushing the envelope with LSD. Little things like the problem of holding down a job in order to earn enough money to buy food and pay the rent. Because it was difficult, after an evening of acid, to motivate oneself to rise with the sun and hustle down to the local Food Mart to unpack crates and stick little price tags on cans, the hippies tended toward part-time jobs like delivery boy and messenger. Thus they had to accomplish in two days what most people did in five.

A burst of concentrated activity followed by long stretches of chemical contemplation—that was the hippie ideal. Whenever anyone chided them for their dissolute lifestyle, they would laugh and claim they were a laboratory for what life would be like in the future, once computers and machines had replaced the need to labor.

Everything was pooled—money, food, drugs, living arrangements. The underlying ethic was that the hippies were all members of an extended family, although the preferred word was *tribe*, a sign of their deep admiration for the Native Americans, whom they revered as an example of how the free live.

Your first night in the Haight was usually spent in one of the many communal crashpads, sandwiched together with a dozen friendly strangers. Your inhibitions and frequently your virginity were the first things to go, followed by your clothes and your old values—a progressive shedding that was hastened along by your first acid trip. Within days your past life in Des Moines or Dallas or wherever was as remote as the school outings you took as an adolescent.

When not working or tripping, which was seen as a kind of work, you could probably be found sunbathing in Golden Gate Park or strolling along Haight Street, stopping at the Drugstore for coffee and the Psychedelic Shop for the latest gossip. Every week there were a couple of new stores to investigate, places like the Weed Patch (drug paraphernalia), the Laughing Raccoon Gallery (crafts), the Blushing Peony (funky clothes), the Print Mint (psychedelic posters), and Quasar's Ice Cream (food). And there was always a new band playing at the Fillmore or the Avalon Ballroom. The Fillmore was the inspiration of Bill Graham, the man who had produced Kesey's Trips Festival. Impressed by the amount of money Kesey had generated with little more than a rock band, some slides, and a drug, Graham had rented an abandoned auditorium in the Black Fillmore district and had begun holding rock dances with local bands, many of whom were living in the Haight.

The Charlatans, who were famous for actually having gotten a summer-long gig, occupied a house at 1090 Page, while the Grateful Dead, Kesey's Acid Test band, were householding a few streets away. In time they would be joined by Big Brother and the Holding Company, the Jefferson Airplane, Quicksilver Messenger Service, and numerous other groupings whose musical half life was too brief to register on the historical consciousness, but whose economic contributions to the Haight were invaluable. With their retinue of hangers-on and their ability to generate sizable sums of cash, the rock bands were one of the linchpins of the Haight-Ashbury economy.

But the bands played another, subtler, role in shaping the hippie ethic. It was thought that rock music was the perfect complement to the psychedelic experience. "It engages the entire sensorium, appealing to the intelligence with no interference from the intellect," wrote former Beat novelist turned hippie philosopher, Chester Anderson. "Rock is a tribal phenomenon, immune to definition and other typographical operations, and constitutes what might be called a 20th-century magic."

Dancing to rock music was a perfect illustration of how two people could do their own thing together.

The outside world rarely impinged. And when it did, it only brought further confirmation of the Establishment's Big Daddy Complex, of which the crusade against LSD was a classic example. Judging from the 123 million prescriptions written for tranquilizers and sedatives in 1965, and the 24 million for amphetamines, America loved its mind drugs. It couldn't live without them. And frequently—three thousand overdoses per year—it couldn't live with them. But tranquilizers and sedatives were ruled okay because they damped down the fires of life, they stupefied the mind rather than opening up its glorious, ecstatic (and sometimes dangerous) depths.

Or consider what happened when a group of hippie entrepreneurs tried to join the local business group, the Haight Street Merchants' Association: they were shown the door. Apparently there was no place for a Psychedelic Shop or a Weed Patch within the parameters of conventional capitalism. Undeterred, the hippies quickly formed a rival business group, the Haight Independent Proprietors, a name that owned much of its existence to the fact that it abbreviated into HIP.

But these were just two entries in an enormous ledger of misunderstanding and suspicion. It seemed to the kids that the parents were always saying NO! That everything about them, their hair, their music, their clothes, the way they talked, their heroes, their dreams, all were considered illegitimate by a generation who couldn't stop patting itself on the back over how democratic and liberal it was.

On the other hand, it seemed to the parents that the kids were always saying "fuck you!" That was expressed in everything about them, their hair, their relationships, the clothes they wore, the cars they drove, etc.

This internecine squabble soon became dignified as the Generation Gap, and while the sociologists and psychologists labored mightily to explain its genesis, the kids couldn't have cared less: they wanted to let the chasm widen until there was sufficient space to create their own alternative culture. This, as the Pranksters would have put it, was the ruling fantasy; the only debate was over which direction this emancipation would take. Would the flow favor the activists or the hippies? Or was there a third alternative?

That this was even a matter for debate testifies to how quickly the hippie ethic was spreading. In March 1966, while its medical section was announcing an LSD epidemic, *Time's* cultural pages were reporting on the proliferation of "oddball cult groups"—the word *hippie* having not yet gained currency. Almost overnight, in every major city, a small community of "acidheads" (*Time's* word) had appeared. And while none of these communities equaled the Haight in terms of cohesion or size, all were remarkably similar, filled with colorfully garbed, college educated contemplatives who talked about LSD with the kind of worshipful fervor last heard in the West during the high Middle Ages.

The activists, at first, were contemptuous. But as the private revolution gathered strength, they became alarmed and began to view the hippie as a dangerous usurper, more concerned with "vibes" than Vietnam. "You've got to straighten out your own heads first," went a famous editorial in the hippies' premier newspaper, the San Francisco *Oracle*: "How can we have a groovy, happy society unless everyone has reached his own nirvana?" This was a worthy point certainly, but it was also one of those endlessly debatable chicken and egg propositions. Can a society of individuals heal its own social ills without first addressing its internal flaws? A century of psychological thinking suggested otherwise. As Leary put it: "If all the Negroes and left wing college students in the world had Cadillacs and full control of society, they would still be involved in an anthill social system unless they opened themselves up first."

The activists were unmoved by this line of reasoning. It was too wimpy, too individual, too whimsically religious (groovy nirvana?). "What about India?" was a stock rejoinder, and one that usually silenced the proponents of the karmic path to social healing. In essence this was a disagreement over materialism. The activists wanted to redistribute the wealth until everyone enjoyed a middle-class standard of living; they wanted to hold the liberal ideal's feet to the fire until it came across. But the hippies wanted none of that. They found the rampant materialism of the middle class repugnant. And although they were hazy on what they preferred instead, it certainly had nothing to do with a rising GNP.

So that was the choice — hippie or activist: a contemplative life predicated on the tenuous possibility of enlightenment, or a worthy struggle that would cleanse America of its racist, imperialistic tendencies, and lead to what seemed to be (in the few rare theoretical formulations) a benign socialism. It seemed impossible, to the activists at least, that any educated person could opt for the first course. Yet they were. And in increasing numbers.

What the activists overlooked, what skewed their expectations, was a misunderstanding of the role LSD was playing in redefining the counterculture's thrust. With LSD, exulted Ginsberg, "technology has produced a chemical which catalyzes a consciousness which finds the entire civilization leading up to that pill absurd." If this was true, then the suggestibility of the psychedelic state, which Leary had studied so intently, made it one of the most potent revolutionary tools of all time, far more powerful than the manifestoes and slogans of the political radicals.

Bonding. (Sculpture by Bruce Carter)

■ ■ ■ ■ ■ ■ ■ ■ ■ ■

In-Country

Richard Currey

First look: sandbags and fog. And quiet. As if the fog itself were the carrier of silence easing among us, touching us, loving our faces. Hundred-pound sandbags stacked fifteen high and four deep until life itself was a simple connection between sacks of dirt and the mudhole ring inside them where we talked and ate and slept.

"No, really, man," Linderman told me, talking quietly. "This is what she said. Her exact fucking words. She will wait for me, and there will be no other guys in between. Not unless she gets word I ain't coming back." Linderman looked out on the fog. "God forbid I buy the farm in this shithole."

"You got any smokes?"

He seemed relieved. "Got some Salems. You can cut the filters off if you want."

"No problem."

We crouched behind the sandbags, lit cigarettes where a match flame could not be seen. Against the perimeter, mortar fire started again, booming distantly.

"How many you think's out there in them hills?" Linderman asked me.

I shrugged, flicked an ash. "Captain Bowers heard something like twenty thousand," I said.

"Jesus fucking Christ."

"Maybe more, is what he was saying. Nobody knows for sure."

"You think they mean to overrun us?"

I drew on the cigarette, blowing a mouthful of smoke between us, and said, "So your ladyfriend says she'll wait for you?"

Linderman nodded slowly, looking at me soberly. "That's what she told me," he said.

2

"I had a cat once when I was a kid," Linderman told me. My field glasses were trained into the hills. The shelling had stopped. I saw nothing but the furrowed green textures of mountainside forest. It was nearly six o'clock. Tuesday. An ordinary time in America, I thought: my mother and father sitting down to dinner with my sisters. My older brother and his wife going out for hamburgers.

Linderman said, "Strange how much I loved that cat."

I lowered the field glasses and looked at Linderman. He was crouched inside our sandbag ring, gazing at the ground. I asked him what made him think of his cat.

Linderman shook his head. "I don't know," he said.

I slid to the ground, back against the sandbags.

"The strangest thing," Linderman said, "is that I didn't know how I felt about that cat until it was gone. Then there I was, crying my goddam eyes out, sitting on the edge of the bed when I knew the cat was gone, going crazy my mother told me, pounding the mattress and all."

"Well," I said, "you know, you were a kid. Those kind of things mean a lot when you're a kid."

Linderman looked at his boots.

"So what happened to your cat?"

Linderman shrugged. "Got lost," he told me. "Stolen. Wandered off." He shrugged again.

"Know what I was thinking about?" I said. "I was thinking about how there's no time in this place."

Linderman stared at me.

"Really, it's six o'clock, dinnertime; back home everybody's sitting down to eat. Then they'll watch the news, kick back . . . but they'll know what time it is, where they are, what they're supposed to be doing. Here, it doesn't matter. There's no such thing as time. No beginning, no ending, no in-between. Just living."

"Until we aren't," Linderman said.

I looked at the ground for a moment and then said, softly, "Come on, man."

"Like my old cat. We're all just here until we're not here anymore, right?"

"Hey," I said, "you don't know about your cat. You say he just wandered off. Took a walk. Went to the Bahamas."

Linderman nodded. "That's what we ought to do. Walk away from this shit."

"You know, Linderman, you're forgetting Sergeant Queen's cardinal rule."

"Yeah?"

"Rule number one: nobody dies. You remember?"

Linderman laughed quietly. "Fucking Queen," he said.

"He told me that when I came on board. He said maybe some people go away, disappear, you don't see them around anymore, but nobody ever dies. Everybody's somewhere."

Linderman looking at the ground, still laughing, and I smiled too, and I said, "Now, really, Corporal Linderman, you got to remember Queen's rule."

When Linderman looked up at me laughing, his eyes were lit with tears. He said, "OK, nobody dies. Not even cats."

I grinned. "Absolutely," I said.

3

You got a girl back in the world?
The oldest opener, a man heard it everywhere in-country. Some carried wallet-size pictures or graduation shots. Some told stories of how fine it was or was going to be. I had a picture but never showed it to anyone. I used to believe the energy of our every moment—Mary's and mine—lived in that picture of her face, every touch we shared, every private murmur. I had decided it was a charm. My personal good-luck piece. If anybody looked at that picture, if I was casual with it, my protection would be lost. A magic at risk. That's how I felt.

Those were the early days in-country. I became less dramatic as time passed. The picture of Mary finally disintegrated in my always-wet hip pocket. I went for it one day, it came out in pieces.

4

"**S**o anyway," Linderman was saying, "we go in this liquor store, it's maybe like two in the morning, all-night liquor store, right? So you know, we're just kids, out on the night and messing around, not a goddam thing to do, and we're thinking we need something to drink. I mean, we've already polished off a couple bottles of Mad Dog Twenty-Twenty between the three of us and we're drunk enough anyways. For kids anyways. And anyway there's only one of us eighteen, old enough to buy a bottle, right? So me and Jackie Franco, we're both underage, we're in this store and our buddy, the guy that's eighteen, he's a little behind us, locking the car or something, right? So we're just looking around, you know, I mean, what do we know from liquor? Store full of the shit and we're probably gonna buy a couple pints of Thunderbird or something, but anyway we're just walking around, talking, bullshitting, and the guy at the counter asks us, you know, big voice, full of authority, *Can I help you boys?* So Jackie shrugs, waves his hand at the door, says something like we're waiting for a friend. So the guy running the place, old Italian guy, bald head except for these two or three hairs he's got combed down into place, he says *Well you can do your waiting somewheres else.* And Jackie says But our buddy's coming right in, he's right behind us. And the old Italian guy says *This look like the goddam bus station? Go wait somewhere else.* Well, I guess we don't move fast enough—I mean, I can see Bobby coming across the lot, he's almost at the door—and the old wop, you ready for this? The old fart pulls a gun on us! No shit. He's got a pistol out and holding it on us and he's saying how we better walk and all, and he's nervous as shit, you know, and about this time Bobby hits the door and stands there a minute, looking at all this, then he says, What the hell is going on? But the old wop is worked up now, he tells us to take a fucking walk, and Bobby goes straight over to the old guy—Bobby was always one real cool son of a bitch—and puts his face up real close to the gun. You know, I'm thinking, Jesus Christ, Bobby! but he's looking at that gun and then he looks at us and then he looks back at the old guy and he starts laughing! And I don't know what the fuck is going on, right? And Bobby says Hey guys, know what? This gun here probably cost about a dollar ninety-eight down to the toy store. And the old guy lets the gun drop, looking disgusted as all get out, and me and Jackie go up there and sure enough. Fucking thing's a toy! Old dude's gonna blow us out of the store with a toy gun. Can you believe that? You know, though, funny thing, we got to be good friends with that old guy. I mean, we ended up going in there all the time, he got all our Saturday night business, we were always laughing, jiving him, you know, about that little toy pistol. He made us promise never to tell anyone, though. Said he'd had to use it a time or two, said it worked both times. So, you know, we said Hey, no problem, right? The secret rests with us. Swear to God. Turns out this guy has a heart attack one night when someone really did rob the place. Weird thing. He was probably going for his toy but was so goddam scared his heart went out on him. He was old and all, but still, weird kind of thing. We missed him. We all went to his funeral up to Little Shepherd. I still think about him, you know? I mean, here I am, corporal in the crotch, and these guns I'm packing sure ain't no goddam toys and if we're stuck in this motherfucking valley much longer I'll probably get so old I'll die of a heart attack too. You know, that old guy was always giving me a load of shit about the nobility of the armed forces, the importance of sacrifice, of serving your country, all that shit. Man, if he only knew. If he only fucking knew."

5

The tent flap lifted from outside. The MP came in, watching us and saying, "You cocksuckers got nothin' but cake."

Howard continued to lay down cards. I was in a hammock to the rear with a month-old *Time* reading how Jackie Onassis was harassed by an enterprising photographer always trying to catch her in the bathroom or sunning in the nude.

The MP turned and said on the way out, "You boys got a shipment."

Howard stood, stretched, picked up his coffee cup, and started for the flap. "You coming?" he called back, so I swung out of the hammock and followed.

Howard stood with the MP at the rear of a military police van. "Check out this shit," he said to me.

"Musta run over a mine," the MP said. "You shoulda seen the jeep." I climbed into the van: shoveled bodies like piles of old hose. One Vietnamese man, a prisoner, had lost his right arm and his pants. A sergeant looked like he was sleeping. A decapitated lieutenant's head had rolled to the front of the van where it stuck, looking at me. "Let's move this inside," I called out, my voice clouding in front of me, and I leaned for support and my hand went through the sergeant's shirt into

his gut that was still warm and the darkness of him froze around my
hand, jerking awake from a nightmare, pushing my arm out, into the
night, folding back a sleeve to reach blind into black, acidic water, his
body talking between my fingers, sending one short gut moan for the
bad light the explosion let in, and I lifted my hand out covered with his
blood and shit.

I looked at Howard. It was raining into his coffee cup, coffee
splashing to his thumb and wrist. "Man," the MP said, "you shoulda
seen that jeep."

6

Lifting off from near Hue, Wednesday dawn. I was born on a
Wednesday, this time of day, laborers rolling to catch the alarm,
blinking in the sudden vacant spot of the bedside lamp.

There is a recurring notion of violin music in the dark. I can't trace
it: a thread of what's recalled or forgotten. Looking at everything I can
see: sun rising out of the Pacific, transcendental magenta and scarlet,
rain forest rowing north into a settled haze and mountain, mythological,
azure and green. Me at the open port of a helicopter dreaming the view
of more than one river at once.

7

The hamlet was ordinary enough, kids chasing us for candy and
powdered chocolate and cigarettes, their parents silhouetted by the
half dark of doorways. Near the end of the hamlet an old woman was
squatting with a skinny, panting dog. We were nearly by when she
spoke, Vietnamese, to no one in particular. The lieutenant looked back,
around the edge of the column to see the woman, then halted the
platoon. He walked within a few feet of her. She did not move.

The lieutenant abruptly shouted "VC?" She stared at his face.

The lieutenant called Corporal Howard out; Howard knew some
Vietnamese. He leaned close to Howard, an illusion of secrets. "Did you
hear what she said, corporal?" Howard looked at the old woman and
did not answer. The lieutenant asked again, louder, more authority,
"What she say, Corporal Howard?" I watched a spider touch its way
along the sill of the hootch doorway behind the old woman. She

squatted and stared at the bridge of the lieutenant's nose.

"Well, sir," Howard said. "She called us . . . uh, dogs, something like that. Maybe like go to hell, something like that."

"Yeah, well." The lieutenant nodded. "You ask her what she knows about Charlie." The lieutenant spit Texas-style, turned sideways looking into the distance, job delegated. Howard hesitated, said something to the woman, and she broke a semi-toothed betel-nut grin. Then she laughed, full-throated, head back.

The lieutenant studied her, reached to unbuckle his holster flap. "Perhaps an understanding can be arrived at," he said, "as to just who the dogs are." He withdrew the .45, clicked the safety off. The blood drained away from my eyes: I stepped toward him, slowly, called his name as calmly as I could. He was leveling the pistol, aiming. He spoke as quietly as I did: "Back in formation, soldier."

Holding the pistol in both hands, arm's length, he fired.

The dog's head turned inside out, splashing the woman, its body bursting like a dropped sack.

8

Dear Mary,
I am enclosing a photograph of myself. The dark stains on my shirt are mostly sweat, a little blood. Not my own, so not to worry. The chain around my neck carries the St. Christopher medal you sent me: even though I am not religious its power seems immense. I wear it with the embossed tags that will identify me in the event of my death.

Please excuse my lack of expression. Forgive the look of fatigue and dull hatred you see in my eyes. *The thousand-yard stare* somebody here called it, and I thought I didn't know what that meant, but here it is, reaching back in my eyes.

The weapon in my right hand is a pirated Ithaca Magnum-10 shotgun, gas-operated, semi-automatic, a full-choke barrel sawed down to ten inches for ease in single-hand handling at close quarters. It was captured from a North Vietnamese officer, later presented to me as a gift.

The bulge in my left hip pocket is a soggy paperback edition of the poems of Emily Dickinson.

Such things live together here, poetry and shotguns. Alive and well in a single body.

The photograph is candid and was not taken with my permission, but once given to me its silence loomed. I send it on not to frighten or disturb but to confirm my existence beyond the transience of my words.

All my love.

9

Memory rode out of its past like a killer on the run, the trance for hire, blues in half tones sung against morning's first light. I would wake to a hand reaching toward me in front of a whispered voice I could not quite hear, and it never mattered if it was only a dream or real as waking up with a start in the warehouse of the night, alive in the jungle mind, light leaking through the seams. I would run my hand across my head, feeling the feel of my body after most of the night on the ground, and morning's first light was always gray before it was blue; the platoon would be up, spitting, blowing noses. I was reasonably good at heating C-rats without burning them: stirred water into the blank pudding of canned ham-and-eggs, turned it to muck, dumped in some of the hot sauce my mother airmailed me, kept it all over low flame. The lieutenant would already be moving through the platoon, general harassment. Part of a lieutenant's job, Sergeant Queen always said.

Got an onion out of the gas-mask bag I kept them in, chopped a little into the heating ham-and-eggs. I traded the mask for onions in a hamlet we patrolled. After a while nobody gave a shit for their protective gear.

10

The little Vietnamese man shadowed the hootch doorway, walked carefully out into a circle of sun, arms straight up. The little man held his arms up and looked at his feet and stood in the circle of sun.

There was a slow wind, birds clacking, monkeys cawing, the wrapped surrender of the little man in his halo.

One soldier spilled a plate of food screaming *Goddammit, hold it!* the little man's feet clearing earth, one arm laid out in the air, chest jerking perforations, body sailing backward, falling in the shadow of his doorway.

The lieutenant jogged around a corner and up to the hootch. "Nice work," he said. "This little bastard is no doubt VC. Gotta be. Write it up, Gunny."

The lieutenant dragged the little man back into the sun circle, kicked the turned-out corpse like he was checking a tire. He opened his Swiss Army knife, sawed off the man's left ear. Blood squirt. "Son of a bitch," he said into the dead face. The lieutenant stood up, called out, "Which one of you good buddies got a camera?"

11

Hey, kid, how about this postcard? Thought you might like a look at the old town right about now. Where the hell are you? Sorry I didn't see you before you left. Hot as Hades here but what's new about that? Not enough rain and the Ohio farmers bitching about profits down and how they can't make their tractor payments—same old story. Mainly want to say sorry we didn't get together before you left and we will when you get back and you're not forgotten here with us. Your grandma sends all her love and BE CAREFUL. Can't say it enough. Don't get much room to write on these things do you? Love, Grandad.

12

Field-stripping weapons: cleaning our pieces, Queen taking down his M-14 as I spread my pistol in parts on a canvas ground cloth, an AMT Combat Government model, .45 caliber semi-automatic: 7-shot clip, 5-inch barrel. All stainless steel construction, target trigger, adjustable combat sights and less than two pounds. I traded a half kilo of marijuana for the gun from an armory sergeant in Pleiku. Queen admired the pistol, more elegant than standard issue, and I offered to sell it to him; shit, I don't need it I told him, grinning. And he laughed, saying, You might, bro, you just might. Tell you what, he said, we get outta here in one piece, that little gun'll be mine. Deal, I told him. When we get outta here.

13

Six months into the tour Private First Class Clovis Taggett of Simpson, Arkansas, shot and killed an old woman advancing into a paddy. Nobody actually saw him fire. We were eating under a copse of

151

banyan, dropped to the ground and saw Taggett on the lip of the dike, lone figure standing black against the sunlight. His rifle was still poised.

The old woman continued to advance, moving away from us. Her arms went up, a hallelujah gesture, and she fell face first into the water. The splash shone brilliant in the light. She was about forty yards out.

"The enemy," Taggett said flatly. "Trying to escape."

"Jesus," the lieutenant said. "Eat your goddam lunch. We're mounting out in fifteen."

Taggett slung his piece, wandered back to the group, sat down and slumped against an exposed tree root. The lieutenant, crouched beside me, resumed his lunch. I looked at Taggett a moment before I turned and said to the lieutenant, "He's lost it. He just snapped."

"Happens all the time, man," the lieutenant said around a mouthful of beans. "You've been here long enough to know that."

I looked again at Taggett, who was staring at the ground, empty-faced. "We gotta get him out of here," I told the lieutenant. "He's a medevac."

"He'll be all right," the lieutenant said.

I took a long breath. "The guy's shooting old women for laughs," I said, "and you're telling me he'll be all right."

The lieutenant looked up at me, letting his spoon drop into the bean can. "He'll *be* all right, man. So give it a rest." He frowned at me before going back to eating. I turned back to Taggett, still sitting on the tree root, looking like a moody child. I stood and threw what was left of my rations into the dirt, kicking dust over the moist mound. Out in the paddy on the surface of the water shining in sunlight the old woman's corpse was adrift. A boy was shouting at her, and began to wade out.

14

Monsoon. Rain five weeks, complete in itself. Nothing beyond it, dreams locked in water. Deadfall from flat sky, constant hiss into mud and drum against tents. Four-thirty a.m. A thickness washing the chest and legs for days.

Mud-suck boots onto elevated wood-slat platform of chow tent. Bare hanging light bulbs. Ambulance driver sitting alone at a bench, mug of coffee cooling as he paged through a glossy magazine. Only a few others in line for the powdered eggs and cold, undercooked bacon. Water seeping into the boards, mildew eating canvas. I sat down across from the driver. At one page he turned the magazine around for me to see. A young girl, maybe fifteen, squatting in full-page color. Her breasts were new and her smile was a benign yearbook grin. She was holding a foot-long dildo in one hand, fingering herself with the other.

He pulled the magazine back and continued flipping pages. He showed me the cover: two teenagers in a sixty-nine with black flags covering the important places. He finished the cold coffee and rolled the magazine into a hip pocket and stomped out.

A chopper came down into the LZ, rotors cutting a space in the rain. The weight that started in my stomach grew in my lungs like a tide.

Contact near Fire Base Louise, no survivors. We bagged the captain and the legless corporal and called Motor T to get the bodies to Graves. I went out behind the tent, feeling it all in slow motion. I was forgetting every detail, could not remember my name. Nausea swam behind my ribs and I could not remember my name.

15

Queen said, "The man has got to go."

We were in a bunker, sharing a joint on a wind-locked night.

I said, "You out of your mind or what? That's called murder where I come from."

Queen rolled his eyes, drawing in a lungful, holding, swallowing smoke, blowing it out through clenched teeth, talking with the smoke. "What you think we be doing, my man, all day every day? That just a popgun you packing?" He spit a seed on the concrete floor, handed me the joint. An ember flew, flared an arc. "Besides," Queen went on, "that dude gonna get us all wasted anyway."

"What I'm saying," I said, "is there's one thing and there's another. And you're talking about the other."

Queen looked at me red-eyed and said, "What I'm saying is I'm gonna blow that peckerwood into China. He be arriving in Peking in small pieces."

Queen and I sat, alone in the bunker, looking at each other, looking. A rain began to spatter, into the mud, hissing. Then the full roar of downpour.

"I mean it, man," Queen said.

"Let it go," I said.

"New guys get you killed, bro."

I studied the glow of the joint between my thumb and finger, and I said, "Let's just hit him over the head when he gets out of hand."

Queen began to laugh.

And I began to laugh. And we laughed and I dropped the joint as I tried to pass it back to Queen, watching Queen howl as the rain roared against the bunker and into the jungle as we rolled on the concrete floor gasping, short of breath and wasted, two soldiers afraid for their lives and laughing.

16

Months passed before the second card from my grandfather. The picture side depicted the gleaming suspension bridge that could be seen from his kitchen windows, CARTER RIGNEY BRIDGE, AN ENGINEERING TRIUMPH, with the message below the legend, six weeks out of date.

My grandmother was dead.

Killed when the car she was riding in — driven by her youngest daughter — left the road near Salem, West Virginia, and slammed into the side of Big Harper Mountain. My grandfather went through the details like a newscaster.

I sat against a sandbag retaining wall, turning the postcard to the picture side, back to the message side. Read it again. Queen sat a few feet away, opening a package from his mother, no shirt and black skin glistening in the open sun.

"My grandmother's been killed," I said.

Queen looked up, studying me. "I'm sorry to hear, man," he said. He studied a moment longer, and said, "I really am. You close to her?"

"Car wreck," I murmured.

"Goddam cars, man." Queen shook his head. "Put away more people than we do in this piss-ant war."

I felt remote, too small for the sky.

"You wanna be left alone or anything?"

"I'm OK," I said. "Gotta be, right?"

Queen said, "I guess."

I asked Queen what his mother had sent him, and he went back to his package.

Eight months in-country. Five to go.

17

Dear Mary,
Coming down the road in the fog and everyone here is a ghost,
changed by mist and a haze of rain, and I think of coming back to this
valley ten years from now, twenty years from now, seeing the past I
belong to: we will all be here still, in this moment we must live and
keep living, walking down the road talking, laughing, complaining,
wishing, finding the way to a latrine, to a card game, to the mail drop.
Hearing, out of sight, the sounds of other conversations, of weapons
being cleaned, keep engines idling and waiting for officers moving from
one useless briefing to another. It will be like it is now, walking down
the road with the rest, except I will seem more real, I will hear the
inside of my heart moving, the rush of blood through the chambers of
my heart. I will remember the smell of this rain as clearly as I am
breathing it now: this is the way it is with ghosts. We look at our own
hands and even in this fog we are real as ever, veins branching, tendons
rising and moving, fingers clenching and spreading and feeling, simply
alive with a whisper of rain and the hours rolled into a map.

18

Night patrol, in a hamlet marked Blueville 5 on military topographical
maps. The platoon securing a village supposedly a VC stronghold.
I was holding in a cleared area with the rest of the unit closing down
around me, my partner gone to pull his radio off the command jeep,
and I leaned against a grass bale hearing pigs root and grunt from some
other part of the settlement, hearing the voices of women, children
crying, soldiers shouting. Across from my position the open door of a
hootch gaped black and I heard movement in the doorway, a soft
scraping. I could see nothing. I felt for my flashlight, remembered I left
it with my pack next to the radio on the command jeep, and there was
another noise, a dry click. I called my partner's name, and again a
sound in the doorway, the scratch of footfall on straw, unmistakable.
There was no cover around me. The jungle a few yards to my rear. I
called for help, going to one knee saying to the doorway, in English,
Anyone there? My voice was a horrified rasp, barely audible, the sound
of it frightening me more than I already was. I unholstered my service
pistol, released the safety, thinking I could turn into the jungle and

cover the doorway until the platoon swept this far in another thirty seconds. Then I thought: Unless that is what is expected of me, and I brought the pistol up in both hands, elbows locked, and said, in Vietnamese as I was trained to do, *Identify yourself or I will shoot.*

Silence. Another rustle in the doorway. Silence.

I fired the pistol into the center of the darkness, the powder burst sparking a clean light that seemed to arc forward from the barrel's tip and back in again. There was the .45's short open roar, echo crushing in behind it, empty air sucked into the vacuum. A fire team was suddenly all around me, submachine guns trained and flamethrowers cocked. The lieutenant turned a high-intensity beam into the doorway, and I saw the man.

He was blown off his feet by the blast and his body was in the distinctive scarecrow disarray that instant death brings. I was still on one knee ten yards from the doorway, and I stood and walked to the body. A Vietnamese man, my age or younger, unarmed, alone, with nothing on but his traditional black silk pants.

I had shot him in the face.

■■■■■■■■■■■

The Vietnam War—Tet

David Caute

TET

South Vietnam, January 30-31, 1968—National Liberation Front (Vietcong) guerrillas, supported by conventional forces from North Vietnam, launch a massive offensive to mark Tet, the Vietnamese New Year. Thirty-six of forty-four provincial towns come under attack. Fierce fighting extends from Da Nang in the north through the Central Highlands to Can Tho in the Mekong Delta. North Vietnamese regulars bombard their way into the ancient city of Hue, at terrible cost to its inhabitants. In Saigon, Vietcong guerrillas penetrate the U.S. embassy; the press carries pictures of American soldiers lying dead within the compound.

On the day the Tet offensive was launched, Defense Secretary Robert McNamara reported to the Senate Armed Services Committee that Vietcong "combat efficiency and morale" were falling. But now fierce fighting extended along a 600-mile front and communist tanks appeared at Langvei, sending South Vietnamese forces and civilian refugees in flight to the American base at Khe Sanh. Here they were disarmed, refused shelter, and driven away. Colonel Lownds, the commander at Khe Sanh, told Newbold Noyes of the *Washington Star*: "This thing can come back to haunt me—all of us. If these people say when the chips were down, after getting us to fight for you, you wouldn't protect them, then the whole civic action business here goes down the drain." Despite the jumbled pronouns, the colonel clearly believed that the South Vietnamese had been fighting for the Americans.

Between January 29 and February 1—four days—the American forces suffered 281 dead and 1,195 wounded. The South Vietnamese dead during the same period numbered 632. The Pentagon lacquered the coffins by announcing that the Communist offensive had been a complete failure. A few weeks later Clark Clifford replaced McNamara as defense secretary, and an additional 10,500 troops were rushed to Vietnam, bringing the American military contingent there to over half a million.

Massive slaughter took place in the ancient city of Hue as it was stormed by the Vietcong and North Vietnamese, then slowly recaptured, inch by inch, by the Americans. According to Gabriel Kolko, American air strikes reduced 80 percent of the city to rubble. The Americans pounded the area around the Citadel to dust with air strikes, napalm runs, artillery, and naval gunfire. By early March at least 1,000 civilians had died, and unburied bodies sprawled on the banks of the Perfume River. Thousands of refugees were in flight from the battle zones. Fires raged in the Cholon district of Saigon. Even Under Secretary of the U.S. Air Force Townsend Hoopes was appalled by the American military response. In Saigon, artillery and air strikes were repeatedly used against densely populated areas of the city. According to Hoopes, on February 7, at least 1,000 civilians were killed and 1,500 wounded in an effort to dislodge 2,500 Vietcong from Ben Tre.

The secretary-general of the United Nations, U Thant, continued to press for a halt to the bombing of North Vietnam. But Lyndon Johnson was adamant. Either Hanoi must suffer the fury of the most powerful nation on earth or it must accept the "San Antonio formula," the president's four conditions for a cease-fire. The Communists would never agree to one of those conditions: that the National Liberation Front evacuate the 20 percent of South Vietnam it currently controlled.

But the American public was deeply shaken, and confidence in the president plummeted. Simultaneously a gold and dollar crisis preoccupied the administration and made it impossible for Johnson to grant the Pentagon's demand for 206,000 more men in Vietnam. The Tet offensive also unleashed the greatest wave of anti-American feeling around the world ever experienced.

THE WAR

The greatest evil of the age was the Vietnam War. Many other furies surfaced in the late Sixties, but it was the systematic destruction of a people and its habitat, the moral collusion of European governments, which "overdetermined" the fusion of other angers, political and cultural, into the international insurrection which is our subject.

The Vietnam War received media coverage more extensive and more intense than any in history. This was the first television war. Reporters from all over the world swarmed in. The army laid on facility trips like a travel bureau. The open society offered an open war—but not quite. Eighteen months elapsed between the massacre at My Lai in March 1968 and its exposure.

The draft brought the war home to the United States, but the impact was primarily moral. Revulsion and rebellion most affected the young members of the social class least affected by the draft. As David Tuck, a black soldier who had served in Vietnam with the 3rd Brigade of the 25th Infantry Division from January 1966 to February 1967, told the Russell War Crimes Tribunal, "In my particular outfit 117 out of 156 were black soldiers. It is a common practice to put the people whom they consider expendable in the infantry. This is (sic) the black soldiers, the Puerto Ricans and the hillbillies." Although the Black Panthers denounced the war, it was not a major issue in the ghettos; indeed, many young blacks volunteered as an escape from poverty.

The absolute necessity and virtue of the global struggle against communism had been planted so deep in the American psyche during the late 1940s and the 1950s that it required a new, disenchanted generation to unravel the surreal logic of fighting totalitarianism by supporting corrupt dictatorships, of combating "aggression" by massive displays of firepower across vast empires of indirect rule. A generation determined to disbelieve the claims of corporate liberalism found itself psychologically incapable of confronting the totalitarian nature of Vietnamese communism, and the repressive facets of Third World liberation movements in general.

France's desperate attempt to retain possession of her Indo-Chinese colony had been increasingly underwritten by the Eisenhower-Dulles administration. However, military disaster finally forced France to the conference table. On May 7, 1954, Dien Bien Phu fell to the Vietminh, who now controlled about three-quarters of the country. Negotiations took place at Geneva from May to July. The Vietnamese Communist delegation called for early, nationwide elections, but the Soviet Union pressed its ally to make concessions—the most fatal one being the provisional zonal demarcation of Vietnam along the 17th Parallel. Thus were born "North" and "South" Vietnam, although the final Declaration of the Conference, issued on July 21, 1954, stressed that "the military

159

demarcation line is provisional and should not in any way be interpreted
as constituting a political or territorial boundary." Indeed, to
consolidate the unity of Vietnam it was agreed that "general elections
be held in July 1956, under the supervision of an international control
commission." The authorities of the two zones, North and South, were
to begin consultations about the elections on July 20, 1955.

In January 1955, the Democratic Republic of Vietnam, led by
President Ho Chi Minh, began pressing for the scheduled joint
elections. In July the American secretary of state, John Foster Dulles,
responded: Neither the United States nor the government of Ngo Dinh
Diem in the South had signed the Geneva Accords or was bound by it.
Dulles claimed that the United States was "not afraid at all of elections,
provided they are held under conditions of genuine freedom . . . " Diem
organized a fraudulent referendum in the South, installed himself as
president, and set about liquidating the pro-Communist National
Liberation Front, whose leader, Nguyen Huu Tho, was imprisoned.
The British and French washed their hands of responsibility and refused
Hanoi's repeated demands for a reconvened Geneva Conference.

Despite Dulles's denial, Washington was, indeed, afraid of nationwide elections. According to President Eisenhower himself, "I have
never talked or corresponded with a person knowledgeable in Indo-
Chinese affairs who did not agree that had elections been held (in
1956). . . possibly 80 percent of the people would have voted for the
communist Ho Chi Minh." The president had explained his position to
a conference of state governors, in Seattle, on August 4, 1953: "Let us
assume we lose Indo-China. . . . The tin and tungsten that we so greatly
value from that area would cease coming. . . . So when the United
States votes 400 million dollars to help that war, we are not voting a
give-away program. We are voting for the cheapest way (to protect) . . .
our security, our power and ability to get certain things we need from
the riches of the Indo-Chinese territory and from Southeast Asia."

By 1958 there were an estimated 40,000 political prisoners in
Diem's jails; by the end of 1961, 150,000. The arrival of the Kennedy
administration in Washington accelerated, rather than reduced,
America's commitment. Meanwhile Roman Catholics, fleeing from
persecution in the North, flowed south.

The NLF proposed a five-point program: independence, democracy,
peace, neutrality, and reunification. But how could the last two items be
reconciled? Interviewing Nguyen Van Tien, chief of the permanent
delegation of the NLF in Hanoi, early in 1967, the radical American

writer John Gerassi asked him, "how he envisaged the 'reunification' of a neutral part of the country with a Communist part." The reply was hardly convincing: "By keeping each section independent in policy but united in a federation. The body at the top will sit over both regimes. Whether it will be an assembly or council or whatever will be discussed later, that is after the reunification. . . . This general policy of ours has been approved by the Government of the North. . . . Each section (of Vietnam) will be independent internally . . ."

Washington and Saigon both knew that a unified Vietnam would be a Communist Vietnam. Determined to thwart this denouement, Kennedy and Johnson poured in aid, advisers, and troops. In March 1962, American troops became engaged in combat with Vietcong guerrillas for the first time. By December 1965, there were at least fourteen major U.S. air bases in Vietnam and 166,000 troops; a year later the manpower had more than doubled.

The policy of removing the rural population from its normal habitat to deprive the guerrillas of support had been practiced by the British in Malaya. It was repeated with new zeal, and on a vaster scale, in Vietnam. Early in 1962, Operation Sunrise was launched with the aim of razing villages and regrouping entire populations. By 1967, the NLF claimed that 14 million inhabitants had been forcibly evacuated into 17,000 concentration camps.

The Diem regime, meanwhile, had fallen to a military coup in October 1963. Diem's personal corruption, his policy of repression, his persecution of the Buddhists, the failure of the strategic hamlet program, and the incompetence of his drafted troops, had all combined to precipitate a crisis and the first of a succession of coups perpetrated by the power-hungry warlords of the South. On December 20, 1964, yet another coup took place in Saigon. By January 1965, the desertion rate within the South Vietnamese army reached 30 percent among draftees within six weeks of induction, and a large proportion of the remainder would not fight. In 1967, Lt.-General Nguyen Van Thieu was confirmed as president of South Vietnam by virtually meaningless elections.

The Johnson administration propounded the "domino" theory; Defense Secretary Robert McNamara described Vietnam as "a major test of communism's new strategy" of local revolution which, if not foiled, might be extended rapidly from one country to the next. Secretary of State Dean Rusk repeated the warning. The logic of this philosophy, and of Washington's claim that South Vietnam was the victim of "external aggression," dictated a major escalation of the war:

the bombing of North Vietnam.

(But "external" aggression? We might imagine that the British had sent in troops to support the Confederate states during the American Civil War. Union troops had moved across the Mason-Dixon line in support of guerrillas loyal to the Union: London had then accused President Lincoln and General Grant—that is, Ho Chi Minh and General Giap—of "external aggression.")

On August 4, 1964, Johnson announced that North Vietnamese torpedo boats had wantonly attacked the U.S. destroyer *Maddox* in the international waters of the Bay of Tonkin; in reprisal he had ordered the bombing of the North Vietnamese installations supporting the torpedo boats. The following day the president requested, and promptly was granted, a congressional resolution authorizing him to take all necessary action "to protect our Armed Forces." Jet planes of the U.S. Seventh Fleet strafed and bombed a number of targets north of the 17th Parallel. The truth of the matter, however, emerged later: on the 30th of July, South Vietnamese patrol boats, protected by the *Maddox*, had raided North Vietnamese fishing vessels and bombarded two islands.

The systematic bombing of North Vietnam began in February 1965, shortly after Lyndon Johnson, the "peace candidate," had won a landslide victory over his hawkish Republican opponent, Barry Goldwater. The major cities of Hanoi and Haiphong were now targeted, the Pentagon insisting that only "military targets" were hit. The distinguished correspondent Harrison Salisbury, of the *New York Times*, personally observed that a significant portion of Nam Dinh had been destroyed: ". . . intensive destruction of civilian housing and ordinary business streets . . . an appearance familiar to anyone who saw blitzed London, devastated Berlin and Warsaw, or smashed Soviet cities like Stalingrad and Kharkov."

In January 1967, John Gerassi visited Nam Dinh. En route he passed through Phu Ly, which "used to be a throbbing little agricultural and artefact centre, a provincial headquarters with 7,600 inhabitants. Today it has none. It used to have 1,230 houses. Today it has 245, and they have been abandoned." The Americans claimed that the town was a rallying point for supplies going south to the NLF. Twelve miles from the sea, and connected to it by small canals and feeder rivers crammed with junks and sampans, lay Phat Dam, a town of 5,700 inhabitants, 4,200 of them Roman Catholic. According to Gerassi's North Vietnamese hosts, Phat Dam had been bombed fifty-seven times between March 1965 and January 1967. On Sunday April 24, 1966, seventy-two

American troops battle with North Vietnamese at Khe Sanh
during the Tet offensive, 1968.
(Photograph by Robert Ellison)

American infantryman
crossing a river in Ia Drang
Valley, Vietnam, 1967.
(Unclassified by USAPA,
photographer unknown)

163

people were killed when bombs struck the church of St. Francis Xavier while mass was in progress.

Prominent among the targets of the American bombers were the dikes, extending for 4,000 kilometers and performing a vital role in the rice-growing economy on the alluvial flats of the Red, Chu, Ma, and Ca rivers. The Russell Tribunal's Second Japanese Investigation Team provided a long, detailed catalogue of bombing attacks on specific dikes and on the teams repairing them. Fragmentation bombs designed to kill or injure human beings were regularly employed. Napalm caused ghastly injuries.

But the suffering of the South was even greater. Nguyen Van Dong of the NLF told the Russell Tribunal that, "Up to 1965, twenty-six out of forty-three provinces in South Vietnam have been submitted to raids which used toxic chemicals. Seven hundred thousand hectares of fields and forests have been devastated, 146,274 persons have been poisoned." A particularly devastating weapon was napalm, a jelly obtained from the salts of aluminum, palmitic or other fatty acids, and naphthenate acids. The acids give a viscous consistency to gasoline so that a highly incendiary jelly results. In 1967, forty-nine members of International Voluntary Services, all of whom had worked in South Vietnam, wrote to Johnson describing the war as "an overwhelming atrocity." They referred to "the free strike zones, the refugees, the spraying of herbicide on crops, the napalm . . . the deserted villages, the sterile valleys, the forests with huge swathes cut out." They spoke of refugees "forcibly resettled, landless, in isolated desolate places which are turned into colonies of mendicants."

Two American reporters, Orville and Jonathan Schell, reported a visit to Quang Ngai Province. "We flew daily with the Forward Air Control. What we saw was a province utterly destroyed. In August 1967, during Operation Benton, the 'pacification' camps became so full that Army units were ordered not to 'generate' any more refugees. . . . Every civilian on the ground was assumed to be the enemy by the pilots by nature of living in Quang Ngai, which was largely a fire-free zone. . . . Village after village was destroyed from the air. . . . Air strikes on civilians became a matter of routine . . ."

The Russell Tribunal heard the testimony of Americans who had fought in the war. The Vietnam veteran David Tuck claimed he had seen a prisoner thrown out of a helicopter, and many others casually executed: ". . . it was the standard policy in my outfit not to take any prisoners" unless they happened to be Vietcong officers. Ears were commonly cut from the dead and collected as trophies. Tuck also described the phenomenon of "the mad minute" when unlimited firepower would be poured into a village.

Another young witness before the Tribunal was Peter Martinsen, who had trained as an interrogator at the Fort Holabird Army Intelligence School in Maryland before being posted to Vietnam in September 1966. Attached to the 541st Military Intelligence detachment (11th Armored Cavalry Regiment), Martinsen described how in November 1966 he interrogated and tortured a prisoner in Long Giao camp, and another such incident in May 1967 during Operation Manhattan, a few kilometers from a Michelin plantation. American officers, said Martinsen, were well aware of the brutal methods used during interrogations, but normally kept out of the way: "I had the man dig his own grave with a gun at his head. . . . I counted off the minutes. . . . I counted them off in Vietnamese so he knew I wasn't kidding. He broke down and cried. . . . I described what death he was going to have. . . . This is what is known as 'breaking the prisoner.'" Electrical torture had been standard for a time, "but was not common towards the end of our assignment." Although Martinsen concluded by reaffirming his own opposition to Communism—"Of course, the Tribunal will be used for Communist propaganda"—he nevertheless wanted to inform his fellow countrymen that "war causes war crimes"— crimes committed by "Mrs. Jones's son down the street."

The last words belonged to President Lyndon Johnson, obsessed by the fear that if he got out of Vietnam he would be judged

> . . . a coward. An unmanly man. A man without a spine. Oh, I could see it coming, all right. Every night when I fell asleep I could see myself tied to the ground in the middle of a long, open space. In the distance I could hear the voices of thousands of people. They were all shouting at me and running toward me: "Coward! Traitor! Weakling!"

Evidently those large ears had closed out "Murderer!"

165

Police assault demonstrator, Democratic Convention, 1968.
(Photograph by Duane Hall)

■■■■■■■■■■■

The Streets of Chicago: 1968

Tom Hayden

I t was Saturday morning, August 24, one day before the official opening of the convention. I was sleeping late. The bedroom door opened. Drowsily, I saw a naked woman, who had risen earlier. Maybe she'll come back to bed, I was thinking, when she said quietly:

"There's a man outside with a gun."

Well. No need for coffee now. She went back to observe him through the front-room curtains while I dressed and composed a plan. Grabbing an apple, I jumped out the kitchen window of the apartment building in Hyde Park, ran several blocks, and hopped the El train to Chicago's Loop. There I made my way through thick crowds of shoppers to our Mobilization offices, high in an office building on South Dearborn.

When I left the elevator at the floor of our office, there was a beefy, casually dressed man with crossed arms, menacing eyes, and greased hair standing against the wall. A hit man, I thought, and quickly entered the office. Rennie was there already and asked, smiling, "Have you met yours yet?" He had first encountered the man now outside the office door on his apartment steps that morning.

Our two plainclothes tails were Chicago police officers named Ralph Bell and Frank Riggio, although they never introduced themselves formally. They were assigned to follow up at the fairly claustrophobic distance of about ten feet wherever we went. We went to the bathroom; they followed. We went to lunch; they sat glowering at the next table. We drove to a meeting; they lurched behind in their car.

When close enough, they made remarks about "getting" us, or "arresting you every time you're in the streets." The larger of them, Bell, had a real habit of losing his temper, getting wild-eyed, moving close, and threatening to do away with me on the spot. A phone call notified us that Jerry and Abbie were being followed too.

If this is a preview, I thought, we are not going to be free to meet or plan, and we will be lucky to survive. The week's events were grim already; now we were being followed by characters usually found in cheap movies about the Soviet Union.

By the afternoon, more and more demonstrators were arriving, filling Lincoln Park, getting to know each other, looking over maps of the city, taking down the phone number for legal aid, mainly waiting apprehensively for some direction. As night fell, the Yippies, who had nominated a live pig for president the day before on a platform of "garbage," were urging compliance with the eleven p.m. curfew. Allen Ginsberg, chanting *om*, believed he could calm the tension with the police. At eleven p.m. promptly, the police surged through the park on motorcycle and foot, removing a few hundred people but with minimal arrests.

As the delegates arrived in their hotels the following day, the twenty-fifth, we felt that the curtain of uncertainty caused by the lack of permits had to be pulled back and tested in daylight. With Rennie carrying a bullhorn and taking the lead, we marched from Lincoln Park all the way to the Loop's hotels— without incident. However, uniformed and plainclothes officers, including Bell and Riggio, strode beside us all the way, quarreling over the details of the route, until we reached Grant Park, across from the Conrad Hilton Hotel, where we dispersed. We were pleased, but no more certain of where the police would draw the line.

Lincoln Park is always dark, but it was absolutely eerie, filled with the silhouettes of young dropouts, militant protesters, McCarthy volunteers, voyeurs, and undercover agents. This would be the night, I sensed, that the battle for Lincoln Park could get out of hand. The convention was beginning the next morning, most of the protesters had arrived, and the police would try to establish dominance. An anticipation of police harassment held the people together, allowing them to forget the relatively low turnout of a thousand or more. If the police had done nothing, the protest might have fizzled, directionless. But it wasn't to be.

On and off during the past two days I had lost my police tails, only to have them show up at the next place or event where they expected me. Tonight they found me in the park and began glaring from behind trees as I wandered through the crowd. If there was going to be a confrontation at eleven, I knew that Rennie and I would not survive it one minute if we were closely tailed. I also knew that I would get little sleep unless I could get away from these pursuers to a safe and quiet apartment for the rest of the night.

A plan took shape: Bell and Riggio had driven their unmarked car into the park before following us on foot. If a tire was deflated, they could be stopped cold. With mingled friends providing protection, I stepped out of sight, circled the park, and approached the darkened car. An accomplice named Wolfe Lowenthal took most of the air out of one tire when Bell and Riggio suddenly appeared out of the trees, saw Wolfe at work, and quickly grabbed him. I ran up, and they turned on me, holding me against the vehicle, trying to shove me inside. What saved me from taking a very rough ride in that unmarked car was a crowd that quickly gathered around the officers, chanting, "Let him go, let him go!" Bell and Riggio, sensing their loss of control, backed away. When I last looked back, they were stooped over fixing their rear tire.

The police waited until an hour past eleven to enforce the curfew that night, then swept Lincoln Park with clouds of tear gas. Our precautions for the gas attack were minor; people were instructed to cover their faces with Vaseline and soaking handkerchiefs or towels, even the sleeves of their shirts if necessary. But the gas cannisters did their job, turning the balmy night air into a jolting, choking, inescapable darkness. It was as if someone held me down and stuffed pepper in my mouth, nose, and eyes. The impact made everyone gradually give way, screaming at the police or throwing rocks at their shotguns, then running blindly in whatever direction promised relief from the clouds of gas. The streets around the park were jammed for hours, as the citizens of Chicago began to feel the presence of confrontation for the first time. Some motorists shouted their sympathy, but most were enraged at the tie-up or immobilized at the sight of police weaving on foot between cars, clubbing longhairs into the pavements. The police also unleashed a volley of hate toward the press, beating many reporters and photographers who were wearing their press badges and attempting to cover the melee.

Temporarily free of Bell and Riggio, I slept a few hours on the couch of Vivian and Richie Rothstein's apartment. The next day, Monday, the twenty-sixth, the convention began formally. McCarthy supporters and dissident Democrats now held out no hope for derailing Humphrey, who, in addition to restating his allegiance to Johnson's policies, was making obsequious statements of support for the Chicago police. The only hope remaining to the progressive delegates calling for an open convention was a Vietnam peace plank they sought to add to the Democratic platform. The platform committee's draft endorsed Johnson's policies, however, despite the fact that a 53 percent majority of Americans in the Gallup poll now thought the war was a "mistake," up from 25 percent two years before. The alternative peace plank, calling for cessation of the bombing of North Vietnam, a mutual troop withdrawal from South Vietnam, and a coalition government in Saigon, would have a lot of delegate appeal, I thought. It would also bring Lyndon Johnson all the way from the Pedernales River if necessary to crush it. "He called me at the convention, where I was with my antiwar friends," Doris Kearns remembered. "He wanted to come, was planning to come. He went on for fifteen minutes about how the country was rejecting him."

I went to Lincoln Park for a meeting of our marshals early that afternoon. Since it appeared that the police would continue their gassing, clubbing, and arrests to drive us away from the convention areas, we needed an emergency response plan. Our exhausted medical volunteers were working on the injured and supplying crucial advice on coping with tear gas. How could we keep the police from arresting them? Our legal teams were similarly swamped, between bailing people out of jail all night and taking down endless affidavits against police brutality. They were frustrated on many levels, for example, by the police practice of covering their identifying badges with tape before the clubbing began. Virtually all communication with city officials, police commanders, and Justice Department liaisons was over.

As we contemplated what to do, I noticed a police wagon and a second vehicle bouncing straight over the grass, coming our way, pulling to a stop less than a hundred feet from us. After a moment, Bell and Riggio, backed by several uniformed and club-wielding officers, jumped out. There was no escape, so I simply said to the marshals, "I'm going to be arrested right now." The officers grabbed me by the arms and marched me into the wagon along with Wolfe Lowenthal, and we took off on a bumpy and rapid ride downtown while a surprised and angry crowd gathered in our way on the grass.

"I oughta kill you right now," Riggio said as we rode in the cramped back compartment of the van. He was nervously dragging on a cigarette and staring at me as if I were an animal. I concentrated on what to do if he starting carrying out his threat. "But you're gonna get it. You're gonna get federal charges and go away for a long time." There it is, I thought. He's already been given the big picture by someone. And this is only day one of Convention Week. They jailed me downtown. Several stories below me I could hear marchers shouting, "Free Hayden!" Another demonstration had been permitted, I happily thought. The rules were changing by the moment. I rested quietly in my cell, trying to plan how I was going to make it through this week on the streets outside. My thinking was interrupted by a jailer who unlocked the cell door, informing me that I was bailed out.

Relieved that it was not yet dark, I quickly left the station—only to discover a new man with a gun leaning against the wall of the precinct. As I groaned to myself, he said, "Well, I've finally caught up with you." He was the original tail, who had waited outside my apartment Saturday morning. I didn't catch his name, but he was indistinguishable from the others, a nastiness seething from and marring his ethnic working-class face. He sauntered close behind me as I looked for Rennie to get a report on the day's events and the night's expected chaos. We reconnected, were surprisingly able to lose my newest tail in the Chicago traffic, and decided to cruise by Lincoln Park as curfew neared.

The second night was worse than the first. In addition to the heavy gas, the police fired salvos of blanks from shotguns at the crowd in Lincoln Park. Allen Ginsberg and his friends seemed to think they could blissfully vibrate the violence away, and I'm sure he was disappointed that so many of us were consumed with what he considered negative energy. At the time I thought, however, that Ginsberg was crazy, sitting lotuslike in the grass, eyes closed, chanting *om* over and over while the police lines tightened. I didn't think our bad karma was particularly responsible for what was happening. In retrospect, I can see now that my own hostility was partly self-fulfilling, but it was also an honest response to being choked by the gas, to doubling up with pain, to crawling or running for safety, and to rubbing blood, dirt, and tear gas into one's eyes.

The scene was totally surreal, a cultural war between thousands of police and protesters just blocks, even doors, away from the exclusive Gold Coast section of Chicago, where the affluent citizens went about their "normal" lives, trusting the police to keep their existence sanitized. It was crazier still in the Loop, where convention delegates wearing straw Humphrey hats, festooned with candidate buttons, were partying in the lounges just a sidewalk away from the police lines and the ominous darkness of Grant Park.

I was watching the delegates return from the amphitheater to the Conrad Hilton about midnight, when I encountered Jack Newfield, Geoff Cowan, and Paul Gorman, the McCarthy speech writer. They described how Hubert Humphrey that night had cemented his pact with the southern Democrats against the antiwar liberals in pushing for the status quo platform plank on Vietnam. I tried to explain how insane it was in the streets, but it was as if we were in two worlds, invisible to each other. They invited me into the Hilton, where they had rooms. I got as far as the revolving door, where a hotel officer held out his arm. "We don't want this man in here," he said. Bemused, my friends started arguing that I was their guest. I became jittery. Just across Michigan Avenue a line of police was confronting a new crowd of demonstrators. Suddenly, Riggio appeared at the edge of our circle, smoking a cigarette, staring at me, his boots pawing the ground. "Forget it," I said and started to cross the street, careful to move away from the confrontation brewing in the park.

Suddenly I felt the hint of a tornado over my right shoulder. Out of nowhere came Bell, charging like a linebacker, crashing both of us to the street, beating my head, dragging me through the kicking boots of other police, twisting my arm in a karate hold, and slamming me into a police car.

It was just after midnight, and I was going back to jail for a second time.

The atmosphere in the detention room was ugly. I noticed among the thirty or so prisoners the faces of many younger SDS members—Bill Ayers of Ann Arbor, Terry Robbins of Cleveland, Jeff Jones from the Columbus strike—who had worked in civil rights and community projects. Whereas my first taste of violence in the South allowed me to *hope* for a response from the national government, their introduction to mindless sadism was coming at the convention of the Democratic party and Johnson administration. In two years, several of them would decide to form the Weatherman Underground and engage in offensive violence. Tonight they were sprawled on the floor, nursing cuts and bruises, listening to raging officers call them scum and threaten to beat them to death. Fortunately, Newfield, Geoff's brother, Paul Cowan, and Jim Ridgeway, all writers for *The Village Voice*, followed me to police headquarters and, after two hours, bailed me out. When I left the jail, it was three or four in the morning, and with my friends I walked the streets trying to get my bearings. It was no time to be arrested again, and I wondered where I could be safe. As Newfield later recalled that night, "Almost every noise was martial: fire sirens, the squawking of two-way radios, cop cars racing from place to place, the idle chatter of police on duty." I felt naked. I could not be me, not on the streets of Chicago.

As we wandered down the street, several prostitutes approached us, asking if we wanted sex. They were black, well dressed, and wore pink sunglasses and large McCarthy-for-President buttons. "No thanks," I said politely. "I just got out of jail."

"You did?" the lady replied. "So did we."

I grabbed a taxi to the *Ramparts* magazine office, where they published a daily "wall poster" on the convention. They would be up all night, and I could find sanctuary, coffee, a couch, and contemplate a solution to my problem.

Late the next afternoon, Tuesday the twenty-seventh, a new Tom Hayden appeared on the streets. Behind the fake beard, sunglasses, neckbeads, and yellow-brimmed hat which I alternated with a football helmet, no one knew me. A friend procured a variety of disguise materials from a stagecrafts store, and by dusk I was ready to rejoin people in the streets. My friends didn't know me until they heard my voice. To others, I looked like an undercover cop or random weirdo. I strolled right by the police. Bell and Riggio were hopelessly lost.

That night, the Unbirthday Party for LBJ was held in the Coliseum, a peaceful sanctuary for bringing together the whole coalition. There were bruised faces and bandaged heads, diehard McCarthy volunteers, the tattered and tired and tenacious listening to Phil Ochs singing "I Ain't a'Marchin' Anymore" and "The War Is Over." At the chorus, somebody lit and raised a match in the darkened theater. Somebody else. And another. Ten. Fifty. Five hundred. A candlelight chorus, everyone singing, crying, standing, raising fists, reaching delirium at the words, "Even treason might be worth a try / The country is too young to die."

T he reformist spirit of the civil rights movement, withered and repressed, had turned into the hardened rhetoric of the Black Panther party, whose chairman, Bobby Seale, flew in from Oakland to address the crowd in Lincoln Park the next day. The Panthers were the living incarnation of Frantz Fanon's "revolutionary native" for whom the acceptance of violence was a purifying step toward self-respect. Formed in late 1966, they carried out the call of Malcolm X for armed self-defense. Like Malcolm, they were street people, "brothers off the block," channeling the chaotic rage into armed street patrols, a newspaper that reached 200,000 people weekly, a children's breakfast program, and a support network that enjoyed massive backing in black communities, especially among young people. Their founder, Huey P. Newton, was a mythic figure on the streets of Oakland; he was imprisoned for a gun battle in late October 1967 that left one Oakland policeman dead, another seriously wounded, and Huey shot in the stomach. Yet because of the Panther presence, Oakland was one of the few black ghettos that never erupted in spontaneous violence in the late Sixties. Even two days after the murder of Martin Luther King, when a Panther named "Little Bobby" Hutton was shot and killed while surrendering to Oakland police along with Eldridge Cleaver, the community remained still. Because of this focus on an almost military discipline, the Panthers initially considered the Yippies foolish anarchists and urged their members to stay away from Chicago during the convention. But under the lyrical spell of Eldridge Cleaver, a convicted rapist whose *Soul on Ice* was a nationwide best seller, the Panthers began to reconsider their stand on Chicago, embracing the notion that a cultural rebelliousness among young white people was a necessary prelude to their becoming real revolutionaries.

Seale flew in to endorse the Chicago demonstrations in the middle of the week. While only there a few hours, he gave a speech rich enough in violent metaphors to lead to his indictment a year later. Cleaver was launching a symbolic presidential campaign with the help of the white members of the Peace and Freedom Party, appealing to the Yippie constituency for his white support. Jerry Rubin eagerly endorsed Seale's remarks about "roasting pigs."

It must have been a truly disorienting sight for the undercover agents: a stern Black Panther in beret and black leather jacket boasting of the necessity of "picking up the gun," together with a hairy Yippie dressed, I recall, in love beads and plastic bandolier. It is a measure of the alienation of the times that what seem now to be caricatures of rebellion could have been taken seriously, but they were. The black underclass was connecting with overprivileged whites in a strange and explosive alliance of resentment and guilt. It was deadly serious, especially to Rubin's personal bodyguard, one of several undercover agents posing as Panthers and the Yippies in the crowd.

Though nothing happened after Seale's appearance, it was only a matter of several hours before the nightly ritual of battle resumed. This time a group of ministers held a vigil around a large wooden cross they carried into Lincoln Park. Over a thousand people sang the "Battle Hymn of the Republic," "Onward, Christian Soldiers," and "America the

Beautiful" before a huge city truck began gassing them more heavily than the previous night. In addition, our medical stations were overrun and smashed, and numerous reporters were again beaten badly. Again the nearby streets were choked with running figures, with rocks, bottles, and police batons everywhere in the air. From Lincoln Park, we began trotting in twos and threes southward, over the several bridges on the way to the Loop and Grant Park, where the delegates were returning from the convention. I remember running the several miles fearing that the police would order the drawbridges lifted to cut us off.

Once outside the Hilton Hotel, we took a dual approach to the returning Democratic delegates. For the most part, we tried chanting "Join us, join us." A number of them actually did, especially as the week went on. But for the LBJ-Humphrey delegates, drinking nightly in the bars, filled with alcoholic disgust for hippies, we had another approach. They became the targets of our secret guerrilla-theater unit, a small group with the goal of exposing, surprising, and confronting delegates with the need to take sides. Mainly women, they dressed smartly and strolled through security lines without incident. Kathy Boudin and Cathy Wilkerson used lipstick to scrawl *VIETNAMESE ARE DYING* on the mirrors in ladies' rooms, and spray painted *CIA* in huge red letters outside an office we believed to be the agency's local headquarters. Connie Brown and Corrina Fales, another former NCUP staffer, along with Kathy, dropped stink bombs in the Go-Go Lounge of the Palmer House, by dipping facial tissues into butyric acid, a chemical that smelled like rotten eggs. Connie, not a very good criminal, was caught red-handed by a security guard. "I don't know what you're talking about," she protested to the guard. But she couldn't explain the foul-smelling odor coming from her purse. She was hustled away; feeling sorry for her, Corinna and Kathy turned themselves in as well. The three were thrown into cells filled with black lesbians and told by furious Chicago police that they would be jailed for twenty years. Kathy was particularly worried because she was planning to enter law school. Months after, on the advice of her father, noted attorney Leonard Boudin, the three pled guilty to malicious destruction of property and served no time. They became "unindicted co-conspirators" in the Chicago conspiracy trial one year later. Kathy never attended law school; two years later she joined the Weather underground, and in 1984, she pleaded guilty to second-degree murder and armed robbery and was sentenced to twenty years to life.

There were far worse ideas circulating spontaneously. For a friend of mine from the New York Motherfuckers, who threw a sharp-edged ashtray at the faces of the police, yelling, "Here goes a provocateur action," this was the apocalypse. Another proclaimed to anyone listening, "You're not a free person until the pig has taken your honkie blood!" At one point I even prepared a tape to be played and amplified from inside the Hilton to embarrass the police into thinking I had penetrated their thick lines. The tape ended by calling on the protesters to "join me." Wiser and more cautious heads decided to throw the tape away before anyone tried to follow me. It was difficult not to be immersed in a frenzy.

About two a.m., the police commander curiously announced on a bullhorn that we could stay in Grant Park overnight, provided we were peaceful. A triumphant cheer of relief went up, and the tension was transformed into a more idyllic collective experience. People were lying on the comfortable grass singing protest songs with Peter, Paul and Mary, the floodlit Hilton in the background. At moments like these, it was perfectly clear how peacefully the protests of Convention Week might have gone.

But suddenly at three a.m., the reason for the relaxed police behavior became stunningly apparent. Down Michigan Avenue in complete battle preparedness came the first units of the National Guard. Not only did they bear M-1 rifles, mounted machine guns, and gas masks, but they were accompanied by vehicles we'd never seen before, jeeps with giant screens of barbed wire attached to their front bumpers, which we came to call "Daley dozers." They abruptly took positions in front of us, menacing but making no move. A few protesters started shouting, "Chicago is Prague!"

While the extreme tension continued, many of our people could take it no more and began lying down on the grass or in sleeping bags to rest before the sun came up. I became worried, as did our marshals, that a preemptive mass street arrest might be launched by the Guard, sweeping us off these streets as the very day of Humphrey's nomination dawned. I took a bullhorn and told everybody to go home. Then I left quickly to get a few hours' sleep myself before the most critical day of the convention.

That night the police carried their vendetta against the media onto the convention floor, where a security officer slugged Dan Rather. On national television, Rather said, "This is the kind of thing going on outside the hall. This is the first time we've had it happen inside the hall. I'm sorry to be out of breath, but somebody belted me in the stomach." Walter Cronkite added, " I think we've got a bunch of thugs here, Dan."

I was exhausted. I asked Bob Ross, who also lived in the Kimbark building, if he would stay with me in the streets the next night. After being arrested and hunted, I told him that I was worried about what the police might do if they caught me again.

With little or no rest, our leadership met the next morning— Wednesday, August 28, the day of Hubert Humphrey's ascension to the presidential nomination and the day long anticipated as the showdown between the protesters and official powers.

Dave, Rennie, and I led a meeting in the empty, gray, paper-littered Mobe office. John Froines attended, as did Irv Bock, an undercover agent from the Chicago Police Department posing as the representative of the Chicago Peace Council. Irv was one of the week's marshals, a big, strong fellow who claimed to have time off from his job with American Airlines. He was suspicious since he didn't fit the stereotype of a protester, but at this point his presence didn't bother us; we had nothing to hide now. Though weary and strained, we had to decide the most crucial questions of the week. Even if the demonstrations were mainly spontaneous, we had the heavy duty of calling the actions, setting the time and place, communicating with the police and press, and making sure that medical and legal help was available.

The dilemmas before us that morning arose from the physical impossibility of achieving our long-standing goal of reaching the amphitheater, about ten miles south of the Loop, at the moment of Humphrey's nomination. We were bottled up in the parks, yet we could not stand by in silence. We did not relish more violence, certainly not after the previous night, but we did want direct moral engagement with the delegates and politicians who we felt were selling out the country.

What, we asked ourselves, were our options? The police were offering the Grant Park Bandshell, near Lake Michigan, about a half mile from the Hilton, for a strictly contrived afternoon rally where we would be allowed to voice our grievances, then be ordered to disperse. This was completely unacceptable from our standpoint. The police wanted our rally to end in the afternoon, while we wanted to demonstrate *during* the nomination proceedings at night. And I suspected that the police were planning to surround us at the bandshell to prevent another night of protest in Grant Park across from the Hilton—the closest thing to demonstrating at the convention site.

We agreed that there should be a rally at the bandshell at noon, to take advantage of the temporary police permit and try to involve those thousands of Chicago citizens who were simply afraid to join us at night. We agreed on music, poetry, and speeches by a cross section of movement leaders and victims of violence. But there were only two choices for those who intended to remain after the "legal" rally. The first, preferred by Dave, was to organize a nonviolent march toward the faraway amphitheater. This, of course, would be blocked promptly by the police and probably end in mass arrests without even getting out of the bandshell area. The second notion was to get out of the park by mobile tactics after the rally and regroup in front of the Hilton by the time Humphrey was being nominated. This would avoid the snare of everyone being arrested in the afternoon. If they were going to make a mass arrest anyway, we could try to delay it to the time of the nomination and make them crush us visibly in front of the Hilton rather than in a remote park.

Feeling honest about the alternatives we would lay before the assembled crowd, we made our way to the bandshell about noon. Irv Bock went to a phone booth to inform his superiors of our intentions.

When we arrived, there were about ten thousand people at the bandshell, mostly an outpouring of Chicago citizens. I remember embracing Mickey Flacks, who came with her newborn baby, Mark, trusting, with so many others, that the rally would be a peaceful one. Vivian Rothstein told her she was crazy, but she wanted to be there. We began at 2:25, with people still filing into the park. Phil Ochs started singing. Dave was chairing. A few speakers from draft-resistance organizations and Vietnam Veterans Against the War were heard. I sat toward the rear with a few savvy marshals, trying to assess the large contingent of police who had arrived and stationed themselves in the corner of the bandshell area that was on the most direct route to the Hilton.

They were handing out a leaflet announcing that "in the interests of free speech and assembly, this portion of Grant Park has been set aside for a rally," then going on to warn that "any attempts to conduct or participate in a parade or march will subject each and every participant to arrest." Meanwhile, Vivian and others were distributing a leaflet appealing to the police. While I fully expected the police to continue their brutal behavior, there was nothing wrong with reaching out to their better judgment. Forty-three U.S. Army soldiers at Fort Hood had just been court-martialed for refusing "riot-control" duty in Chicago; why not some of Chicago's finest? The leaflet was poignant in its entreaty to the police:

Our argument in Chicago is not with you.

We have come to confront the rich men of power who led America into a war she voted against. . . . The men who have brought our country to the point where the police can no longer serve and protect the people—only themselves.

We know you're underpaid.

We know you have to buy your own uniforms.

You often get the blame and rarely get the credit.

Now you're on 12-hour shifts and not being paid overtime.

You should realize we aren't the ones who created the terrible conditions in which you work. This nightmare week was arranged by Richard Daley and Lyndon Johnson, who decided we should not have the right to express ourselves as free people.

As we march, as we stand before the Amphitheater, we will be looking forward to the day when your job is easier, when you can perform your traditional tasks, and no one orders you to deprive your fellow Americans of their rights of free speech and assembly.

By now the convention itself was unraveling from the strain of the week's events. Many of the delegates were joining our nightly protests as they returned to the hotels. Idealistic McCarthy workers, who turned "clean for Gene" from New Hampshire to Chicago, were heartbroken, alienated, radicalized. The effort to nominate their hero was only a matter of going through the motions. On this night, Hubert Humphrey would inevitably be nominated, the wheels of the party machine relentlessly turning regardless of the political consequences. However, a spirited fight would be taking place over the Vietnam platform plank in the afternoon. The Johnson-Humphrey position would prevail numerically, but the size of the peace bloc would measure how far the antiwar movement had reached into the Democratic mainstream.

Suddenly there began a commotion by a flagpole situated between the bandshell and the police line. A shirtless longhair was climbing the pole toward the flag. Nothing seemed to madden the police more than affronts to the American flag, although their hearts never seemed to melt when we sang "America the Beautiful" or "This Land Is Your Land." On this occasion, the teenager on the flagpole intended to turn the Stars and Stripes upside down, an international distress signal, though no one knew his intention at the time. People at the foot of the flagpole were yelling their approval or disapproval. Led by Rennie, our marshals headed over to keep order. A column of police waded in with clubs to make a forcible arrest. A few people threw stones and chunks of dirt at a police car. Dave urged calm over the microphone. The vast majority remained in their seats as Carl Oglesby, the SDS president, was introduced. Carl was an extraordinary orator, and was saying that while we tried to give birth to a new world there were "undertakers in the delivery room" when thick lines of police, clubs in position, began forming in front of the flagpole, facing off against our marshals, who had largely succeeded in calming people down. Rennie later remembered taking the megaphone and telling the police it was under control, we had a permit, and they should pull back to avoid further provocation. "On that last word," Rennie said, "they charged."

The police started forward in unison, then broke ranks, running and clubbing their way through the marshals and into the shocked people sitting on their benches. Human bodies flipped over backward. Others staggered into the benches and fell. Some police stopped to beat again and again on their helpless forms, then moved forward into the screaming, fleeing, stumbling crowd. Tear gas was wafting into the air, and I saw Mickey Flacks running off with her baby's face covered. The police were the Gestapo to her. She approached several of them, screaming, "Here, do you want the baby? Take him, take my baby!" Gaining her control, she began shuttling injured demonstrators to the university hospital on the south side, with the baby asleep in a backseat carrier.

Somebody yelled to me that Rennie was hit and lay bleeding, trampled, and unconscious. Oglesby kept speaking, describing the police state unfolding even as he tried to exercise his freedom of speech and assembly. I was not disguised, so I took my shirt off to change my appearance for the moment. Then I turned over and piled up several park benches to slow the charge of the rioting police. Next I circled around the melee toward the flagpole area to check on Rennie. He was being attended to by our medics and readied for an ambulance. His head was split open and blood was flowing over his face and down his shirt. The man standing over him with a microphone and tape recorder, I later learned, was from Naval Intelligence. Rennie was taken to the

Daley dozers engage protesters at Democratic Convention, Chicago, 1968. (Photograph by Duane Hall)

hospital by our own medics. Within a short while, the police arrived at the hospital to arrest Rennie, who was beginning to recover from a concussion and abrasions. The hospital staff hid him under a sheet, rolled him on a gurney through the police lines, and placed him in a cab. He was driven to South Kimbark, where he watched the rest of the night's events from the Flackses' couch, his aching head heavily bandaged.

Somehow the insanity subsided after half an hour. The police pulled back to their original position, but now they were reinforced by new units and helicopters from every direction. National Guardsmen were moved into place by the bandshell as well, also taking up visible positions on nearby bridges and the roof of the Chicago Museum. Bleeding, gassed, and disoriented, we were now surrounded on all sides. A full force of twelve thousand police, six thousand army troops with bazookas and flamethrowers, and five thousand National Guardsmen with Daley dozers stretched from the bandshell back to the Hilton and the Loop.

Surprisingly, the rally went on, with Allen Ginsberg, Dick Gregory, and several other speakers. But eventually it came to a final focus. Dave Dellinger announced that there were options for people: first, joining himself in a nonviolent parade attempting to go to the amphitheater; second, staying in the bandshell area; and third, moving out of the park for "actions in the streets." He then introduced someone from the Peace and Freedom Party who made the out-of-place proposal that we go picket with the striking Chicago transit workers. Next came a bizarre Jerry Rubin, with a live pig, which he wanted to enter in nomination for the presidency. A little flustered by these suggestions, Dave reiterated that his proposed nonviolent march would begin in the far corner of the park, and then he introduced me. I was reaching a climax of anger and, curiously, freedom. It didn't matter what happened now. "Rennie has been taken to the hospital, and we have to avenge him," I began, repeating it twice to get people's attention. I pointed out the police, guardsmen, and droning helicopters, and warned that we were now surrounded as twilight approached. I urged people not to get trapped in the park, to find their way out and back toward the Hilton: "This city and the military machine it aims at us won't allow us to protest in an organized fashion. So we must move out of this park in groups throughout the city and turn this overheated military machine against itself. Let us make sure that if our blood flows, it flows all over the city, and if we are gassed that they gas themselves. See you in the streets."

Seconds later, I disappeared from the park with Bob Ross, heading for my Kimbark apartment and a new disguise. A *New York Times* reporter drove with us. I heard on the car radio that the Vietnam peace plank was rejected by the convention by a 1,500-1,000 margin and that a protest rally had begun on the convention floor. In about an hour, I was back at the bandshell with a fake beard and helmet to cover my face. It was late in the day, perhaps five o'clock. Dave's march of over a thousand people was half sitting, half standing, blocked by a line of police who would not let them out of the park. Meanwhile, individuals and small groups of demonstrators were headed north along the lakeshore chain of parks looking for a bridge to cross onto Michigan Avenue and access routes to the central downtown area. Each of the crossings was occupied by troops employing mounted machine guns and Daley dozers.

By some miracle, our trotting, winding crowd finally came to an open bridge at Jackson Boulevard, north of the Loop, and with a great cry of liberation ran over the short space and into Michigan Avenue, turning left to head the mile back toward the Hilton. There were over five thousand people cheering, running, shaking fists or making V-signs, flowing like a peasants' army toward the castle of the emperors. Seemingly from nowhere, the mule-drawn Poor People's Caravan, which Dr. King had intended to lead before his death, materialized in our ranks with Ralph Abernathy leading it as we headed down Michigan Avenue. It was seven-thirty, nearly time for Humphrey's nomination. The streets were open, as the police were forced to regroup in the face of our surprising initiative. The Dellinger march disintegrated, and everyone found their way toward the Hilton.

It was nearly dark, the city lights turning on, as we reached the corner of Michigan and Balboa, where all the swirling forces were destined to meet. Lines of blueshirts were in front of us, clubs at the ready. The protest column filled the street and swelled with unity as we moved straight ahead now. The first lines sat down.

As if by magic, hands were suddenly in the evening air, and we began chanting, "The whole world is watching, the world is watching, the whole world is watching."

We saw smoke and heard popping noises a split second before tear gas hit our front lines and began wafting upward into the Hilton and nearby hotels. We stopped, choking, trying to bite into our shirts. Then the blueshirts charged, chopping short strokes into the heads of people, trying to push us back. They knocked down and isolated several people, leaping on them for terrible revenge. One very young longhair was caught in the gutter, four or five police cutting his head open with their clubs. A reporter took a famous picture of him, face bleeding, holding up the V-sign, before he passed out. Medics wearing Red Cross armbands, who tried to get to him and others, were clubbed, choked, and kicked down in the street. Mace was squirted in the face of any others who approached, including the photographers. The mass of people fell back, stunned but orderly, helping the injured, to regroup for another march forward.

Bob and I got through the front lines and around the police to the very wall of the Hilton, where a mixed group of fifty or so McCarthy workers, reporters, protesters, and—for all I knew—plain ordinary citizens, were standing frozen against the wall, between the hotel and the police, who were facing the oncoming marchers. When the marchers fell back, the police turned on our trapped crowd, moving in with a vengeance, clubs and Mace pointed at our faces. We instinctively joined arms. They started pulling off one person at a time, spraying Mace in their eyes, striking their kidneys or ribs with clubs, and tripping them. Their eyes were bulging with hate, and they were screaming with a sound that I had never heard from a human being. Someone started shouting that a woman was having a heart attack. We were so beseiged that I couldn't turn around to see what was happening. Then, as people started staggering backward, someone kicked in the window behind us, and we fell through the shattered street-level opening to the Hilton's Haymarket Lounge (named, strangely enough, in memory of Chicago police killed by an anarchist's bomb during a violent confrontation between police and protesters in 1886). The police leaped through the windows, going right by me, turning over tables in the swank lounge, scattering the drinkers, breaking glasses and tables.

Now, the *inside* of the Hilton was a battleground. Trapped demonstrators were trying to sit inconspicuously—in Levi's and ripped shirts—in chairs in the lobby until it was possible to get out safely. Bloody victims were walking about dazed, looking for help, as bellboys and clerks stared in shock. Reporters were rubbing their heads and trying to take notes. The McCarthy forces started bringing the injured to a makeshift "hospital" on the fifteenth floor, where they had headquarters. It had been a very bad night for them. The candidate's wife, Abigail, and children were warned by the Secret Service not to attend the convention; she assumed this was because they could not be protected from the Chicago police.

Upstairs now, the staff members of the defeated presidential candidate were ripping up bed sheets to serve as bandages. Many of the wounded were their own. Some flipped-out political aides were throwing hotel ashtrays at the police down in the street; others were trying to pull them away. Lights all over the McCarthy floors of the Hilton were blinking on and off in solidarity with the protesters in the streets below. Soon, the police cut the phone lines to the McCarthy suites and, in a final orgy of vengeance, stormed the fifteenth floor, dragging sleeping volunteers out of bed and beating them up as well.

At the convention, Humphrey was being nominated, but not without resistance. Senator Abraham Ribicoff, in nominating Senator George McGovern, stated that "with George McGovern, we wouldn't have Gestapo tactics on the streets of Chicago." Mayor Daley, in the first row, was interpreted as screaming, "Fuck you, you Jew son of a bitch, you lousy motherfucker, go home."

After Humphrey's nomination, which took until midnight, the McCarthy contingent vowed to march back to their hotels. About three in the morning, we welcomed them, a funeral column of tie-wearing delegates, each somehow holding a candle against the foul night air. Robert Kennedy had been fond of quoting a Quaker saying in his brief presidential campaign: "Better to light a candle than curse the darkness." Now it had come to this: While I welcomed these candles in the park, I wanted to curse the darkness.

I had reached exhaustion; so had the protest. So too had the hopeful movement I had hoped to build only a few years before. Over the course of the next day, the defiance wound down. Dick Gregory led a march halfway to the amphitheater before it was stopped by more arrests, this time of many convention delegates themselves. We heard Eugene McCarthy, with gentle dignity, urge us to "work within the system" to take control of the Democratic party by 1972. He was harangued embarrassingly by SDS leader Mike Klonsky as a "pig opportunist." Ralph Abernathy spoke from an impromptu stage, an upside-down garbage can, calling it a symbol of Martin Luther King's last cause.

I lay on the grass, pondering the alternatives. Reform seemed bankrupt, revolution far away. We had taught the pro-war Democrats the lesson that business as usual was a formula for political defeat and moral self-destruction. But was anybody listening?

I felt drawn into a tunnel of our own, with no light at its end.

The National Commission on the Causes and Prevention of Violence, appointed by President Johnson, concluded that a "police riot" was to blame for the disaster. In his introduction to the report, *Los Angeles Times* reporter Robert J. Donovan described the Chicago police behavior as nothing less than a "prescription for fascism."

Drawing on twenty thousand pages of witness statements, most of them from the FBI and the U.S. Attorney's offices, and 180 hours of film, Walker's team came to conclusions at great variance from Daley's accounts. There were 668 arrests during Convention Week, most of them involving individuals under twenty-six years of age, the vast majority being young men from Chicago with no previous arrest records.

About 425 persons were treated at the movement's makeshift medical facilities. Another 200 were treated on the spot by movement medics, and over 400 received first aid for tear gas. A total of 101 required treatment in Chicago hospitals, forty-five of those on the climactic night of the twenty-eighth.

There were twenty-four police windshields broken, and seventeen police cars dented (by whomever). In addition, 192 of 11,000 officers checked themselves into hospitals. Of this number, 80 percent were injured in the spontaneous events at Michigan and Balboa on the twenty-eighth. Only ten police, according to their own affidavits, said they were kicked, six said they were struck, and four said they were assaulted by crowds.

In contrast, of 300 press people assigned to cover the street actions, sixty-three (over 20 percent) were injured or arrested. Fifty (including Dan Rather) were struck, sprayed with Mace, or arrested "apparently without reason," in the words of the Walker Report. The Daley machine had tried to sharply limit television access to the convention and streets; when that failed, the whole world was watching their tactics.

When the convention was over, Richard Daley offered his personal explanation for the violence in an interview with Walter Cronkite. Rennie, Dave, and I were communists, he darkly hinted, and that somehow explained it all. The mayor's words recall the blind mendacity of those times:

Daley: *Well, there really isn't any doubt about it. You know who they are.*

Cronkite: *No, I really don't actually.*

Daley: *Well, you know Hayden, don't you, and what he stands for?*

Cronkite: *I don't know that he's a communist.*

Daley: *You sure know Dellinger, who went to Hanoi. Why don't, why isn't anything said about these people? They're the people who—go over now, see if your cameras will pick them up in Grant Park. Rennie Davis. What's Rennie Davis?*

Cronkite: *Well, I don't know that they're communists.*

Daley: *Well, neither do I, but . . .*

I suppose it was fitting that such a bad year would end with the election of Richard Nixon to the presidency. The Democrats never recovered from the convention cataclysm and, more fundamentally, from Vice President Humphrey's continued allegiance to Lyndon Johnson. In retrospect, it is almost inexplicable that Humphrey did not distance himself from the president until late in the campaign, and then ever so timidly. The president's long-standing position was that there could be no American bombing halt without a "reciprocal" North Vietnamese military response. On September 30, Humphrey proposed an unconditional halt of bombing to clear the way for diplomatic progress, though he reserved the right to resume the air war. Immediately, there was a subtle shift of new support toward Humphrey. As Theodore White's history noted, there were no antiwar hecklers after that. A newspaper photo showed a student with a sign reading IF YOU MEAN IT, WE'RE WITH YOU. The McCarthy forces began supporting Humphrey actively. At the same time, support for third-party candidate George Wallace was eroding.

The Gallup poll of October 21 showed the depth of Humphrey's problem. Richard Nixon, pledging both law and order and a "secret plan for Vietnam peace," was leading by a 44-36 margin. In late October, Hanoi agreed to sit at the same table with the Saigon regime if the bombing stopped. On October 31, with the election less that a week away, Johnson played his trump card, announcing the bombing halt. On November 2, both the Gallup and Harris surveys shaved Nixon's lead to a perilous 42-40. According to White, "had peace become quite clear, in the last three days of the election of 1968, Hubert Humphrey probably would have won the election."

There has been much political conjecture that Hanoi wanted a victory at the American ballot box. Yet if any Vietnamese party meddled in American politics in 1968, it was the Saigon regime. By all accounts, they hoped for a Nixon victory to improve their bargaining position. As several histories of the 1968 election have indicated, staunch Republicans, such as Mrs. Anna Chennault, intervened to persuade General Thieu, on behalf of candidate Richard Nixon, not to join the new Paris talks. Hold out for a Nixon presidency, they implied, and a better strategic position. Thieu agreed, and Johnson's peace initiative fell through at the last minute.

Nixon's victory was by 0.7 percent: 43.4-42.7.

This was the concrete explanation for Humphrey's defeat, but the broader question lingers: Did the radicalism of Chicago elect Richard Nixon? Having struggled with this question for twenty years, I find there is no "neat" answer. For years afterward, I tried to deny it, not wanting to take any blame for Nixon's victory. It would have been easier for me to accept blame if I truly believed the differences between Nixon and Humphrey were meaningless, or if I subscribed to the view that electing Nixon would "sharpen the contradictions" and accelerate the process of change. But I did not. I do not know if Humphrey would have ended the war sooner or differently than Nixon. I would like to think so, but it would have required Humphrey to break with the basic liberal anxiety of two decades about "losing" countries to communism. However, I am certain that a Humphrey administration would have avoided the scandalous Watergate conspiracies of the Nixon years, directed as they were against so many mainstream Democrats, and I doubt that Humphrey would have indicted the Chicago conspirators.

But it is too simple to place the primary blame for Humphrey's defeat on the New Left or the demonstrators in Chicago. I still believe that Humphrey would have won the November election if he had separated himself from Johnson's policies and spoken out for a negotiated Vietnam settlement earlier. To blame the protesters in Chicago, and student radicals in general, unfairly absolves the Johnson White House and the Democratic leadership from primary blame for their own self-destruction. Our cause was both just and rational, even if all our methods were not. Our values were decent ones, even if we could not always live up to them. We were not responsible for the killing in Vietnam or the segregation in Chicago. We arrived at a confrontational stance not out of political preference but only as a last resort. In repudiating our demands, the national Democratic leadership was cementing an alliance of expediency with its conservative and militarist southern wing against the more progressive ideals of its student, black, and peace constituencies.

The movement that had begun on the back roads of Mississippi saw

188

its dreams napalmed by Vietnam; similarly, we who proposed political realignment found ourselves after 1964 and 1968 still excluded from a Democratic party that meanwhile upheld such affronts to peace and justice as allowing segregationist Mississippi senators to remain entrenched as chairmen of the Judiciary and Armed Services committees in America's highest legislative body. Mississippi blacks had been excluded in 1964; now the entire reform wing of the party was out in the streets. Emotionally scarred by eight years of battle, politically convinced that the party was beyond reform, I found it unimaginable that in just four years there would be a triumph of reform, that George McGovern would be nominated or that Richard Daley would lose his status as a convention delegate. My belief in the system was in critical condition.

I believe that, had he lived, Robert Kennedy would have been elected president in 1968. I interviewed several people in 1987 to determine whether this conclusion was wishful. I asked former U.S. attorneys Tom Foran and Richard Shultz, allies of Mayor Daley, who prosecuted the Chicago conspiracy trial; and Mike Royko and Studs Terkel, two famed Chicago journalists who were critical of the police and Mayor Daley. They all felt, with myself, that Robert Kennedy would have persuaded Mayor Daley to defuse the convention confrontation and would have been nominated in August.

Seeking the opinion of someone with a truly inside perspective, I went to Steve Smith, a Kennedy in-law and top campaign adviser to all three Kennedy brothers. Smith had kept his knowledge to himself for two decades. "Who can say with certainty?" he replied to my question. "But we were full of confidence. I don't know that Daley agreed with Bobby. There may have been some concern. But the relationship was left full of promise. 'Stay at it,' Daley told us. New York was next. I think we'd have won it. We were of a mind that if we won New York, Daley'd have been there."

Assuming Kennedy had won the nomination, I believe he would have been elected in November. He could have retained Humphrey's basic vote, cut into Wallace, and turned out large numbers of disaffected voters that Humphrey could never rouse.

But it was not meant to be. Instead, 1968 ended as a Greek tragedy. I understand why Robert Kennedy found meaning in the ancient Greeks. Tragedy involved folly, and every mistaken folly of politicians was recorded by Thucydides 2500 years earlier. "Love of power, operating through greed and through personal ambition, was the cause of all these evils," Thucydides wrote in his *History of the Peloponnesian War.*

"Revenge was more important than self-preservation" among the rulers of the time. The doomed policy of Pericles could have consoled U.S. leaders: "All who have taken it on themselves to rule over others have incurred hatred and unpopularity for a time; but if one has a great aim to pursue, this burden of envy must be accepted." Blind arrogance made Chicago and the disaster of Vietnam seem inevitable.

But tragedy has another dimension, a noble one. Edith Hamilton described the "suffering of a soul that can suffer greatly" and the experience of loss for an entire generation that began with its soul fired with great hope. The two great periods of tragedy in Western culture, she pointed out, were Periclean Athens and Elizabethan England. Both were times, like the Sixties, "when life was seen as exalted, a time of thrilling and unfathomable possibilities." Tragedy takes place only amid such possibilities of greatness.

Rarely, if ever, in American history has a generation begun with higher ideals and experienced greater trauma than those who lived fully the short time from 1960 to 1968. Our world was going to be transformed for the good, we let ourselves believe not once but twice, only to learn that violence can slay not only individuals, but dreams. After 1968, living on as a ruptured and dislocated generation became our fate, having lost our best possibilities at an early age, wanting to hope but fearing the pain that seemed its consequence.

As Jack Newfield wrote, after 1968, "The stone was at the bottom of the hill and we were alone."

■ ■ ■ ■ ■ ■ ■ ■ ■ ■ ■

Twisters and Shouters

Maxine Hong Kingston

The couple waved to somebody, urgently, and they were off. A long-time-no-see friend has at last made the scene. Mix. Circulate. So, talking to him didn't count as circulation? Ditched. Don't anybody notice who's friendless at the party. He fought his shoulders' hunching up and his feet's shuffling, and his eyes' hunting for who was noticing that he was unpopular. If he could stand by himself alone, him and his cigarette, he would have perfected cool. In another corner, an overexcited party-goer had shut his eyes and was holding his hands in salaam position, his lips ohming and mumbling, trying to calm the space in and around him. How rude. Go home, why don't you? When you meditate, meditate; when you party, party. If Wittman were married, he and his wife, the two of them, would probably be standing here with nobody coming up to talk to them, both peeking from downbending, wine-sipping heads on the look-out for rescue socially.

Well, here's a "pool of acquaintanceship" of two to three hundred. According to friendship experts, the average American has seven "friendship units," couples counting as one unit, that is, from seven to fourteen friends. How many does he have? Below average. In making up his short-list, he's going to cut everybody except his equals, those who felt lifelong.

Over by the fire, people suddenly burst out laughing, apparently at something the chattering fire did. "Oh, no!" "Oh, yeah!" Silence. Then many of them spoke at once, trying to get the rest to listen. "We could get arrested for watching that." "There are people who want to arrest other people for watching that." Giggles. Quick lookings around by the paranoid to check out who meant what by "that." "They want to arrest people for feeling good." Gleeful laughter. Scornful laughter. The glee winning out. Then they were all smiling calmly, gazing into the now silken flames. They were swimming in hallucinogen, ripped but appearing as ordinary as pie. So this is how the psychedelic state looks from the outside, that is, through the vantage eyes of a head straight from ear to ear at the moment. The stoned heads didn't look especially strange, a little high and red-eyed maybe, but they were smoking too, and topping mescaline and/or lysergic acid with god knows what else—combinations, asmador and Stelazine, carbogen and laughing gas, Romilar C.F. and bella donna from Vicks inhalators, wippets and whipped cream and aerosol. If peyote, the messy stage was over. They were not outwardly extraordinary; they were not actually flying around the room or going through the changes from amoeba on up. They were looking Neanderthally at the fire because we were cavemen for a long time. Then it will be a campfire on the lone prairie because we were cowboys for a generation (and two more generations, counting the movies). And then—atomic flashes. The ages of man, though, did not visibly ripple up and down their faces. Their hair was not standing up on end as antennae for the aurora borealis. Now, all of them were calm, breathing in unison; they must be on that trip where the margins between human beings, and between human beings and other creatures, disappear, so that if one hurts, we all hurt, so that to stop war, all we have to do is drop lysergic acid into the water supply, but we don't even need to do that—because all human beings of all time are in connection—the margins didn't disappear, there aren't any margins— psychedelics only make you know about things, and do not cause a thing to be—it is—it already is—no need to reconnoiter the reservoir at Lake Chabot over beyond the Canyon and the one you can see from the MacArthur Freeway, climb the dam walls and elude guards and drop L.S.D. in the water supply after all. The pleasure of acid was in knowing ideas as real as one's body and the physical universe. A girl with long hair brushed her face; the webs were bothering her. A couple of people suddenly sat up and looked around, alert. Somebody knelt like church, arms and face raised like stained glass cathedral. Wittman did not dash over to ask what anybody saw. They were not a lively bunch. He and his compadres may not have actually flown, but when they turned into fenris wolves and dire wolves in a pack on the roam through the wilds, they had actually run barefoot through Berkeley, running to the Steppenwolf one night, having also dropped rauwolfia serpentina—"What's the trip?" "Fear and panic, man." —the fun of pure fear—and on another night, landing at the laundromat, as you do, that laundromat on Telegraph Avenue, coming down with green paint on their faces. And recalling talking to a Black man, who was saluting a tiny American cocktail flag on top of a pyre. And they had talked, evolving language from growls to explanations of life in the Universe. It must be that people who read go on more macrocosmic and microcosmic trips—biblical god trips, *The Tibetan Book of the Dead, Ulysses, Finnegan's Wake* trips. Non-readers, what do they get? (They get the munchies.)

Wittman went over below the tall black windows, where a group were talking politics. "At the rate the Masai are killing elephants," somebody was saying, "elephants will soon be extinct. Forever. From off the face of the planet Earth." "Fuck the Masai," said this scientist girl, whom he had met before. "If I had a choice which—Masai or elephant— to conserve, I'd choose the elephants. There are too many people and not enough elephants. Elephants are peace-loving creatures, and faithful to their families and to their tribes their whole lives long. That's more than you can say for people. You must've noticed, there's a lot of anti-elephant propaganda. The movies are brainwashing us against non-human species. We have pictures in our heads of stampeding herds of elephants—rogue elephants on the rampage—man-eating elephants— trampling villages. Well, the fact is: elephants can't run. They walk. Remember in 'Dumbo the Flying Elephant' when Timothy Mouse scares the circus elephants, and they tear down the tent? Walt Disney couldn't do a 'Living Desert' type movie with elephants acting like that; he had to use animation." Oh, yes, she's the one doing her doctoral dissertation on Walt Disney with an emphasis on "The Living Desert." "I say Fuck the Masai. The brain energy of human beings goes into thinking up ways to kill whatever there is that moves. Fuck the Masai. Sure, I mean it. I'm on the side of life. When I shop at the Co-op, I choose the tomatoes with the bug bites and worm holes. I do." "Yeah, yeah, I'm hip. Fruit and vegetables want to be eaten," said this guy with a rep as a heroin addict. "Oranges drop out of trees and say, 'Eat me. Eat me.'" Strange how heroin addicts are always eating health food. Somebody else, who had majored in Africa, said that the Masai were hardly the elephantine consumers the Disney scholar was making them out to be. They don't cut up their cattle into hamburger and sirloins but only bleed and milk them. "The same way that Indian medicine women harvest parts of plants, some leaves from each plant, a branch, a section of a tuber system, rather than pull up the whole plant by the root."

"How come Masai men are really good-looking," said a girl who
traveled a lot, "and Masai women aren't?" "They seem that way to you
because you're extremely hetero and not attracted to any kind of
woman." "No, no, I'm speaking objectively." "What do you mean by
'good-looking'?" "Masai are like fraternal twins. Take a boy twin and a
girl twin who look so alike they'd be identical if they were both boys or
both girls. The boy always looks good for a boy, but the girl looks like
a boy." "Yeah, like the Kennedys all look alike, but the men look good,
and the women are homely." "If you watch elephants closely, you'd see
that they are individual in looks and personalities." "Maybe you have a
warped standard of beauty. Who amongst us in this room looks like a
Masai woman? Come on, pick one out, and we can decide for ourselves
whether she looks good or not." The scientist girl and the traveler girl
looked at this one and at that one, turned around to look, and said that
nobody there looked as ugly as a Masai woman. "Keep looking."
Putting them on the spot. "You're being fooled by make-up and
fashions. The range of human looks can't be that far apart. Of all the
people here, who looks the closest to a Masai woman?" They waited,
nobody letting the white chicks off the hook. There was a tall Black girl
in the group, getting taller, and nobody was about to say it was her, and
nobody was going to point out any other Black woman either. Wittman
wasn't shining; time to maneuver a getaway. A newcomer was looking
over shoulders, and Wittman stepped back, made room for him, and
walked off, his place taken. He was getting good at shed-and-dump.

And he ran right into the most boring guest at the party, this left-
wing fanatic who can't tell the difference between a party and a
meeting. Each time they'd ever met, he carried on about injustice in a
country you never heard of, and invited you to a "demo" in front of a
hotel or post office, which is Federal property. The "demo" would be
sponsored by "The Ad Hoc Committee to Save Whatever," founded by
its only member, this left-wing fanatic. If you got a word in edgewise, he
put it in his Marxist bag, and let you have it for not being radical
enough. He had urged students to take R.O.T.C. to learn practical skills,
such as shooting guns, that can be useful in making revolution. "You
mean you want me to *kill*?" Wittman had asked, to agitate him; "I'll
join R.O.T.C. if you join the Tibetan Brigade." Remember the Tibetan
Brigade drilling on the soccer field near Bowles Hall? What happened
to them? Did they ever get to Tibet? A man of principle has to hear a
leftist out. It's very brave of him to picket Nob Hill all by himself,
vexing delegates of governments and corporations who stay at the Mark

194

Hopkins, the Fairmont, the Stanford Court. Tonight, the leftist was
dragging around an old and tired lady. "This is Doña Maria Francesca
De Ortega y Lopez" — a longer name than that — from Sud América.
Wittman, a nobody, was not introduced by name. She didn't look at
him anyway. One moment she was silent, and the next, she was spieling
from deep inside, barely audible. He hoped that she was not saying
what he was hearing, ". . . political torture . . . every man in the
village . . . ," and names, Dons and Doñas. She rolled up a sleeve; there
was a dark indentation in the bruised fat of her arm. "Bullet wound?"
he asked. "Soldiers?" She shook her head, "Si"; she does that yes-no
under interrogation. Please don't be saying that soldiers killed kids —
niños y niñas — in front of parents. "Rapid," she said. "Rapid." As in
rapo, rapere? He should come to the rescue; this doña is his summons
to political responsibilities. "Listen," he said. "I have to tell you — could
you tell her for me please — that I am — that we have to make — that I
believe that there's a story to our lives that we have to make? And I am
working hard for the plot of my life, that it not be taken over by a war. I
don't want to give my life over to you. Comprendes? I don't want
politics to make my life. I can't go off on somebody else's trip. Could
you translate that for me?" The leftist rolled his eyes — a me-ay of
exasperation — and took the lady by the unwounded arm over to
another listener. Enlisting Norte Americano consciences one by one.
She said, "Gracias." Wittman said, "Mucho gracias." Well, now he
knows: the more one has suffered, the less affect when telling about it;
fakes and actors jump up and down emoting.

He hurried to pass a set of modular sofa-chairs, arranged invitingly
by the married women, who were sitting safely together. They were
newlyweds, young matrons, who last year were dates, but now they
were wives. The adventurous girls had left for New York. The husbands
were getting loaded with the boys, or dancing with the Pan Am stews.
He'd gotten stuck with the wives before — stopped to say howdy-do and
couldn't get away. Not a one of them were like Anna Karenina or
Constance Bonacieux or Lady Connie Chatterley. Nobody bursting
with sexy dissatisfaction. They were unappealing and blobby — well, two
were pregnant. It was true about "letting herself go." They might as well
have blackened their teeth. He had asked, "What have you been up to?"
After they say they're housewives, there is nothing for him to say next.
He had nodded and nodded, as if interested in "my stove," "my dinette
set," "my floors," "my husband," "our pregnancy." A husband would
come by and ask his wife to dance, but afterwards he brought her

straight back here and left her. Surely, wives hate being stuck with wives. But how to party without being unfaithful? Why hasn't his lively generation come up with what to do with wives at parties? "Hi, Lisa," he said. "Hi, Shirley." That turning of wives' faces to him, troping him as he hurried by to join the men and single girls, wasn't because of his attractiveness; they didn't have anything else to do. They'd been sitting here like this since the last party. Watch to see when Lance starts parking Sunny.

His host and hostess were in the middle of a group that seemed to be having the best time, but he couldn't very well go over there when he'd been conferred his turn.

"Excuse me," said a little woman beside him. She was unusual in that she seemed older and straighter than anybody. "Have you seen Sam? I've been looking all over for him."

"Sam who? I don't know anybody named Sam."

"I better go look for him. I'll be right back." And she took off. Another hit-and-run.

"I can't find him." Whaddaya know. She had said, "I'll be right back," and she was back.

"You're smart to keep track of him. Sam's a plainclothes narc."

Her eyebrows flew up, and she laughed, delighted. "Sam? You've got to be kidding. Not Sam. Oh. I'm not *with* Sam. I have been going out with him, though. I don't think it's going to work out. He's a health-food freak."

"Is he a heroin addict?"

"Oh, no, of course not. He's a health nut."

"Every heroin addict I know is on health foods. They're always trying to feel better. Another sign of the addict is strange smelling piss. It must be the asparagus they eat."

"The only food I've seen Sam eat is lettuce with beige stuff. He took me sailing on the Bay, and we landed on Angel Island for a picnic. When he opened up the cooler, there were napkins, and his tacklebox with fifty-six kinds of vitamin pills, and this salad, which he drizzled beige stuff on top of. He talks about grinding up raw almonds in his blender. I guess that's what that beige stuff is. There were deer and raccoons; they went over to other people's picnics. He and I have no future."

"Want another drink?" asked Wittman. "Here I am letting you stand there with an empty glass. Let me freshen it up." He was getting good at party brush-offs. You ask if you can get them a drink, and dig out.

Testing them, do they want to talk to you further? If so, they'll say, "No, thanks," in which case you can say, "I think I'll get myself one," and cut out before you get bored or boring.

"Yeah, sure."

"I'll be right back," he said, and headed toward the refreshments. There. He'd never used those manners before. Something must be happening to him. She hadn't even been uninteresting, and he had ducked her. He could go back there and talk to her some more if he wanted. They're not supposed to feel hurt. Nothing personal. Circulating. Calculating.

He went straight out to the porch, and up some stairs to a balcony—no other party escapee here—smoked, considered hanging it up, half-ass gibbous moon in the sky—and reentered to a corridor of closed doors. The Steppenwolf at the entrance to the Magic Theater. Lu Sooon surrounded by the eight slabs of rock doors at fishbelly Holm. "For Mad Men Only. The Price of Admission—Your Mind." He opened any old door and entered. Movies. Also pot-luck doping going on. And they were showing a short co-produced by his own self with a stop-and-go hand-held camera. He crawled under the lightbeam and sat on the floor beneath the projector. The technique he'd help invent was to try for a cartoon effect using face cards—you shoot a few frames, stop, move the cards, shoot again. And there they were, very bright, the Queen of Hearts, the Knave of Diamonds, the King of Spades running about on the wood table. The Knave is driving a toy pick-up truck, in the bed of which the King is being hauled away. The Queen is backing off into the distance. And—deus ex machina—a black Hand (in a glove) clacking a pair of scissors beheads the Knave, picks up the King, chases the Queen, and carries them into the air. They'd filmed extreme close-ups of all three beheadings, and during the editing, decided which royal head would have the en scene star focus death. A new king and a new queen parade with the heads on pikes by torchlight. The grande finale—a cauldron of swirling water and red paint, and toy dinosaurs falling in by the Handful, and the pieces of the King, Queen, and Knave turning, and, what the hell, the rest of the pack, everything dizzying in the vortex of time. The End.

People were clapping, and they had laughed. "Not bad." "Not bad." The movie was different from when he'd run it; it was the music. There had been dirge music—the royal family moved majestically. But now there was Loony Tunes music, and the playing cards were rushing nuttily about, though the speed was actually no faster. The same story

197

can be comedy or tragedy, depending on the music. Bad noises roaring overhead and in the streets, the world gets crazier.

Then up on the screen popped a slide of the sun setting beyond the mud flats of the Bay, the sun to the right, a branch of driftwood in the foreground on the left. Somebody said, "Sunset"; otherwise, would you know (if you weren't from around here) whether the sun at a horizon were in the east or the west, a sunrise or a sunset? In real life, there's no doubt. "Sh-sh. Look." Lance at the projector. He ejected the slide, and flipped it over, now the sun on the left and the black stick on the right. It gave off a different emotion—a shift inside the mind and chest. I felt safe, and now I am desolate. Because the first was the image as it occurred in nature? And in this reversal the stick sticks out more lonely on the salt marsh. Lance flipped the picture again, and the sun was again important and warm. Because we saw it this way previously? The audience, patient on dope, and never tiring of taking out a somewhat aphasic brain and playing with it, were wowed.

At airport parties, Lance would stand at the revolving postcard rack, and arrange cards in some kind of sequence. "Do you think somebody will come along and read what I've done?" And the next time at the airport, he checked out whether he'd been answered. "Did anybody answer?" "Nope." "You mean those cards are in the same order that you left them in?" "Oh, no, people have been shuffling through them to buy." Just so, Wittman looked for some kind of a meaning to the order of the slides.

Then there was talk about F-stops, camera numbers, apertures, etc., and he went into the next room.

Where the tube was on. He sat himself down, intercepting a joint, passed it on, eschewed taking a hit. Contact high already all over the house. The picture wasn't coming in, but the viewers were entranced, chuckling, commenting. "Wow." "Oh, wow." "Do you see what I see?" "Beautiful, yeah." Wittman had not tried the snow show straight before. What you do is turn the knob to a channel that's not broadcasting, and you stare at the snow. Try it. Pretty soon, because the mind and eye cannot take chaos, they will pull the dots into pictures of things—in color even on a black and white set—confetti jumping and dancing to music. Snow is not white. Regular TV programs are for zombies who allow N.B.C., A.B.C., and C.B.S. to take over the sacred organizing of their brain impulses into segments, sitcoms, the news, commercials. Look, where it comes again! It works both stoned and straight. There, across the bottom of the screen, rolls a line of new cars like off an assembly line in an auto plant. But each car a different make and color. And there are drivers behind the wheels. Nobody tailgating or passing anybody else. They're on an eight-lane freeway. Some people drive with their elbows out the windows, and they make hand signals in another language. Girls are poking their heads out of the sunroofs, drying their hair. Can you control what you see by thinking? Wittman sped up his mind, and, sure enough, the cars speed up. A Volkswagen flips over, spins on its back, and slides along among the onrushing race. You can sort of control the pictures; they are not strict mirrors of your thoughts. They'll do things you don't know what they'll do next. Look. A row of cars has come to a corner. Where are they going, zipping around the corner? People too, running round this edge. Wittman tried hard to see the other side, but was distracted by the girls with long hair, who fly out of the sunroofs, and become a row of feathery angels at the top of the screen. Oh, more space up there. He had been concentrating on a few rows of dots down at the bottom. There are more stars in the Universe. Every jumping dot can be one of the three billion people on this planet, each one of whom you will not have time to meet, and everybody up to something. And, furthermore, there are animals. Elephants. Wild elephants. And elephants with fringe and leis and sounding bells and other adornments. A fire truck. A float with a queen and princesses. You cannot make something stop running to study its details. Majorettes. A marching band passing a garage band. An Indian band riding a flatbed truck. The sitar music was coming from the phonograph. It felt like Ravi Shankar was playing one's spine bones — the note off the top vertebra shoots into outer space forever. Bicycles and tandems with silver spokes spinning, Gandhi wheels. Clowns gyrating on unicycles. It's a parade. No tanks, please. No drill teams presenting arms. No nationalistic flags. Every single thing different and not repeating. Cars speeding up, black-and-whites behind. Car chase. Here comes the Highway Patrol. A row of pink piggies with patent-leather hoofs roll all the way across the screen. Yibbidy. Yibbidy. Some of them are wearing police hats. One of them is hodding bricks. Then the piggies are driving black-and-whites with stars on their doors. Ouch. The horizontal bar rolled up through the screen. Straight Wittman felt it smack him in the brain. That same hit as when riding the glass elevator at the Fairmont or the Space Needle in Seattle — while you're looking at the view, a crossbeam comes up, and whomps you in your sightline. "Ow," said the other people too. "Ouch. Oh, my head." The stars shoot off from the police cars and the Highway Patrol cars and the pig hats. Ah, a line of shooting stars, each with a golden tail. Cycle wheels of many sizes are spinning silver mandalas in the heavenly skies. The stars are making formations and constellations—flag stars, wing stars, sheriff's stars. Stars and stripes, and flags of other nations, stars on wings and epaulets, kung fu stars. There goes a badge with a bullet ding in it where it saved a lawman's life. The sitar plinks, reverberating on and on and on, forever spacious. Wittman pinned his mind power on one star, made it move to the center of the screen. It grows magnificently. Is this satori? Am I going to reach it this time? And it doesn't go away? The star blows up—smithereens of stars. Explosions massage the brain. Here we observers sit, detached as Buddhas, as the Universe blows up. What was that? Just before the bang, did you see Captain America with a star on his forehead and one on his shield, and Doctor Zhivago/Omar Sharif attach jets to Planet Earth and blast it crazy off its axis? Wittman picked up (with his mind) one of these iota stars, and pushed it to the middle of the galaxy, where it pulsates intensely, and bursts again, a dizzy of birds—tweet tweet—wun wun day—and stars orbiting around a cat's head with X'd eyes. The pink pigs in top hats and patent-leather hoofs roll by. Yibbidy. Yibbidy. That's all folks.

"Wow." "Oh, wow." "Wotta trip that was." People got up, some went out, some changed seats. Did all of us get to the same place at the same time? Did we really see the same things? "Did you see the pigs roll away?" "Yeah. Yeah." "Pigs? What pigs?" Somebody has got to be scientific about all this; lock everybody up independently in separate lead-lined rooms to draw what he or she sees, and then compare.

"Look. There's more." Mushroom clouds. It was the last scene in "Dr. Strangelove"—the graceful puffing of H-bombs. Poof. Poof. Poof. "We'll meet again. Don't know where, don't know when, but I know we'll meet again some sunny da-a-ay." Electricity was shimmering between the thunderheads and the ground. A row of human brains on stems. The End. The End. The End. The End means the end of the world.

The monkey brains had tuned themselves in to an open channel to a possible future. If this many bombs were to fall, light would flash through time, backwards and forwards and sideways. Images would fly with the speed of light years onto this screen and onto receptive minds. Future bombs are dropping into the present, an outermost arrondissement of the Bomb.

A second row of mushroom clouds bloomed, and the two rows of them boiled and smoked. Their viewers tried to shape them into other things, but the winds were dead. The Bomb, the brain, and magic mushrooms—fused. How to unlock them? Give us some peace. Some peas rolled across the screen. Helplessly, the heads watched: A parade of freaks gimped and hobblefooted across the screen—nuke mutants. See that baby attached to its mother's back? She's been running with it, carrying it piggyback along the Civil Defense route mapped out in the phone book, and it got stuck to her permanently. Werecoyotes—Los Angelenos are going to bond with the coyotes that come down from the hills and cross Ventura Boulevard into the suburbs of Studio City. Those minotaurs used to be dairy farmers and cows, or rodeo riders and toros. We're going to have a mutating generation. Nature will sport at an accelerated rate. The reason we make bombs is we want to play with Nature, so we throw bombs at her to make her do evolution faster. Nature panics. She throws handfuls of eyes at babies, and some sports will catch three or four, and some none. See that baby with sealed eyes? Before it was born, radioactivity zapped through its mother and lit up her insides. Blind calves have already been born in Nevada. Furry eyes protect them from too much light. Bees and flies will especially suffer when the light hits their many eyes and lenses. Nothing left but insects buzzing crazily. Those may be our own electrified ashes we're looking at. We won't be able to bear the touch of one another's fingertips on our faces. We'll walk blindly through the streets of unrecognizable cities. We'll be able to hear, though. Those who can see must keep talking and reading to the others, and playing music and ball games for them on the radio. After the bombs, there will be beautiful music, like the pod-picking scene in 'Invasion of the Body Snatchers.' We won't have orchestras and bands; the music will be on tape. Fingers will melt together. Spadehands. Spadefeet walked across the screen. Languages will have a lot of vowels like "Aaaaaaah!"

"Remember in the days before the Comic Code Authority," said Wittman, "there was an E.C. comic book about this mad scientist who invented a potion that he gave to his big girlfriend, and she split in two. I don't mean like sides of beef. She became identical twins with red lips and long blue-black hair. Each woman was half the size she used to be, shorter but in proportion, still a normal enough height for a woman. Matter can neither be created nor destroyed. And clothes don't tear when anybody changes identities, according to comic books. Both of her had on a tight red dress and black high heel shoes, just as before. The mad scientist takes one of her aside, and kills her. No tort case because there's still the other one alive. But that one wants to get even with him for killing her, see? She steals into the laboratory and downs some more of the drug. She's two again. Her plan is to kill him, and only one of her would have to pay for the crime. The two women gang up on the mad scientist, and he's fighting them off, when, because she O.D.ed on the chemicals, and because the two little women need reinforcements, they divide into four. No sooner does he kill one or knock one down than more form. Eight. Sixteen. Thirty-two. Geometric fucking progression. But, don't forget, everytime the women multiply, they become smaller, each one half her former size. Pretty soon, there are hundreds and thousands—sixteen hundred—thirty-two hundred—of these little women in red dresses swarming at him from all over the room. They're attacking from the shelves and tables and curtains and floor. He's tromping on them and swatting them, but they come at him again and again with these little bitty screams, 'Eeeeek. Eeeeek.'"

Thousands upon thousands of tiny teeming black-heeled women—a natural for the snow show. Wittman would like to be able to consolidate the dots into the picture of one face, but he was getting a hold on an order.

"The artists drawing the E.C.s were skin freaks. They loved to draw viscous flesh dripping. Remember the one about the guy who asks a witch to destroy his evil half? 'I want to be good,' he says. She warns him, 'Are you sure that's what you want?' He can't see how you can go wrong getting rid of your evil self. The last panel took up a full page: he staggers into a mortician's office with his right side healthy, and his left side decaying and dropping worms. His wordballoon says, 'Do something. I can't stand the smell.' And remember the funnybook with this girl who had blue doughnuts erupting almost out of her skin? Something at the amusement park had gotten her. I don't remember the story to that one. Only this picture of her in a bathing suit, lying in the sawdust, while in the background, the ferris wheel and the merry-go-round and the hammer turn and turn." Blue rings—ringworms—the Worm Ouroboros—rolled across the screen.

"Okay, here's an especially disgusting one: There were these parents who punish their kid by locking him in the closet. The kid screams repeatedly that there's a thing in there, but they shove him in. Pretty soon he makes friends with it. They hear the kid talking to somebody. 'Were you talking to yourself in there?' they ask. No, the kid says, he has a friend named Herman, and they better not be bad to him anymore, or Herman will get them. Just for that, his parents throw him in the closet again. The kid's saying, 'No! No! Herman's going to hurt you.' And, in the penultimate panel—oh, yeah, the dad's a butcher, and they live above the butchery—there's this meat grinder with its long handle up in the air, and ground human meat is pouring out of the blades, all over the table and down the legs to the floor. And the Keeper of the Crypt, the narrator-witch who gives the moral of the story, cackles, 'Hee hee hee, kiddies, the next time you eat hamburger, don't look too carefully. You might find a gold tooth. Hee hee hee.'

"Those comic books were brainwashing us for atomic warfare that causes skin cancer and hamburger guts. They were getting us inured so we could entertain the possibility of more nuclear fallout. Chain reactions aren't that bad, they're saying; that lady in the red dress doesn't go extinct. And they tried to make us despair of ridding ourselves of evil. I mean to keep heightening my squeamishness and horror."

Snow jumped and stormed on the screen. Every mind was exhausted of images. Most people stood up and left—"You're better than the story lady at the library." Those remaining selected a regular channel and talked back to the commercials. Wittman left too.

SDS "Days of Rage," Chicago, 1969.
(Photograph by Duane Hall)

The Implosion

Todd Gitlin

E nter the Weathermen. The 16,000-word position paper from which they took their name, called "You Don't Need a Weatherman to Know Which Way the Wind Blows" after a little-known Bob Dylan line, argued that you *did* need one after all, and they were it. It swooped from giddy Third Worldism to a call for "antipig self-defense" movements and "cadre organization" on the way to a "Marxist-Leninist party" and "armed struggle." From Chinese defense minister Lin Piao's famous 1965 polemic came the notion that just as the Chinese revolutionaries had first mobilized the peasantry and surrounded the cities, now the Third World revolution was going to surround the imperialist metropolis; it was just a matter of time before the United States — the imperialist mother country itself — was engulfed in revolution. The Weathermen closed with Lin Piao's title, "Long Live the Victory of People's War."

Who knows how many of SDS's hundred thousand or so members actually read this clotted and interminable manifesto, which raised obscurity and thickheadedness to new heights? But the Weathermen didn't recruit through force of argument so much as through style. Their esprit was undeniable. They were good-looking. They had panache. They radiated confidence as if to the manner born. Nor did it spoil their mystique that, like some of the PL leaders, several of the Weathermen came from wealth: Bill Ayers, the son of the chairman of the board of the Commonwealth Illinois electrical combine; David Gilbert, the son of a toy manufacturer; Diana Oughton, the daughter of a small-town Illinois banker and Republican state legislator, and great-granddaughter of the founder of the Boy Scouts of America. Most of the Old Guard, by contrast, were children of public-school teachers, professors, accountants, and the like; a higher proportion of the prairie-power group came from working-class families. But contrary to popular impression, most of the Weathermen were not the spoiled children of the rich. What drove them was not so much class origins but magical fury. Theory permitted them to abase themselves before a stereotyped Third World, and yet hold on to their special mission. They presented themselves as the refutation of PL, which was tactically stolid, morally stodgy (no drugs, no living in sin), and shockingly unenamored of the Black Panthers and Ho Chi Minh. In accord with the prevailing sociology of the Fifties and Sixties, they thought the bulk of the American working class—all but the young angries—had been bought off. They scorned the notion "that there is a magic moment after we reach a certain percentage of the working class, when all of a sudden, we become a working-class movement. We are already that if we put forward internationalist proletarian politics." Presto! Who needed the working class?

At the core of the Weathermen mystique stood SDS' interorganizational secretary, Bernardine Dohrn, who combined lawyerly articulateness with a sexual charisma—even more than her chorus line looks—that left men dazzled. At SDS's 1968 convention Dohrn picked up a national following when she declared she was a "revolutionary communist" with a small c. She fused the two premium female images of the moment: sex queen and streetfighter. (Indeed, of all the factions, the Weathermen were the most alluring to women, who could prove themselves now by slinging revolutionary jargon and kicking ass with the best of the men.) Once installed in the SDS office, she agreed to put aside feminism for The Revolution. Compared to Bernardine Dohrn, the famous Mark Rudd was a minor Weatherman adornment, if a major one by media lights.

These hip outlaws made revolution look like *fun*. One of the signers of their manifesto, Gerald Long, had raved about *Bonnie and Clyde* for the *Guardian*, likening the "consciousness-expanding" outlaws to Frantz Fanon and the NLF hero, Nguyen Van Troi. The Weathermen relished LSD. They liked orgies. Although their formal position papers were as leaden as all the other factions', they were not allergic to wit, on which they placed heavy hands. They were given to headlines like "Hot Town: Summer in the City, or I Ain't Gonna Work on Maggie's Farm No More." In *New Left Notes* (soon renamed *Fire*) they ran pictures and articles celebrating the presumed guerrilla exploits of a five-year-old child named Marion Delgado, who had once derailed a train. Their top command was—what else?—the "Weatherbureau." Proud of their roots in youthful innocence, they sang songs like "I'm dreaming of a white riot" (to the tune of "White Christmas"), and from *West Side Story*, "When you're a red you're red all the way / From your first party cell till your class takes the state," and to the tune of "Maria": "The most beautiful sound I ever heard / Kim Il Sung. . . / I've just met a Marxist-Leninist named Kim Il Sung / And suddenly his line / Seems so correct and fine / To Kim Il Sung / Say it soft and there's rice fields flowing / Say it loud and there's people's war growing / Kim Il Sung / I'll never stop saying Kim Il Sung." Giggling at their own fanaticism, they also affected themselves superior to it. During the People's Park battle, for example, a visiting Weatherman delegation criticized the Berkeley wallposter group I belonged to because we had failed to conclude our editorial with a resounding "Power to the People!" A few days later, I heard two of them at a party, stoned, going on about Chairman Mao having said this, Chairman Mao having said that. "Where did the Red Book come from?" I finally exploded. "Heaven?" They exchanged a look of stoned knowingness, and rolled their eyes. The blond Jeff Jones, formerly of Antioch College, cherubic as the Southern California surfer he had once been, smiled at me and hissed, "Yesssss!" Then the two of them cracked up at the straight-man rube.

"They knew they were crazy," said Carl Oglesby (who knew them better than anyone else of the old SDS) years later. "Terry [Robbins] and Billy [Ayers] had this Butch Cassidy and Sundance attitude—they were blessed, they were hexed, they would die young, they would live forever, and at their most triumphant moment they would look over their shoulders, as Butch and Sundance looked back at their implacable pursuers, and say more in admiration than in dread, 'Who *are* those guys?' I believe they thought they looked cute, and that everybody would know it was basically a joke. The next minute, they were lost in it and couldn't get out."

Although the Weathermen loathed the old New Left—they lashed out at "so-called 'Movement People'" as "this kind of right-wing force, this weirdness that's moving around," infected by pacifism and morality—

they still cried out to be taken as sole heirs of the original SDS. They had credentials, mostly from the SDS of 1966 and after—SDS campus travelers like Washington's Cathy Wilkerson (ex-Swarthmore) and the Midwest's Terry Robbins (ex-ERAP); the onetime Columbia chapter influentials John Jacobs, Ted Gold, and Dave Gilbert, as well as the media shooting star Mark Rudd; the longtime civil rights and ERAP organizer (turned August 1968 Chicago Hilton stink-bomber) Kathy Boudin; the Ann Arbor Children's Community School organizer Bill Ayers ("CHILDREN ARE ONLY NEWER PEOPLE," read their happy-face button). Many of them had been swept away at staggering speed: A mere two years earlier, Gilbert had been one of the authors of the "Port Authority Statement," Boudin an organizer of welfare mothers in Cleveland, Ayers a campaigner for an anti-war resolution in the American Federation of Teachers. . . . On the movement's breakneck timetable, they could claim to have tried everything short of revolutionary violence.

SDS's 1969 convention, its last, met in the cavernous Chicago Coliseum, amid a veritable counterconvention of reporters (excluded), FBI agents (equipped with long lenses on the third floor of a vacant building across the street), and hundreds of police milling around, in and out of uniform, snapping pictures. Of the 1500 delegates, perhaps a third were controlled by PL. Perhaps another third were divided between the Weathermen and their short-term allies, the upholders of a rival version of a Revolutionary Youth Movement—RYM II for short, in the arcane jargon of the time. (Among the RYM II supporters was a Bay Area faction passing out a pamphlet called *The Red Papers* adorned with portraits of Marx, Engels, Lenin, and Stalin.) The remaining third were baffled newcomers, dazed rank-and-filers, and other tendencies casting anathema on all the leading factions—most inventively a grouplet of anarchists passing out Murray Bookchin's corrosive pamphlet *Listen, Marxist!* with its cover pictures of Marx, Engels, Lenin, and Bugs Bunny. The rest of the organization—tens of thousands of national members, and who knew how many members of individual chapters—voted with their feet and stayed away. So did almost all the old and middle-period hands of SDS. Reports filtered back from Chicago as if from another planet—or rather, from a moon in orbit around one's own, for that bone-white light, that silver deathliness, had the familiar look of reflected light.

The funeral had its farcical aspects. To score points against PL, the Weatherman-RYM II coalition trundled out Third World allies:

208

representatives of the Young Lords, Brown Berets, and finally, of course, the Black Panthers, whose Illinois minister of information in the course of a diatribe against the "armchair Marxists" of PL suddenly launched into a celebration of "pussy power," proclaiming that "Superman was a punk because he never even tried to fuck Lois Lane." (The anarchists' Bugs Bunny cartoon turned out more realistic than they could have imagined.) Another Panther took the stage to endorse "Pussy Power" and to add, à la Stokely Carmichael, that the correct position for women in the movement was "prone." The crowd, aghast, hooted. The next day, the Panthers returned and read an ultimatum: PL had to change its line or "they will be considered as counter-revolutionary traitors and will be dealt with as such." It sounded like a burlesque of the left-wing mumbo jumbo of earlier decades, but no one laughed. PL chanted, "Smash redbaiting, *smash redbaiting*," "Read Mao, *Read Mao*." But these were only curtain-raising preliminaries to the grand climax: the Weathermen and RYM II caucused, then decided to expel PL and its allies for being "objectively anticommunist" and "counter-revolutionary." "Long live the victory of people's war!" were Bernardine Dohrn's parting words before leading 700 fist-waving delegates out of the convention hall, chanting, "Ho, Ho, Ho Chi Minh," into their own rump SDS. The Weathermen had no qualms about dismantling the largest organization of the New Left, indeed, the largest American organization anywhere on the Left in fifty years. The rest of an agonized, bewildered movement could be sloughed off like old skin. They reveled in the thrill of cutting loose—true outlaws at last.

H ilarious, this debacle, but no one could laugh it off. There was too much at stake, and tragedy that repeats itself too often becomes numbingly banal. In the course of the previous year, namecalling had become SDS's premium style. Whole issues of *New Left Notes* were filled with columns of factional denunciation, written in clumsy Marxoid code, "Brother-fucking," I called it, and wrote to a Cuban friend that "these fights among brothers depress me enormously. The Left is its own worst enemy here . . . and often I'm glad we're in no position to take power: if we did, the only honorable sequel would be abdication." One small but exemplary moment: the arraignment of almost 500 demonstrators, including my civil-libertarian self, who had gone to a January 1969 rally banned by fiat at San Francisco State College. I had been skittering around the edges of the campus strike for months, writing articles, working on a campus wallposter, comforting the wounded, outside-agitating in an effort to organize an alternative to the PL caucus in the SDS chapter, and then, during the bust, watching a cop blithely steal my address book for my pains. Now, in court, I heard the clerk call my name. As I walked to the front of the courtroom one of the PL people hissed, "Revisionist!" A small thing, but demoralizing. All the veterans had stories like that. "On every quarter of the white Left, high and low," as Carl Oglesby wrote, "the attempt to reduce the New Left's inchoate vision to the Old Left's perfected remembrance has produced a layer of bewilderment and demoralization which no cop with his club or senator with his committee could ever have induced."

Still more demoralizing, it dawned upon Oglesby and me and others of our ilk that the sectarian furies were more than an epidemic of nasty manners. The intellectual squalor and moral collapse of the SDS leadership followed, in fact, from their common and long-growing commitment to revolution from on high—which was the only place it could have come from in this decidedly unrevolutionary circumstance.

True sectarians are in the habit of disputing one another's positions in earnest, endlessly, humorlessly, as if the concepts deserve to be taken at face value; too little attention has been paid to sectarianism as a phenomenon in its own right, a force capable of fueling wild energies on behalf of positions that seem, to all but partisans, incomprehensible. Political sectarianism is the fight for possession of a sacred thing, i.e., The Revolution. The more appealing the fantasy, the more vicious the sectarian ravages. For the force of sectarianism is one result of an inflated belief in the power of revolutionaries. The silent reasoning goes like this: (1) The need or the situation is revolutionary. But (2) behold! The Revolution is not upon us. Therefore (3) it follows that the masses (workers, students) are being misled by bad revolutionaries—who must be as powerful as we would like to be, as we *would* be if not for *them*. In 1969 the revolutionaries' only property was the idea of The Revolution embodied in The Organization. Thus the overriding importance of taking over SDS. Thus the ferocity of the factional struggle.

Tom Nairn put it well in an analysis of the May '68 movement in France:

Where ideas are all, the upholder of a contrary thesis becomes automatically an enemy—indeed, the most vicious of enemies, since his 'position' is the most direct contestation of the vital truths. Where the revolution is reduced to this poverty, every scrap matters: every opinion, every attitude, every individual adhesion to this or that idea must be fought over like a bone. Antagonism becomes hatred, and polemic is turned into degenerate abuse.

When history is not performing the way the script decrees, then the sectarian conceives

> a bottomless faith in organization, in the ability of the group to accomplish by sheer drive and hard energy all that 'history' is failing to do. The fierce, arid tension of this subjectivity is then interpreted as the revolutionary spirit, the right fighting atmosphere. . . . This and all the other traits of sectarian Marxism indicated—its arrogance, its violent elitism, its instant and cutting condemnation of all deviations from the 'line,' its chronic substitution of insult for argument, its mystique of exclusive worker militancy, the cult of organization—reflect the basic, precarious defensiveness of such movements. That is, its underlying historical task of. . . keeping alive the consciousness of revolution across the 'Hell-black night' of the last decades.

Language became a cudgel in this shadow play—which is why PL's and the Weathermen's pronouncements, mind-numbingly derivative and frequently self-contradictory, far from damaging their claims to revolutionary virtue actually certified them. Each side agreed there was a "primary contradiction" in the world; they disagreed only about what it was. Simpleminded on the surface, obscurantist on further inspection, these pronunciamentos read like encrusted imitations of Stalinist polemics from bygone decades, or bad translations from the Chinese. *That they were bad writing was essential to their purpose.* Their leaden abstraction served to distract from intractable realities—above all, the widespread public distaste for revolutionary violence. Murk enabled the sectarians to mask (even from themselves) what they intended to do. As George Orwell noted, it is easier to speak of killing someone if you muffle the intention in a batting of polysyllabic abstractions. The clumsily translated quality of Weatherprose also certified that the writers belonged to the club of successful revolutionaries. I open the "Weatherman" document at random and find this sentence: "As a whole, the long-range interests of the noncolonial sections of the working class lie with overthrowing imperialism, with supporting self-determination for the oppressed nations (including the black colony), with supporting and fighting for international socialism." The prefabricated phrases spare the trouble of genuine thought, but more: they are easily parroted by those who want to feel privy to Important Questions. They are like a tourist's handbook phrases, instantly conveying a false sense of membership in an alien culture—in this case, the culture of World Revolution. (Thus too, the Weathermen's postschism document embraced the People's Republics of North Korea and Albania. Ignorance wasn't an excuse—it was a requirement.) Impenetrable outside the charmed circle of believers, the phrases amount to ritual incantation for the cadres. They ratify the division between vanguard and ignorant mass—the vanguard, by definition, are the people who can read, or abide, the priestly phrases. The Weathermen quickly learned to spice their proclamations with snappier exhortations to "kick ass" and "kill the pig," but they never shed the belief that political power in The Revolution grows out of a barrel of grandiose slogans.

The Weathermen proceeded to launch theory into practice. Their first project was to inspire white working-class youths to join The Revolution. They organized squads to barge into blue-collar high schools in Pittsburgh, Detroit, Boston, and other cities, pushing teachers around, binding and gagging them, delivering revolutionary homilies, yelling "Jailbreak!" The kids were bewildered; in Boston, 500 high school students countermarched on Northeastern University to fight *against* the revolutionaries. Some 200 Weatherman organizers spent the summer trying to convince tough white teenagers in Detroit, Columbus, Pittsburgh, Boston, and elsewhere that they were tougher, hence deserved to be followed into battle against "the pigs"—as if all that was holding the young multitudes back from an uprising was the fear of losing. They carried National Liberation Front flags through July Fourth celebrations, planted them in the sand at lakeside beaches, barged into hamburger joints and schoolyards, talked about "kicking ass" and "getting us a few pigs," and dared the local kids to fight. In the fall, ostensibly to impress Harvard-hating high schoolers, twenty Weathermen marched on Harvard's Center for International Affairs— known for counterinsurgency research—and smashed windows, yanked out phones, shoved secretaries, and beat three professors, for which the ringleader was subsequently sentenced to two years in prison. If the Weathermen stuck it out—as one of them, Shin'ya Ono, a former Columbia graduate student in political science, wrote—the kids would learn that "their only choice is either joining the world revolution led by the blacks, the yellows, and the browns, or being put down as U.S. imperialist pigs by the people of the Third World, as has already happened to 300,000 working-class Amerikans in Vietnam."

Not being Vietnamese peasants, working-class kids did not think they had to choose. A handful joined up for the chance to vent some class spleen, but the rest thought the Weathermen were maniacs. They threw punches at them, even drove them out of their neighborhoods — and still the Weathermen claimed victory. The children of the upper classes were gleeful about the taste of blood, even if it was their own. To be outnumbered and martyred testified to their vanguard status. Their RYM II allies soon abandoned the alliance and went off to find their own working-class base — the first of a series of factional splinterings that culminated, years later, in the founding of a minuscule Revolutionary Communist Party.

Unfazed, the Weathermen plunged on toward a grand October assault in Chicago under the slogan, "Bring the war home!" The Pentagon and Chicago August '68, they said, marked "the conception and birth of a white mother country anti-imperialist movement. A movement conceived in battle and willing to die in battle." Now it was time to act "not only against a single war . . . but against the whole imperialist system that made that war a necessity," to plunge into a new style of "anti-imperialist action in which a mass of white youths would tear up and smash wide-ranging imperialist targets such as the Conspiracy Trial, high schools, draft boards and induction centers, banks, pig institutes, and pigs themselves." The point was "not primarily to make specific demands, but to totally destroy this imperialist and racist society." Fighting in the streets would train the fighters, would take "the first step toward building a new Communist Party and a Red Army," would "do material damage so as to help the Viet Cong." It would even reinforce the mass antiwar movement: "The ruling class would have to consider the probability that the longer they drag their feet in admitting defeat and getting out of Vietnam, the more the candle-holding type [of peace marcher] will join the ranks of the crazies on the streets." After several such actions, they thought they could "build a core of ten to twenty thousand anti-imperialist fighters" who would stir up still more "local and national mass kick-ass anti-imperialist street fights" and "give the ruling class a tremendous kick" — so tremendous that, in combination with the Vietcong's victories, the U.S. would be forced to pull out of Vietnam within six months. In July, a Weatherman group met with North Vietnamese and NLF delegations in Cuba and came away convinced that the Vietnamese had thrown away their customary caution and endorsed the streetfighting tack.

Each Weatheraction could be interpreted, bent, in such a way as to redouble the Weathermen's giddiness. There were no limits. "If it is a worldwide struggle," the cocky twenty-four-old Bill Ayers told a Weatherman gathering in late August, "if Weatherman is correct in that basic thing, that the basic struggle in the world today is the struggle of the oppressed peoples against U.S. imperialism, then it is the case that nothing we could do in the mother country could be adventurist, nothing we could do, because there is a war going on already, and the terms of that war are set." The snag was that they were too tiny, and the United States too vast and recalcitrant, for the American phase of the seamless world revolution to offer much "material aid" to the people's armies of the Third World. If working-class youth weren't hip enough to recognize the Weathermen as their vanguard, so much the worse for them. "The more I thought about that thing 'fight the people,'" said Ayers, "it's not that it's a great mass slogan or anything, but there's something to it." You could win over the toughs by being tougher—beating white privilege and male supremacy out of them and "out of ourselves" in the process. Polarization was good. Those who doubted were "movement creeps," "right-wingers," "these old 'Movement people'." Students were "wimpy," said a boot-stomping Mark Rudd to an unimpressed audience at Columbia. "I hate SDS," said Rudd that fall, "I hate this weird liberal mass of nothingness."

Children of privilege were rediscovering the virtues of command. They relished the "ass-kicking" their childhoods had denied them. "We began to feel the Vietnamese in ourselves," wrote Shin'ya Ono. "We're bullets in the guns of the Third World," another Weatherman bragged. But the way they toughened themselves was more like a Fifties horror story of juvenile delinquency: one collective, sealed off behind chicken wire, proved itself by smashing tombstones in a cemetery, and killing and eating a cat. On one occasion, Illinois Black Panther chairman Fred Hampton called the Chicago action "Custeristic," worried that it would bring the wrath of the police down on the ghetto, called Mark Rudd "a motherfucking masochist," and knocked him to the ground. For years the movement had been cultivating a hierarchy based on sacrifice. It suffered from what Jerry Rubin called "subpoena envy." Wounds were credentials. The Weathermen pushed this middle-class notion one step further, concluding that the old "parlor game" movement had been "defeatist" because it feared that winning a battle would bring down the heavy hand of repression. "It was as if the movement made a secret, unspoken agreement with the ruling class not to struggle beyond certain limits," Ono wrote. The Weathermen thought they had freed their minds for "a life-or-death revolutionary struggle for power."

The "mass of white youths" failed to materialize in Chicago on October 8 for what was now known as "Four Days of Rage." The two or three hundred people who showed up in Lincoln Park to "bring the war home" were almost all students and ex-students, equipped with helmets, goggles, cushioned jackets, and medical kits, armed with chains, pipes, and clubs, the men outfitted with jockstraps and cups. They had convinced themselves, and aimed to convince everyone else, that the movement was precisely the nightmare which the police had fabricated a year before. ("They looked exactly like the people we [the Conspiracy defendants] were accused of being," thought Tom Hayden.) They psyched themselves up with *Battle of Algiers* war whoops and chants of "Ho Chi Minh," and to the astonishment of more than 2,000 police—who must have known that the vast majority of the demonstrators of August 1968 had been peaceful until roused—they charged onto the upper crust Gold Coast, trashing cars and windows, smashing into police lines. "Within a minute or two," Shin'ya Ono wrote, "right in front of my eyes, I saw and felt the transformation of the mob into a battalion of 300 revolutionary fighters." The police fought back in kind, shooting six of the Weather soldiers, arresting 250 (including forty on felony charges), beating most of them, sticking them with $2.3 million worth of bail bonds requiring $234,000 in cash bail. The fighters injured enough cops (75), damaged enough property, precipitated enough arrests and headlines ("SDS WOMEN FIGHT COPS," "RADICALS GO ON RAMPAGE"), and outlasted enough fear to talk themselves into a fevered sense of victory.

In the aftermath, they were shaken by casualties and defections—and revved themselves up yet again. Their most thorough published account, by Shin'ya Ono, blithely contradicted itself: "Militarily and tactically, it was a victory"; then, in the same paragraph, "mass street action is a necessary, but a losing, tactic." But again the Weathermen found a way to finesse their confusion: the sharpness of the clash confirmed that the apocalypse was impending. They were awed by their own audacity and by the thrill of having lived out their fantasy, having "done it in the road." To be against the war was too easy, too namby-pamby, they argued: "THE VIETNAM WAR ISN'T THE ISSUE ANY MORE. Mainly because the war is over. . . . What we say when we demonstrate about the war isn't that the U.S. should end the suffering or brutality. We tell people about how the VC have won. It's not so much that we're against the war; we're for the Vietnamese people and their victory."

Meanwhile, the mass antiwar movement was showing its strength, commanding the spotlight. A week after the Days of Rage came the immense October 15 Moratorium. A November 15 Moratorium was in the works, coupled with a mass demonstration in Washington. Bill Ayers and three other Weathermen—"flat and grim in their shades and work clothes and heavy boots," as Jeremy Larner, an eyewitness, described them—told Moratorium leaders that a $20,000 payment toward their Days of Rage legal expenses might avert violence in the Washington streets. The Moratorium organizers, who had the impression they were being blackmailed, said no. On November 13, the Weathermen went into the streets, led a splinter march on the South Vietnamese embassy, fought with the police, trashed store windows, garnered headlines. On November 15, 1969, perhaps three-quarters of a million people, the largest single protest in American history, a veritable mainstream, flowed through the streets to the Washington Monument. Senators George McGovern and Charles Goodell gave speeches; John Denver, Mitch Miller, Arlo Guthrie, and the touring casts of *Hair* sang; Pete Seeger led the throng in choruses of "Give Peace a Chance." But the breakaways wanted more. Led by Jerry Rubin and Abbie Hoffman—then on trial as part of the Chicago 8—several thousand militants marched on the Justice Department, complete with NLF flags. Smoke bombs, rocks, and bottles brought forth the obligatory tear gas. The "Amerikan" flag came down, the NLF flag went up. The militants dispersed through a gassed city, building barricades and setting fires. Attorney General John Mitchell, gazing out upon the spectacle, said it "looked like the Russian Revolution." (Movement militants liked to cite that quote to certify their path—as if the attorney general was an expert on revolutions.) The Nixon White House, which had tried for weeks to tar the entire antiwar movement with the brush of violence, was delighted. Over the protest of the news staff, the Justice Department sideshow took the lead over the mass march on the *CBS Evening News*.

But unlike the other sects, forever selling their newspapers on the fringes of the crowd, the Weathermen were not willing to settle for parasitical influence. Martyrdom could not satisfy them forever. They were impressed by the Tupamaros, the Uruguayan urban guerrillas who robbed banks and kidnapped the rich to finance their movement; they reveled in the terror tactics displayed in *The Battle of Algiers*. To push on to the next phase, and abort doubt, they had to forge, at white heat, a world apart. So they withdrew from friends and former comrades, and sealed themselves off airtight. The world having failed their analysis, they rejected it. The whole movement had been self-enclosed for a long time, progressively more so into the late Sixties, for turning toward revolution usually meant turning away from family and the wrong friends, dropping contact with disquieting ideas, confounding books, critical magazines. Of course, the more insulated we were from counterarguments and complicated reality, the easier it was to hold onto abstract revolutionary schemes. The Weathermen developed this hermetic tendency to a coarse art. The revolutionary loop closed.

In the furious Weathergroups, inconvenient individualism got reduced to pulp; battered egos were welded into the Weathermachine. Couples were disbanded by fiat; everyone was to sleep with everyone else, women with men, women with women, men with men. Weatherwomen wrote articles celebrating their victories over monogamy. The point was to crash through the barriers to revolution by creating a single fused life: "People who live together and fight together fuck together." Collective drug sessions, and protracted rounds of "criticism-self-criticism," adapted from Maoism, broke down "bourgeois" inhibitions. (The LSD ritual was also intended to flush out police infiltrators, but at least one FBI informer succeeded in passing the "acid test.") And then, having "smashed monogamy," the Weathermen turned around and experimented with celibacy, as if to prove they were will incarnate, more powerful even than sex.

All summer and fall of 1969, what remained of the New Left buzzed with rumors and dismay and horror about the Weathermen; and while most of the movement was appalled ("You don't need a rectal thermometer to know who the assholes are," was a Wisconsin SDS slogan), and the Weather ranks never grew beyond a few hundred, they held the rest of the Left enthralled. Freelance collectives split over whether to join or imitate them. At just the moment when antiwar action was peaking, most SDS chapters broke apart, floundered, or collapsed. Imitators formed their own collective: "Mad Dogs" in New York, "Juche" (the North Korean slogan for self-reliance) in Cambridge, Massachusetts. Sympathizers in Washington and New York met to figure out what beliefs they shared with the Weathermen and to wonder aloud if they had the guts to run with them. (Some humor surfaced in Berkeley, though: Frank Bardacke, Sol Stern, and friends formed a commune called "Fisherman." Their slogan: "You don't need a fisherman to know something's fishy." Their T-shirt showed a hand gripping a fish—a "clenched fish.") Those who disappeared into the

Weathermachine spoke bitterness to recalcitrants who wouldn't follow. "If you don't do it our way, you're up against the wall"—that was how Kathy Boudin told off one of her old comrades, himself a self-described "militant internationalist." ("You're so hostile and fucked-up," he yelled back. Those were the last words they exchanged.) They convinced themselves that other activists would be inspired "to re-examine the nature of their revolutionary commitment . . . and to struggle harder," but most of the "struggling" took place between, and within, the movement's battered psyches.

To go with the Weathermen was to take flight from political reality. To go against them was to go—where? Women could take refuge, find community and political purpose in the women's movement. But most of the old New Left men—those who weren't on trial or immersed in defense committees—felt paralyzed. In the name of what compelling strategy for ending the war could we oppose the Weatherpeople? The weather felt as though it had become the climate. We could not imagine any life without the movement, but the movement no longer held any life for us. The demonstration rituals felt stale and—for militants—increasingly dangerous. Anyway, the occasional demonstration, whether nonviolent or not, could not satisfy our need for an insurgent life all of a piece. What we wanted—what we had lived for the better part of a decade now—was a movement which was both a whole way of life and the cutting edge of change. Now the sects, the Weathermen most of all, had run off with the cutting edge. Some veterans, burned out by the infighting, brooding with visions of impending apocalypse (concentration-camp roundups, urban riots), found this a propitious moment to slip off into communes in Vermont, Mendocino, and their equivalents. They talked about offing the pig and joked about "liberated bases"; what they did was feed their livestock. Beneath the rhetoric, they kept up their whole way of life by relinquishing any illusion that they could shape history.

On the intellectual's premise that to comprehend was to feel liberated—or was comprehension only the next best thing?—I worked on and off for months on a long essay about the movement's crisis. But the harder I looked at the movement's history, the less I saw simple error, the more I saw the Weathermen embodying the worst of both poles of the movement's long-standing built-in dilemma. Their guilty Third Worldism was a caricature of the "politics-for-others" stance, their arrogance an extension of "politics-for-selves." The white movement had been guilty of a "failure of nerve"; now it should take its "postscarcity" identity seriously while recognizing its limits, all the while disowning the false solution of Leninism. In the meantime, I criticized "assuming you are the revolution if you say so; getting to like the taste of the word 'dictatorship' (of the proletariat, over the proletariat, over anyone); getting so pleased with being correct that you don't like being corrected; substituting rhetoric and slogans for analysis and appeals; kicking your friends as practice for your enemies." In columns for the *Guardian* and articles for the underground papers, I railed against sectarianism in the name of a cooler anti-imperialism. If *only* the movement would wise up! All well and good, but appeals to movement will amounted to ineffectual moralism, and I half knew it.

All my thinking had been predicated on the intelligence of the movement itself as the embryo—like the classical Marxian proletariat—of a new society taking shape in the shell of the old. Now the premise decomposed. Therefore, the more predestined the Weathermen and the SDS crackup seemed, the more depressed I felt. "Can't separate things," I wrote Chris Hobson: "grief over SDS & all that; sense of displacement from 'the movement'—which seems to require quotation marks now; . . . discovering that I had believed in the movement *itself* (you're right: an elitist belief) as embodiment as well as instrument of dreams; having lost faith, I don't know just what I believe in now." Around the country, my comrades were making their own agonizing reappraisals. One spent days building wooden model airplanes. Whenever I brought up the subject of SDS's collapse, to see whether anything could be resurrected by old-timers, he threw up his hands. I couldn't blame him. But we were not much good for each other. Our exhaustion and impotence congealed into yet another political fact. The sects had triumphed by default—and our defeat became one more bludgeon with which to beat ourselves.

Some argued rationally against particulars in the Weatherman manifesto—who exactly *was* the hypothetical vanguard, for example? Carl Oglesby pointed out the Weathermen's incoherence: "Sometimes the vanguard is the black ghetto community, sometimes only the Panthers, sometimes the Third World as a whole, sometimes only the Vietnamese, and sometimes apparently only the Lao Dong [North Vietnamese Communist] Party. Sometimes it is a curiously Hegelian concept, referring vaguely to all earthly manifestations of the spirit of revolution." Some endorsed the Weatherman notion that imperialism was a system from which all white (and why only white?) Americans benefited, and picked away at the Weathermen's backfiring tactics, their romance with the Third World, their male chauvinism. But the counterarguments, deep or shallow, were beside the point. The Weathermen were a scourge, not an argument. They were the foam on a sea of rage. The same rage disarmed their opponents. Worst of all, in the revolutionary mood, no one could imagine how to translate compelling refutations into a compelling political practice.

No alternative theory or action crystallized from the murk of the collective despair. Too much of the criticism came in the name of some less melodramatic but still abstract vision of The Revolution. *They're crazy*, one heard, *but you have to admit they've got guts. Anyway, are you quite so sure they're wrong? And what is going to bring down American imperialism? And what are you, we, going to do about it?* It was hard to summon up the standing to criticize. Were not critics tainted by their love of private life? Did not many white New Leftists feel, in the ferocity of their political frustration, that private life was a niche protecting what Tom Hayden too called "the pseudo-radicalism of the white left"? Hayden, for one, concluded that "the New Left was rapidly becoming the old left, a comfortable left, with too many radicals falling into the ruts of teaching and monogamy, leaving Che and Malcolm and Huey only as posters on their walls." With Malcolm and various Cuban posters on my own wall, I took it personally.

Thousands in the movement's most experienced networks bled from the bludgeons of Weatherguilt. "Gut-checking"—scrutinizing one another for leftover "bourgeois attitudes"—became the movement's favorite parlor game. And what one didn't do to one's comrades, one could do to oneself. There was a tale about an activist in Santa Barbara who wondered aloud whether it was counterrevolutionary to watch the sunset. I remember telling a friend that even if American prosperity did rest on the exploitation of the Third World—a cardinal movement premise in 1969—a politics built on guilt was not to be trusted. "Where would we be without guilt?" was his retort, and that stopped me. We, the collectively privileged—he himself was the son of a wealthy doctor—could not be trusted. Touché, I thought, though my own parents were high school teachers. A modest tuna sandwich had the power to remind me that I'd read somewhere that the tuna catch came from the waters of countries like Peru whose people didn't have enough protein to eat. I dreamed about the Weathermen and the Conspiracy defendants. In dreams, they weren't berating me; old comrades were partners again. They were *doing something*. What was I doing?

"Do you find the word incredible is no longer useful?" I wrote Chris

Hobson after the Days of Rage. The sheer facts were stupefying. Kathy Boudin and I had been good friends in the mid-Sixties, when she was neither stupid nor foolhardy. I knew many of the other Weathermen. They were not geniuses but not dopes either—at least not any dopier than any of the other sectarians. Big consequences surely required big causes, but my common sense failed to comprehend their wildness. Casting about, I turned to *When Prophecy Fails*, the classic of social psychology published in 1956. Leon Festinger, Henry W. Riecken, and Stanley Schachter investigated a millenarian cult which believed that on a certain date a great flood would engulf the land, but they would be carried off in time by flying saucers. When the great day came and neither flood nor saucers materialized, many believers fell away, but some devotees found a way to make sense of the "cognitive dissonance." The absence of saucers became a signal that they were coming later—and so the believers redoubled their commitment. Around this time, I ran into a friend who had also been a friend of Bernardine Dohrn. She told me she had found a book that made the Weathermen comprehensible: *When Prophecy Fails*.

The Weatherlogic ground on, relentless. In blind faith and paranoia, the barbarians made ready to go underground. "We have to create chaos and bring about the disintegration of pig order," proclaimed their invitation to a Christmas 1969 "National War Council" in Flint, Michigan. America was Rome and they talked of changing their name to the Vandals, again taking inspiration from Dylan: "the pump won't work 'cause the vandals took the handles."

Inside Flint's ghetto ballroom, a huge cardboard machine gun hung from the ceiling. A twenty-foot poster depicted bullets attached ecumenically to the Weathermen's enemies' list: Mayor Daley, Humphrey, Johnson, Nixon, Ronald Reagan, the *Guardian*—and Sharon Tate, recently murdered by Charles Manson's gang while eight months pregnant. The slogans were "Piece Now," "Sirhan Sirhan Power," "Red Army Power." The sessions, amid whoops and karate displays, were dubbed "wargasms." Bernardine Dohrn apologized for the Weathermen's having gone "wimpy" after the Days of Rage. Three weeks before, the Illinois Black Panther leader Fred Hampton had been murdered in his sleep during an armed assault on the Panther apartment by Chicago police; the Weathermen should have burned Chicago down, said Bernardine. She recommended a new attitude: "We were in an airplane and we went up and down the aisle 'borrowing' food from people's plates. They didn't know we were Weathermen; they just knew we were *crazy*. That's what we're about, being crazy motherfuckers and scaring the shit out of honky America." Mark Rudd contributed this pensée: "It's a wonderful feeling to hit a pig. It must be a really wonderful feeling to kill a pig or blow up a building." "JJ," a onetime Columbia strategist, said: "We're against everything that's 'good and decent' in honky America. We will burn and loot and destroy. We are the incubation of your mother's nightmare." The more theoretically inclined Ted Gold said that "an agency of the people of the world" should be set up to run the United States once imperialism went down to defeat; when a critic objected that this sounded "like a John Bircher's worst dream," Gold replied: "Well, if it will take fascism, we'll have to have fascism." Charles Manson, exulted Bernardine Dohrn, truly understood the iniquity of white-skinned America: "Dig it! First they killed those pigs, then they ate dinner in the same room with them, then they even shoved a fork into the victim's stomach. Wild!" Flint's favored greeting was four slightly spread fingers—to symbolize the fork.

Flint's "group psychosis"—so one participant later called it—was a public rite to exorcise the Weathermen's last doubts. Their experiments in ego-smashing had succeeded. Having unmade and remade themselves, they had resolved to disband what was left of SDS and go it alone. After Flint, their collectives broke into smaller groups, Debrayist "focos," the better to weed out infiltrators and faint-hearts. They dropped from sight, about a hundred people in all. Only loosely connected, the affinity groups made their plans.

Over the next few months, Weatherpeople rarely surfaced among unbelievers. When they did, one of their themes was that all white babies were tainted with the original sin of "skin privilege." "All white babies are pigs," one Weatherman had insisted in Flint. Robin Morgan recounts that one day a Weatherwoman saw her breastfeeding her baby son in the *Rat* office. "You have no right to have that pig male baby," said the Weatherwoman. "How can you say that?" said Morgan. "What should I do?" "Put it in the garbage," was the answer.

On March 6, 1970, Cathy Wilkerson's father, a radio-station owner, was vacationing in the Caribbean. Cathy had grown up without her father, grown up without much money, in fact, a bit of a juvenile delinquent. Then her father had paid her way to Swarthmore College, where she'd joined SDS. Now, in what she later called "a sort of guerilla action," she had made off with the key to his West Eleventh Street townhouse, just off Fifth Avenue. There, a group of Weathermen were manufacturing pipe bombs and bombs studded with roofing nails—makeshift copies of antipersonnel bombs like those the United States was dropping in Vietnam. Someone connected the wrong wire. The house blew up, igniting the gas mains. Cathy Wilkerson, Kathy Boudin, and several other Weathermen staggered out of the rubble and disappeared. That night, Ted Gold's crushed body was identified. Diana Oughton's had to be identified from the print on a severed fingertip. There wasn't enough of Terry Robbins's body left to identify; only a subsequent Weatherman communiqué established that he was the third who died. Enough dynamite was recovered, undetonated, to blow up a city block. By some reports, including the police's, the roofing-nail bombs were intended for use at Columbia University; the Weathermen deny it. There is another claim that they were planning to bomb an army noncommissioned officers' dance at Fort Dix, New Jersey. The Weathermen have never said—they insist they will never say—what the target was going to be.

I t was, and is, too pat: "the Sixties blew up." If the townhouse had blown up on February 1, it could have rounded out an exact decade since the Greensboro sit-ins. Indeed, the quest for precise symbolism might back up to the wee hours of New Year's Day, 1970, when three Wisconsin activists stole an ROTC plane and dropped three bombs—which failed to explode—on an army ammunition plant outside Madison. ("The Vanguard of the Revolution," they called themselves.) The habit of thinking in decades is hard to break. So is the sense of inevitability, and the search for a neat lesson. What conclusion would be commensurate with this disaster? That what goes up must come down? What begins in ideals ends in destruction? If nonviolence is dead, anything is permitted?

The turn toward deliberate violence against property was already well along, the explosions amplified, as usual, by the mass media. By conservative estimate, between September 1969 and May 1970 there were some 250 major bombings and attempts linkable with the white Left—about one a day. (By government figures, the actual number may have been as many as six times as great.) The prize targets were ROTC buildings, draft boards, induction centers, and other federal offices. As far as is known, almost all these acts were committed by freelance bombers and burners, though the Weathermen, the most organized phalanx, were probably some inspiration to greener terrorists. For every bomber and arsonist there were several who mulled over the idea. The members of one Berkeley commune liked to go out at night, for example, randomly trashing Safeways (in support of striking farm workers) or banks (against imperialism); massive retaliation might be imminent, they thought, and for that contingency they kept a Molotov cocktail in the basement, designed to the specifications of the *New York Review of Books* cover of 1967. A San Francisco grouplet, impressed by the attention the media paid to political explosions, hoarded dynamite and talked seriously about blowing up Grace Cathedral (which had been a refuge for antiwar meetings) as an act of protest.

As antiwar militants turned against imperialism, attacks turned to the headquarters of multinational corporations. On February 4, a riot in Isla Vista, outside Santa Barbara, in protest against the guilty verdicts in the Chicago Conspiracy trial, culminated in the burning of the local branch of the Bank of America. (A student explained, "It was the biggest capitalist thing around.") Five nights after the townhouse explosion, bombs went off in the Manhattan headquarters of Socony Mobil, IBM, and General Telephone and Electronics; a note to the press denounced "death-directed Amerika." No one knows how many people committed all these acts; probably only a hundred or two, including police agents. (The most famous was Thomas Tongyai, "Tommy the Traveler," who expertly posed as an SDS organizer in upstate New York and taught militants how to make Molotov cocktails to burn down a campus ROTC building.) Many antiwar militants were reduced to cheerleading. "The real division is not between people who support bombings and people who don't," wrote Jane Alpert, herself a secret member of a freelance bombing collective, "but between people who will *do* them and people who are too hung up on their own privileges and security to take those risks."

The West Eleventh Street disaster sobered the surviving Weathermen and probably saved more lives than it cost. Just afterward, the network of Weatherman groups convened for an emergency summit meeting. In a supercharged atmosphere, they rejected any further antipersonnel tactics and decided to centralize. They tried appointing themselves the vanguard of the freak culture; in September they tried to secure that reputation by helping Timothy Leary escape from the California federal prison where he was serving a drug sentence. The twenty or so bombs they set off subsequently (including one that blew up New York police headquarters and another a U.S. Capitol bathroom) killed no one; the Weathermen (now feminized as the Weather Underground) phoned warnings. Dwindling numbers of cheerleaders went on rejoicing. But the townhouse shook the ground under the whole movement. The freelance bombings up to that point had killed no one. The Weathermen, like it or not, were national figures; three people were dead; and New York was the world's media hub. As word spread about what was being manufactured in the townhouse, there was the toll of an ending, the subliminal sense that what blew up was not just three people but the movement's innocence and its larger logic.

But still there is a missing link. How exactly does one get from murky theory about the world revolution to blasting caps and roofing nails? Not just through a wrongheaded political analysis. Not just by mistake, or the malignant habit of abstraction, or hermetic self-enclosure. It asks too much of any strictly political logic, either the Pentagon's or the Weathermen's, that it should explain the building of bombs whose use is to kill civilians at random. Nor can individual biographies account for the way revolutionaries can shade into nihilism. There is something not quite explained by the notion of forcing an impossible revolution. For even if one is willing to sever means from ends, it is not easy to forget the practical fact that the State possesses the vast majority of the guns. The war had kindled a loathing for "Amerikkka," but the Weathermen were traveling to the far reaches of loathing. The immensely bad ideas and dreadful tactics must have had a root in some larger upheaval of the movement's collective psyche. Charles Manson, the fork, the Weathermen as vandals and scourges—we have stumbled into the realm of the demonic.

A curious slogan, "Bring the war home." Curious too, the particular slant Ted Gold gave it in a talk with an old Columbia comrade he met in the West End Bar on Broadway not long before he died. As things stood, Ted Gold said, the Vietnam war was an abstraction; liberals could afford to sit back and let it happen on the other side of the world. "We've got to turn New York into Saigon," he said.

"Smashing the pig means smashing the pig inside ourselves, destroying our own honkiness": so went their last aboveground communiqué. They wanted to be "bad"—"We are the incubation of your mother's nightmare"—the way the Vietcong and the Panthers were "bad." As the movement had felt from the start that it had to give birth to itself, so had the revolutionary child metamorphosed into its own harsh parent, out to "smash" the retrograde, hesitant self. Revolutionary logic, tied in knots, led to a bad imitation of Pentagon logic. They could not see that the dread "pig inside ourselves" that had to be "smashed" was not just "male chauvinism, individualism, competition," but the imperial attitude which insisted that villages had to be destroyed in order to save them. The best to be said for the Weathermen is that for all their rant and bombs, in eleven years underground they killed nobody but themselves.*

The townhouse was the flash point for an implosion still greater and more horrendous. The Weathermen heightened the general self-hatred, darkened the darkness that already spilled over the Left. No end to the war, no end to the trials, no end to being white or American; no end to guilt for not being on trial, or dead, or for not being a Weatherman, or for not having stopped them. . . . It was as if the whole of the Left, and the counterculture as well, discovered bottomless guilt and death around them and inside them, not always able to tell which was outside and which inside. In the poisoned, sectarian atmosphere, even political trials—those time-honored occasions for solidarity— ceased to unify. With so much harshness and suspicion and death in the air, it was not easy to find a life-principle. Beneath the billowing clouds of rhetoric, the Left's real-life problem was simplifying down to a single earthy one: how to keep the terror at bay.

Everyone had a casualty roll call in 1969-70. Here is mine:

■ Early in May 1969, a man who called himself a reporter telephoned my old SDS friend Dick Flacks, then an assistant professor of sociology at the University of Chicago, and asked for an interview. Flacks, who had been visibly active against the war, agreed to meet the man in his office. He had never seen him before. After a few moments of conversation, the man took a crowbar and smashed Flack's skull and his right wrist. A student found him by chance, lying in a puddle of blood, his hand almost severed. Newspaper editorials had been fulminating that radical professors were responsible for student rebellion.

■ The day after the Weathermen's Days of Rage, the police arrested Charles Manson outside Los Angeles and charged him and his harem-commune with the grisly Tate-LaBianca murders. Monstrous, but what did it mean? In those plummeting days, every stark fact was pressed into world-historical significance: teenage vandalism became "Blows Against the Empire," guerrilla attacks permuted into fronts of the single world revolution. For the mass media, the acidhead Charles Manson was readymade as the monster lurking in the heart of every longhair, the rough beast slouching to Beverly Hills to be born for the next millennium. At year's end the Weathermen too boasted a family resemblance, never mind that Manson's gang tried to pin the murders on blacks, hoping to foment race war. Jerry Rubin caricatured the caricature, paid Manson a visit in prison, and wrote: "I fell in love with Charlie Manson the first time I saw his cherub face and sparkling eyes on national TV. . . . His words and courage inspired [me] . . . and I felt great the rest of the day, overwhelmed by the depth of the experience of touching Manson's soul . . ." The Los Angeles *Free Press* let Manson write a column, and ran free ads for a recording he made; another underground paper, *Tuesday's Child*, depicted him as a hippie on the cross.

Marvin Garson looked at the hypnotic-eyed photo of Manson on the cover of *Life* magazine and proclaimed the portent: "Charles Manson, *son of man*." I argued with him, but the media image was not altogether dismissible. Not so long before, long hair had portended good. Even politicos like me, who pooh-poohed the hippies' pretensions, were glad they were there, pleasant and peaceable if not smashers of the State. Manson was a unique monster. But around that time, visiting a friend in Mendocino, I heard a couple of cowboy-booted longhairs·whoop it up about going into town to find whores, and suddenly realized that the yahoo streak in the counterculture was the resumption of one of the less salutary of American traditions.

■ Meanwhile, on Halloween night, 1969, my bony Jewish-Afro'd freak friend Marshall Bloom, the cofounder of Liberation News Service, sat in his beat-up Triumph Spitfire in western Massachusetts, reading the paper, running exhaust through a hose, and died. Marshall Bloom, twenty-five years old, former editor of the Amherst student paper, leader of student revolt at the London School of Economics, was the incarnation of counterculture whimsy. Ripoffs were his art form. Once he drove across the country in his Sgt. Pepper-style frock coat staying at motels, saying that he was the advance man for a rock band which would arrive the next day, and they would settle the bill together; then waking up at four in the morning and driving off. Ripoffs became habit. In the summer of 1968 he and cofounder Raymond Mungo and their hang-loose hippie faction of LNS wearied of the Marxist half of their collective, made a down payment on a farm, and absconded with money, printing press, and mailing list from bad-vibes New York. ("The movement had become my enemy," Mungo wrote later. "The movement was not flowers and doves and spontaneity, but another vicious system, the seed of heartless bureaucracy, a minority Party vying for power rather than peace.") The New York faction raided the farm, terrorizing and beating Marshall, but after the dust settled, LNS/N.Y. and LNS/Mass. started publishing their separate weekly mailings, Mass.'s polyform, less gray, hippier than New York's. In his droll way Marshall told me that the proper strategy for revolution in America, since America lacked a peasantry, was to populate the countryside with an artificial peasantry—ourselves. Over the next year, the farm and the neighboring farmers became the main preoccupation of the LNS/Mass.

I visited Marshall in the rolling hills near Amherst in September 1969. We picked cucumbers, fried slices of eggplant, drove to nearby Amherst College, his alma mater, to inspect a piece of equipment for his possible acquisition, and talked about the movement turning ugly. Marshall said it was important to distinguish between "opinions," which were cheap, and a "point of view," which came with accretion, preferably in the country. Even if the bucolic image was overripe, I was willing to find peace and wisdom in unlikely places. I was more of a rationalist and a politico than Marshall, less of a hippie, but we appreciated each other.

So on my return to California I started fiddling with a poem for him, rhapsodizing about the cucumber harvest by folks "who a year ago didn't know a furrow / From a hole in the ground." Late in October I mailed it. A few days afterward, a friend called to say that Marshall was dead. The communards found nude-boy magazines in his room; people said he was a closeted and shamefaced "gay celibate," and speculated that the implications of the Stonewall gay riot, the new message of gay pride, hadn't sunk in. Some said he had never recovered from the violent LNS schism. For me, Marshall Bloom died of the movement's sins.

■ Early on the morning of December 4, on the West Side of Chicago, the police shot down Fred Hampton and Mark Clark of the Illinois Black Panthers. Hampton, the state chairman, was killed in his bed. Although the police claimed the Panthers had instigated the shootout, it quickly became clear that the Panthers had fired at most a shot or two while the police riddled the walls with a hundred bullets.

■ Woodstock, in June, had been the long-deferred Festival of Life. So said not only *Time* and *Newsweek* but world-weary friends who had navigated the traffic-blocked thruway and felt the new society aborning, half a million strong, stoned and happy on that muddy farm north of

New York City. If youth culture was too squishy to become a people's army, surely it was at least a luminous prefiguration of the cooperative commonwealth, Abbie Hoffman's "Woodstock Nation," People's Park writ large, that possible and impending good society the vision of which would keep politicos honest. And so when the Rolling Stones announced their own West Coast free concert, at Altamont, near San Francisco, I had to go.

The tale has been told many times of how, at Altamont, among three hundred thousand fans, the Hell's Angels, serving as semiofficial guards, killed a young fan, black, who had a white date and the temerity to offend the Angels (by getting too close to them, or their motorcycles, or the stage), and then, at some point, pulled a gun — all the while Mick Jagger was singing "Under My Thumb." I heard about the killing that night, on the radio, having left before the Stones took the stage. But by the time I left, in the late afternoon, Altamont already felt like death. Let it sound mystical, I wasn't the only one who felt oppressed by the general ambience; a leading Berkeley activist told me he had dropped acid at Altamont and had received the insight that "everyone was dead." It wasn't just the Angels, shoving people around on and near the stage, who were angels of death. Behind the stage, hordes of Aquarians were interfering with doctors trying to help people climb down from bad acid trips. On the remote hillside where I sat, stoned fans were crawling over one another to get a bit closer to the groovy music.

Afterward everyone was appalled and filled with righteous indignation. But exactly who or what was at fault? On a practical plane, there were movie-rights squabbles; greed had played its part in preventing adequate preparations. But the effect was to burst the bubble of youth culture's illusions about itself. The Rolling Stones were scarcely the first counter-cultural heroes to grant cachet to the Hell's Angels. We had witnessed the famous collectivity of a generation cracking into thousands of shards. Center stage turned out to be another drug. The suburban fans who blithely blocked one another's views and turned their backs on the bad-trippers were no cultural revolutionaries. Who could any longer harbor the illusion that these hundreds of thousands of spoiled star-hungry children of the Lonely Crowd were the harbingers of a good society?

That night, lying in bed, I was struck by a bolt of panic so strong, it felt as if my mind were trying to blast away from my body. Too much Altamont, too much bad politics, too much grass added up to a bad "set" and a worse "setting." A few days later, in fear and trembling, I wrote a piece for Liberation News Service called "The End of the Age of Aquarius." "If there is so much bad acid around," I asked, "why doesn't this contaminated culture, many of whose claims are based on the virtues of drugs, help its own brothers and sisters? Why do the underground papers leave it to the media narcotizers to deplore the damaging possibilities of bad drugs? . . . Freedom, in the aggregate, turned out to be a spectator sport. . . ." The star-struck crowd was "turned on, not to each other, not to the communal possibilities, but to the big prize, the easy ticket—the 'good trip.' The age of Aquarius was invented by the same hypesters who believe that television invented the 'global village.' Maybe it did, but then it was the same mean village which Sinclair Lewis wrote to death, a town of petty gossip and quiet desperation." I wondered "whether the youth culture will leave anything behind but a market."

People's Park, even if not the outskirts of Eden, had been an attempt to create; Altamont—even Woodstock—was a ritual consecrated to consumption.

■ In March 1970, three days after the townhouse explosion, in the small Maryland town of Bel Air, a bomb blew up the car carrying Ralph Featherstone and "Che" Payne of SNCC, and killed them. According to their comrades, Featherstone and Payne had gone to Bel Air to set up security for Rap Brown, about to go on trial for inciting to arson; the bomb had probably been intended for Brown, who promptly went underground. The FBI and Maryland state police claimed that Featherstone and Payne had intended to plant the bomb in the courthouse. I hadn't seen Featherstone since Cuba, and I knew people changed, but I couldn't imagine him anything other than sweet-tempered, a cooling influence. It was reasonable to surmise that SNCC was heavily infiltrated by informers, perhaps by agents provocateurs. At the time, at least it was reasonable to think Featherstone had been murdered. In any case, to mourn.

■ On August 24, 1970, a bomb planted by the Madison, Wisconsin, New Year's Gang blew up the army's mathematics research building, killing a graduate student who was working late: the movement's first innocent casualty. This headquarters of war research had been a focus of Madison's nonviolent protest for years. The bombers were veteran activists—a tiny minority, true, but they played out a logic. In the illumination of that bomb the movement knew sin.

Anxiety and despair were most of what I knew. My world had exploded, ten years of the movement; I had lost the ground I walked on. Two nights after the townhouse explosion, I dreamed I was with the Conspiracy defendants, arguing against bombs, while blacks threw boomerangs at our rally; and I was not the only one to keep dream-appointments with the disaster. In the movement rhetoric of that hour, *we* were life and *they* were "the death culture," "Amerika," the Combine out of control, its death lust having surged beyond any rational political motives. The movement core were Manichaeans as well as utopians; our sense of innocence required all-or-nothing thinking, and innocence was the motor of our collective passion. What Altamont was for the counterculture, the townhouse was for the student movement: the splattering rage of the "death culture" lodged in the very heart of the "life force." Whence the shock when it proved impossible to draw a hard and fast line between the two. The revolutionary mood had been fueled by the blindingly bright illusion that human history was beginning afresh because a graced generation had willed it so. Now there wasn't enough life left to mobilize against all the death raining down.

*In the late Seventies, several schisms later, most of the Weather Underground — including Dohrn, Ayers, Wilkerson, and Jones — surfaced and turned themselves in. But on October 20, 1981, a remnant underground group including David Gilbert, Judith Clark, and Kathy Boudin robbed a Brink's truck in Rockland County, north of New York City, killing a guard and two police (including the county's first black policeman) in the process. Gilbert and Clark were found guilty of murder and sentenced to seventy-five years in prison; Boudin, pleading guilty of robbery and murder, was sentenced to twenty years to life.

■■■■■■■■■■

Young Men Fighting or Playing with Green Poles

Diane Wakoski

The secret
has always been
what men find
to do
with each other. Those great
majority of moments which, like football
and jock itch, and mining,
exclude women.

We have so
little.
The hut
where we go
when we're bleeding, and the moon
is swimming or being washed from out between our
thighs.

> Water polo,
> a big sport,
> at my Southern California high school,
> favored by rich kids who lived in The Heights
> with swimming pools,
> boys
> who drove new Fords when they were juniors,
> after their sixteenth birthdays, boys
> who closed their eyes when they touched
> us in those wet places, all
> of us hoping their hands
> would not come away bloody. But the

lips
always were,

whether we sang, "Bar-bar-bar
           Bar-bar-braAnn" or
           "My Little Deuce Coup,"
whether we drank cherry cokes
or milk, or wrote poetry or watched
movies, we walked in our starched crinolines
and lacy blouses once a month to
segregated rooms, smelling like fish
under our deodorant.

But the boys, they had fun
when they were segregated;
when they were alone together
they touched,
   —with jokes
     or greetings,
          "hey, man,"
as we never did;
they talked,
as we still cannot;
they found out how to run the world,
as,
   of course,
we do not.

And water polo, those boys
     hitting that big white ball around
     in the green-like-emeralds water
     of the FUHS olympic-sized pool;

oh, they even knew our secrets;
that the moon they tapped and spun and slapped
around the water was just like the one
pushed out between our thighs each month
     —if we were good,
     —if we were lucky,
     —if we were smart.
oh, don't tell me, EVER,
that women have secret lives,
or treasures
that no one except other women
know about.

     Tell me
      instead,
that the secret is,
and always has been,
why
men find so much pleasure in each
other's company; why women
when they are segregated and together with
each other, have only the menstrual hut,
the old rusty, monthly blood
to share?
or its taboo opposite:
the little clone of ourselves
forming inside our bodies,
etching its face and shape on the moon,
which will then disappear for nine even lonelier
months.

The Awful Power of Make-Believe

P. J. O'Rourke

WHAT I BELIEVED IN THE SIXTIES

Everything. You name it and I believed it. I believed love was all you need. I believed you should be here now. I believed drugs could make you a better person. I believed I could hitchhike to California with 35 cents and people would be glad to feed me. I believed Mao was cute. I believed private property was wrong. I believed my girlfriend was a witch. I believed my parents were Nazi space monsters. I believed the university was putting saltpeter in the cafeteria food. I believed stones had souls. I believed the NLF were the good guys in Vietnam. I believed Lyndon Johnson was plotting to murder all Negroes. I believed Yoko was an artist. I believed Bob Dylan was a musician. I believed I would live forever or until 21, whichever came first. I believed the world was about to end. I believed the Age of Aquarius was about to happen. I believed the *I Ching* said to cut classes and take over the Dean's office. I believed wearing my hair long would end poverty and injustice. I believed there was a great throbbing web of psychic mucus and we were all part of it. I managed to believe Gandhi and H. Rap Brown at the same time. With the exception of anything my parents said, I believed everything.

WHAT CAUSED ME TO HAVE SECOND THOUGHTS

One distinct incident sent me scuttling back to Brooks Brothers. From 1969 to 1971 I was a member of a "collective" running an "underground" newspaper in Baltimore. The newspaper was called, of all things, *Harry*. When *Harry* was founded, nobody could think what to name the thing so we asked some girl's two-year-old son. His grandfather was named Harry and he was calling everything Harry just then so he said, "Harry," and *Harry* was what the paper was called. It was the spirit of the age.

Harry was filled with the usual hippie blather, yea drugs and revolution, boo war and corporate profits. But it was an easygoing publication and not without a sense of humor. The Want Ad section was headlined "Free Harry Classified Help Hep Cats and Kittens Fight Dippy Capitalists Exploitation." And once when the office was raided by the cops (they were looking for marijuana, I might add, not sedition), *Harry* published a page one photo of the mess left by the police search. The caption read, "Harry Office After Bust By Pigs." Next to it was an identical photo captioned "Harry Office Before Bust By Pigs."

Our "collective" was more interested in listening to Captain Beefheart records and testing that new invention, the waterbed, than in overthrowing the state. And some of the more radical types in Baltimore regarded us as lightweights or worse. Thus, one night in the summer of 1970, the *Harry* collective was invaded by some 25 blithering Maoists armed with large sticks. They called themselves, and I'm not making this up, the "Balto Cong." They claimed they were liberating the paper in the name of "the people." In vain we tried to tell them that the only thing the people were going to get by taking over *Harry* was $10,000 in debts and a mouse-infested row house with overdue rent.

There were about eight *Harry* staffers in the office that evening. The Balto Cong held us prisoner all night and subjected each of us to individual "consciousness-raising" sessions. You'd be hauled off to another room where ten or a dozen of these nutcakes would sit in a circle and scream that you were a revisionist running dog imperialist paper tiger whatchama-thing. I don't know about the rest of the staff but I conceded as quick as I could to every word they said.

Finally, about six a.m., we mollified the Balto Cong by agreeing to set up a "People's Committee" to run the paper. It would be made up of their group and our staff. We would all meet that night on neutral turf at the Free Clinic. The Balto Cong left in triumph. I breathed a sigh of relief. My air-head girlfriend, however, had been actually converted to Maoism during her consciousness-raising session. And she left with them.

While the Balto Cong went home to take throat pastilles and make new sticks or whatever, we rolled into action. There were, in those days, about a hundred burned out "street people" who depended on peddling *Harry* for their livelihood. We rallied all of these, including several members of a friendly motorcycle gang, and explained to them how little sales appeal *Harry* would have if it were filled with quotations from Ho Chi Minh instead of free-love personals. They saw our point. Then we phoned the Balto Cong crash pad and told them we were ready for the meeting. However we asked if their Free Clinic was large enough to hold us all. "What do you mean?" they said. "Well," we said, "we're bringing about a hundred of our staff members and there's, what, twenty-five of you, so . . ." They said, uh, they'd get back to us.

We were by no means sure the Balto Cong threat had abated. Therefore the staff photographer, whom I'll call Bob, and I were set to guard the *Harry* household. Bob and I were the only two people on the staff who owned guns. Bob was an ex-Marine and something of a flop as a hippie. He could never get the hair and the clothes right and preferred beer to pot. But he was very enthusiastic about hippie girls. Bob still had his service automatic. I had a little .22 pistol that I'd bought in a fit of wild self-dramatization during the '68 riots. "You never know when the heavy shit is going to come down," I had been fond of saying, although I'd pictured it "coming down" more from the Richard Nixon than the Balto Cong direction. Anyway, Bob and I stood guard.

We stood anxious guard every night for two weeks, which seemed an immense length of time back in the 1970s. Of course we began to get slack, not to say stoned, and forgot things like locking the front door. And through that front door, at the end of two weeks, came a half-dozen hulking Balto Cong. Bob and I were at the back of the first office. Bob had his pistol in the waistband of his ill-fitting bellbottoms. He went to fast draw and, instead, knocked the thing down in the front of his pants. My pistol was in the top drawer of his desk. I reached in and grabbed it, but I was so nervous that I got my thigh in front of the desk drawer and couldn't get my hand with the pistol in it out. I yanked like mad but I was stuck. I was faced with a terrible dilemma. I could either let go of the pistol and pull my hand out of the drawer or I could keep hold of the pistol and leave my hand stuck in there. It never occurred to me to move my leg.

The invading Balto Cong were faced with one man fishing wildly in his crotch and another whose hand was apparently being eaten by a desk. It stopped them cold. As they stood perplexed I was struck by an inspiration. It was a wooden desk. I would simply fire through it. I flipped the safety off the .22, pointed the barrel at the Balto Cong and was just curling my finger around the trigger when the Maoists parted and there, in the line of fire, stood my air-head ex-girlfriend. "I've come to get my ironing board and my Herman Hesse novels," she said, and led her companions upstairs to our former bedroom.

"It's a trap!" said Bob, extracting his gun from the bottom of a pant leg. When the Balto Cong and the ex-girlfriend came back downstairs they faced two exceedingly wide-eyed guys crouching like leopards behind an impromptu barricade of overturned bookcases. They sped for the exit.

It turned out later that Bob was an undercover cop. He'd infiltrated the *Harry* collective shortly after the first issue. All his photos had to be developed at the police laboratory. We'd wonder why, every time we got busted for marijuana, the case was dropped. Bob would always go to the District Attorney's office and convince them a trial would "blow his cover." It was important for him to remain undetected so he could keep his eye on . . . well, on a lot of hippie girls. Bob was in no rush to get back to the Grand Theft Auto detail. I eventually read some of the reports Bob filed with the police department. They were made up of "_____ is involved in the *Harry* 'scene' primarily as a means of upsetting his parents who are socially prominent," and other such. Bob is now an insurance investigator in Baltimore. He's still friends with the old *Harry* staff. And of the whole bunch of us I believe there's only one who's far enough to the left nowadays to even be called a Democrat.

WHAT I BELIEVE NOW

N othing. Well, nothing much. I mean, I believe things that can be proven by reason and by experiment, and believe you me, I want to see the logic and the lab equipment. I believe that Western civilization, after some disgusting glitches, has become almost civilized. I believe it is our first duty to protect that civilization. I believe it is our second duty to improve it. I believe it is our third duty to extend it if we can. But let's be careful about the last point. Not everybody is ready to be civilized. I wasn't in 1969.

IS THERE ANYTHING TO BE GAINED BY EXAMINING ALL THIS NONSENSE?

I like to think of my behavior in the Sixties as a "learning experience." Then again, I like to think of anything stupid I've done as a "learning experience." It makes me feel less stupid. However I actually did learn one thing in the 1960s (besides how to make a hash pipe out of an empty toilet paper roll and some aluminum foil). I learned the awful power of make-believe.

There is a deep-seated and frighteningly strong human need to make believe things are different than they are—that salamanders live forever, we all secretly have three legs and there's an enormous conspiracy somewhere which controls our every thought and deed, etc. And it's not just ignorant heathen, trying to brighten their squalid days, who think such things up. Figments of the imagination can be equally persuasive right here in clean, reasonable, education-choked middle America. People are greedy. Life is never so full it shouldn't be fuller. What more can Shirley MacLaine, for instance, want from existence? She's already been rewarded far beyond her abilities or worth. But nothing will do until she's also been King Tut and Marie of Romania. It was this kind of hoggish appetite for epistemological romance that sent my spoiled and petulant generation on a journey to Oz, a journey from which some of us are only now straggling back, in intellectual tatters.

Many people think fantastic ideas are limited to the likes of Harmonic Convergences, quartz crystals that ward off cancer or, at worst, hare-brained theories about who killed JFK. Unfortunately this is not the case, especially not in this century. Two of the most fecund areas for cheap fiction are politics and economics. Which brings me to Marxism.

Marxism is a perfect example of the chimeras that fueled the Sixties. And it was probably the most potent one. Albeit, much of this Marxism would have been unrecognizable to Marx. It was Marxism watered down, Marxism spiked with LSD, and Marxism adulterated with mystical food coloring. But it was Marxism nonetheless because the wildest hippie and the sternest member of the Politburo shared the same day-dream, the day-dream that underlies all Marxism: that a thing might somehow be worth other than what people will give for it. This just is not true. And any system that bases itself on such a will-o-the-wisp is bound to fail. Communes don't work. Poland doesn't either.

Now this might not seem like much to have learned. You may think I could have gleaned more from a half dozen years spent ruining chromosomes, morals, and any chance of ever getting elected to political office. After all, the hippies are gone and—if *glasnost* is any indication—the Communists are going. But there is a part of the world where politico-economic fish stories are still greeted with gape-jawed credulity. It's a part of the world that pretty much includes everybody except us, the Japanese, some Europeans and a few of the most cynical Russians. You can call it the Third World, the Underdeveloped World or just the Part of the World That's Completely Screwed.

Over the past four years, working as a foreign correspondent, I've spent a lot of time in the part of the world that's completely screwed. It's always seemed a comfortable and familiar-feeling place to me. The reason is, Third World countries are undergoing national adolescences very similar to the personal adolescence I underwent in the Sixties. Woodstock Nation isn't dead; it's just become short, brown, distant, and filled with chaos and starvation.

Marxism has tremendous appeal in the Third World for exactly the same reason it had tremendous appeal to me in college. It gives you something to believe in when what surrounds you seems unbelievable. It gives you someone to blame besides yourself. It's theoretically tidy. And, best of all, it's fully imaginary so it can never be disproved.

The Third World attitude towards the United States is also easy to understand if you think of it in terms of adolescence. The citizens of the Third World are in a teenage muddle about us—full of envy, imitation, anger and blind puppy love. I have been held at gunpoint by a Shi'ite youth in West Beirut who told me in one breath that America was "pig Satan devil" and that he planned to go to dental school in Dearborn as soon as he got his green card. In Ulundi, in Zululand, I talked to a young man who, as usual, blamed apartheid on the United States. However, he had just visited the U.S. with a church group and also told me, "Everything is so wonderful there. The race relations are so good. And everybody is rich." Where had he gone, I asked. "The south side of Chicago."

We are a beautiful twenty-year-old woman and they are a wildly infatuated thirteen-year-old boy. They think of us every moment of the day and we take no notice of them whatsoever. If they can't have a chance to love us, a chance to pester us will do—by joining the Soviet Bloc, for example. Anything for attention.

Isn't this very like the relationship we "drop-outs" of the Sixties had to the "straight" society of our parents? Weren't we citizens of our own Underdeveloped World, the world of American teenage pop culture?

So what are we supposed to do about all this? How do we keep the disaffected youth of the West out of mental Disney World? How do we keep the poor denizens of Africa, Asia and Latin America from embracing a myth that will make their lives even worse than they are already? How do we keep everyone from falling under the spell of some even more vile and barbaric phantom such as religious fundamentalism? We have to offer an alternative to nonsense, an alternative that is just as engaging but actually means something.

Maybe we should start by remembering that we already live in a highly idealistic, totally revolutionary society. And that our revolution is

based on reality, not bullshit. Furthermore it works. Look around us. It
works like a son of a bitch. We have to remember it was this revolution,
not the Bolsheviks', that set the world on fire. Maybe we should start
acting like we believe in it again. That means turning our face against
not only the Qaddafis, Khomeinis, and Gorbachevs, but also against
the Dengs, Pinochets, and Bothas.

The President and his advisors will not have to sit up late working
on a speech to explain this policy shift. There's a perfectly suitable text
already in print:

> *We hold these truths to be self-evident, that all men are
> created equal, that they are endowed by their Creator
> with certain inalienable Rights, that among these are
> Life, Liberty and the pursuit of Happiness. That to
> secure these rights, Governments are instituted among
> Men, deriving their just powers from the consent of
> the governed.*

And that is a much spacier idea than anything which occurred to me
during the 1960s.

■■■■■■■■■■

Building

Gary Snyder

We started our house midway through the Cultural Revolution,
The Vietnam war, Cambodia, in our ears,
   tear gas in Berkeley,
Boys in overalls with frightened eyes, long matted hair, ran
   from the police.
We peeled trees, drilled boulders, dug sumps, took sweat baths
   together.
That house finished we went on
Built a schoolhouse, with a hundred wheelbarrows,
   held seminars on California paleo-indians during lunch.
We brazed the Chou dynasty form of the character "Mu"
   on the blacksmithed brackets of the ceiling of the lodge,
Buried a five-prong vajra between the schoolbuildings
   while praying and offering tobacco.
Those buildings were destroyed by a fire, a pale copy rebuilt
   by insurance.

Ten years later we gathered at the edge of a meadow.
The cultural revolution is over, hair is short,
   the industry calls the shots in the Peoples Forests.
Single mothers go back to college to become lawyers.

Blowing the conch, shaking the staff-rings
   we opened work on a Hall,
Forty people, women carpenters, child labor, pounding nails,
Screw down the corten roofing and shape the beams
   with a planer,
The building is done in three weeks.
We fill it with flowers and friends and open it up to our hearts.

Now in the year of the Persian Gulf,
Of Falsehoods and Crimes in the Government held up as Virtues,
   this dance with Matter
Goes on: our buildings are solid, to live, to teach, to sit,
To sit, to know for sure the sound of a bell—

This is history. This is outside of history.
Buildings are built in the moment,
   they are constantly wet from the pool
     that renews all things
    naked and gleaming.

The moon moves
Through her twenty-eight nights.
Wet years and dry years pass;
Sharp tools, good design.

■■■■■■■■■■
The Movement

Casey Hayden

The movement was everything to me: home and family, food and work, love and a reason to live. When I was no longer welcome there and then when it was no longer there at all, it was hard to go on. Many of us in this situation, especially the Southern whites, only barely made it through. I count myself lucky to be a survivor. But that is another story.

Some felt that what we were doing was the most natural and proper thing in the world, that we were heroines from the very beginning, that each move was carefully planned. Actually, as I recall, one thing led to another and it was all quite underground, illegal, dangerous and on the road. There was a lot of bumming of cigarettes from each other and long cross-country drives in the night to meetings and a lot of going home with someone afterward, or taking someone home. It was outrageous, really. Exciting, liberating, spicy, when we were young and in the South. Sometimes I have longed for the movement so profoundly. The only nostalgia that compares is for my grandmother's backyard when I was a child—the pomegranates and ripe figs, roses and sweet peas, ferns and irises and crepe myrtles and oleanders, pecans and walnuts and swings and wet grass on little bare feet in the summertime. The movement was rich like that. And in like manner there is no going back.

There was a comfort in that time that was born of the absolute certainty that what I was doing was the right thing to be doing. Nothing compares to that except the carrying, bearing and nursing of my children. When we were young and in the South we were so beautiful and naive. It was a children's crusade, really. We were the fairhaired girls and nothing could touch us. Looking back we marvel at our courage, but at the time there was no courage, no fear. We were protected by our righteousness. The whole country was trapped in a lie. We were told about equality but we discovered it didn't exist. We were the only truth-tellers, as far as we could see. It seldom occurred to us to be afraid. We were sheathed in the fact of our position. It was partly our naiveté which allowed us to leap into this position of freedom, the freedom of absolute right action.

I think we were the only Americans who will ever experience integration. We were the beloved community, harassed and happy, just like we'd died and gone to heaven and it was integrated there. We simply dropped race. This doesn't happen anymore. And in those little hot black rural churches, we went into the music, into the sound, and everyone was welcome inside this perfect place.

We were actually revolutionists, in my opinion. We loved the untouchables. We believed the last should be first, and not only should be first, but in fact were first in our value system and it was only the blindness of everyone else not to recognize this fact. They were first because they were redeemed already, purified by their suffering, and they could therefore take the lead in the redemption of us all. We wanted to turn everything not only upside down, but inside out. This is not mild stuff. It is not much in vogue now. We believed, pre-Beatles, that love was the answer. Love, not power, was the answer. All the debates about nonviolence and direct action and voter registration, in my view, were really about whether love or power was the answer. And we did love each other so much. We were living in a community so true to itself that all we wanted was to organize everyone into it, make the whole world beloved with us, make the whole would our beloved, lead the whole world to the consciousness that it was our beloved and please come in to the fire, come in here by the fire. This is where it is truly safe.

The movement in its early days was a grandeur which feared no rebuke and assumed no false attitudes. It was a holy time. This is, of course, just my personal experience, as is all of life.

Some of us were radicals. We liked to think of being radical as going to the root of things. Of course, I was with the New Left folks a lot, the rowdies, although they were quieter and more scholarly then, before the war. Unfortunately radicals of the right came up with clearer answers to the questions we raised than we did. And better P.R. The failure of liberalism which we correctly identified has in fact issued forth in a right swing. I don't know any left-wing radicals today, really.

The following approach to the women's movement is an example of

245

the style in which we thought, mostly at the time about race. Even for those of us who do not pretend to be politically involved it is good to do these exercises now and then for old times' sake, to keep the fort intact: Traditionally, the notion that women are trapped by and need to be liberated from their childbearing function, their biology, is widely accepted in the women's movement. I think it's incorrect. If carried to its logical extreme this position would result in the eradication of the human race.

Why not take biology, the body, as positive and see the problem in the society, the culture's attitude toward birth? No one talks about labor much anymore, and never about labor as a source of value and seldom about labor as in bearing children. Both are undervalued and their place in the rewards of the culture are not reflective of the truth of their value to the experience of being human. Anyone who is present at a human birth, and especially the conscious mother, knows a great secret. Freedom is not a question of the control of the birth function (although certainly that is useful to have at our command) so much as recognition and dignification and reward of this function and the child-rearing function that follows from it. This line of reasoning carries one into deep waters, of course. We used to think like this all the time, these radical approaches with astounding implications.

We used to hold hands and stand in a circle to sing "We Shall Overcome." When we were debating how to continue to work and create together at Waveland after the summer of 1964 (which was a momentous time and a time when we couldn't seem to get at deciding what to do anymore) I remember talking about circles. Instead of lines and boxes and hierarchy in the diagrams of how to organize SNCC, I was drawing circles indicating people working together and the circles overlapping other circles as we all generated programs and things to do together. That was how the movement really was. Our side lost. But we were right. Hierarchy could not replace the circle dance.

Bob Moses changed his name to his mother's maiden name, around this time of the women's memos. It was going back to something else to make the present full, to reach an understanding. He was the only one who knew what to do. Bob wanted to do his doctorate at Harvard on the philosophical differences in Swahili and English, I understand, after he and Janet and the kids got back from Africa. After the SDS reunion there was some money left over which came to the New York group and we used it to throw a party to raise some more money for a film on Ella

Baker. At the party Bob spoke and he talked about a Swahili word which meant the mother of the tribe, the spiritual guide of the community. He said Ella was that. He told about when he was a kid in Harlem and his family was very poor and the only way they could afford milk was through a milk co-op. Years later in the South he learned that this milk co-op had been organized by Ella Baker.

Things do not always fall apart. Sometimes what looks like falling apart is only part of a coming full back around. I think we have to hope for that, for a time when the truths women and old organizers know will be honored and the secret compassion we have secured in our hearts will find value in the population, among the people. Or that the people will find we have shared this all along. Somewhere in the questions that the Swahili/English text would raise must be the question of whether history is linear or circular, or maybe spiral. What is progress, really? How is history to be served? How do we serve each other? What is to be done?

When I was working several years ago with Elaine Baker, another Tougaloo Freedom House grad, on an oral history project in a remote part of southern Colorado, we came up with this idea of putting tape recorders and tapes in the local library. Then we had the idea to get a grant and do it all over the country, so anyone anywhere could come in and record their life history and put it in the local oral history archive. We were working on an old SNCC axiom that everyone is as valuable as everyone else, and so is everyone's experience as valuable as everyone else's. Radical equality, like a mother's love which sees each of her children as equally valuable. We can seize the time and make it our own, make our story our own, in our own style and fashion. For instance, a book about my life would look like a Sixties comic book and be called "The Amazing Life of Casey Cason Hayden: How She Escaped Death and Lived To Tell About It." Getting it published or broadcast is not the main thing. We all remember the discrepancy between reality as we experienced it in the movement and what we read about that reality in print. We know that publication does not validate experience, nor do we need it for our experiences to be valid. What you record will be used, be useful, someday. It will be a service to the future. Save it for your grandchildren.

For the Zen teacher body and mind are one. So for a brief time in history, in our very own lives, art, religion and politics were one. Those of us with SNCC in the South in those days were political, it is true, but

247

more radically, we were observers, participants, and midwives to a great upheaval, uprising, outpouring of the human spirit. This was the spirit of the thousands and thousands of poor Southern blacks who were in fact the movement. The form, the style, the very life of the movement was theirs. They were there when we got there and there when we left. Many of them could not read or write and they could barely speak the English language. They will never see this writing. They, and not we were the heroes, the heroines. I was privileged to have been their servant for a while. To them, for all I learned from them and for all the beauty I witnessed, I extend my most sincere and humble thanks.

■ ■ ■ ■ ■ ■ ■ ■ ■ ■ ■

The Angel of Dad

Fred Pfeil

Max the Rad, galumphing home, saw his dead father strolling down the other side of the street. "Rad" here is short for Radical; Max was 35; his father, who'd died of an embolism eight years before, at the end of his fifties, looked connotatively not at all like his old living self, although the flushed face and heavy body were unmistakable. In mortal life a rumpled figure in nondescript suits shiny with synthetic fiber and prolonged wear, he now appeared a virtual fop in gray wool slacks and blazer, white shirt open at the throat, limber walking stick (rattan, perhaps?) atwirl in his left hand. And the sly good nature of his glance across the street, amused assessment, droll tip of the head—none of this was in character, none at all.

Max the Rad nodded back, monkey see monkey do; his father smiled, walked on. Around Max, to his left and right on this tree-lined street of the smug college town where he lived, a woman flapped her elbows in a gray sweatsuit, a scrubbed squad of young Republican males ambled past fresh from their latest class in death-bound rationality, business or engineering; across the street, as an older couple in matching beige sweaters looked on, his father turned his face over his shoulder and winked back.

"Jesus," exclaimed Max the Rad under his breath, the sound no more than part of the jolt his whole self had just received; and, as instinctively, he turned and walked away. Through the first bleak and then bleaker Seventies into this new ice age he has had to learn how to bracket anomalies, small miracles of political will, squeaks of collective transcendence, without either wholly discounting them or getting too charged up. The result, what this all boiled down to, was a cautious skepticism made of equal parts of plodding on and tune-in-later, muted milleniarianism and despair—which attitude could, with some stretching, cover even the sight of one's dead father heading south on Emerson Street.

So Max turned his attention elsewhere, off over his head to the yellow leaves stirring in the breeze pulled off the ocean and over the coastal range each evening of late summer, early fall, to bank down the heat of these baked plains. *It's okay,* thought Max the Rad to the cuticle of moon at the sky's edge, *Wait and see;* and without pausing for a reply, he bent his dogged long steps home.

T his happened on a Tuesday night, the night of the Women's Study Group, as he was reminded mid-meal by Angela. "Out by seven," she said, leaning forward, resting her arms on the table. "Don't forget."

Her face was hard, her dark brows knit, conveying the same kind of no-nonsense she could dish out at the end of any meeting, when it came time to divvy up tasks. Once, just after hitting town, Max himself had found her humorless and high-handed, back when they'd first met as fellow members of a group opposed to CIA recruiting on campus. Since that time, five years ago now, it had been god knows what all—doomed community coalitions, public employee strike support groups, delegations and committees against cutbacks, for jobs, for economic justice, you name it and Angela was there doing the work, making things go. Since so was Max, at a certain point a few years later it only made sense for them to link up as housemates with Carol and Jill, two other members of La Causa and her friends, in this funky frame house at the student ghetto's dilapidated edge. By that time, of course, he had long since come to understand her brusqueness as a function of an intense focus on the long and short run both, a desire to make (finally) a revolution and to wrap the business up fast before it drove you out of your mind. Yet just now, sitting down to eat, looking forward to telling them all about seeing (or hallucinating) Dad, have a light, caring laugh and letting it go, that same abruptness felt like a slap.

Max took a spoon of glop—cheese-beans, it was called—washed it down with a glug of milk. No good; the rage kept wriggling around, a hot hunched shape low in his chest. Slowly he raised his eyes to his three housemates, dark poised Angela looking back wide-eyed, waiting for his answer, Jill and Carol dipping spoons to and from their bowls, detached as cats. Problem was, everyone still remembered the night six months ago when he barged into the living room having clean forgotten, thus interrupting the group at a particularly sensitive moment, in the midst of their sharing of all their stories of sex with men ever endured against their wills. His grin slowly fading in the face of their appalled collective outrage, the two lesbian separatists, Mickey and Jodey from north of town standing stiffly, brushing past him, walking out in protest—a bad scene for all concerned, which no one wanted again. *Macho shit*, he was thinking even now, stroking milk from his mustache, *just the very kind of thing* but came out with it anyway, knowing someone at their next house meeting would call him on his sulking and be fully in the right. "I know that, Angela," he said. "I'll be out of here on time, dear ladies, never fear."

To his surprise Angela herself said nothing, merely leaned back and lifted a corner of her mouth. It was Jill who put down her spoon and took over instead. "Seems to me," she said, softly enough, "like I'm hearing some hostility there, Max. Want to talk about it some?"

"No," he said, picking his own bowl back up. "Thanks anyway, but no."

"It's okay then?" said Carol, off to his right. "You feel all right about it then?"

Another swallow of milk. Still the anger, but now blended with some guilt. "I feel all right. Thanks for asking. I feel fine."

He finished the meal quickly, and went upstairs to his room for his coat. By the time he came back down they were done too. So he helped Carol pick up while Angela washed and chef du jour Jill went off upstairs, probably to watch her TV. "I'm looking at the Community Calendar," Angela announced as if not a second had passed since the conversation had broken off, and proceeded to read from the pink chart drawn up and distributed monthly by the local DSA folks, posted on the corkboard over the sink. "You can go to the County Commission meeting at the Law Enforcement Building at 7:30. Or to Christians for Peace at the Methodists at 8 o'clock."

She put a glass in the drainboard, wiped her hands on her worn khakis, turned around and smiled at him her dry humorous smile. "Hot dog," he said, trying to respond in kind. "Developers or warm hearts." But he was sure they could both hear the edge still in his voice; he could watch the good will wither, their faces closing down. Carol looked over at Angela; Angela shrugged; Max looked down at the frayed collar of his denim jacket, white with age. "Well then," he said, "have a good meeting. I'm off to the Roost."

And strode down the hall as fast as possible without running, back outside into the sunlight's glaring finale for the day, skid of swallows, clamor of finches hopping in the mangy shrubs up against the dingy house. Destination set, boot heels chunking the pavement; Max the Rad, six feet tall, ginger hair flowing over his collar, marching purposefully off straight ahead. East on 1st, past Emerson, Hawthorne, Dana, Irving, etc.—there was always some such system in these college towns. For almost a year in the mid-70s, back when environmental seemed the only action around, he had lived in a Northern California town where the north-south streets were hardwoods, east and west explorers, trappers, big-name knaves and brigands from a century ago. Another place, this one in Nebraska, simply lettered east-west and gave north-south to former Secretaries of State. Blaine, and H, Dulles and A, Crockett and Cherry, Huntingdon and Oak. Shoe clerk, CETA trainee, dishwasher, nurses' aide. And the Revolution still ain't happened yet.

"Exactly," said his father. "So what've you got to show?"

As if he had simply stolen up, reached your side, and matched his step to yours. All of which (how natural it seemed) being what made it so bizarre; that and the note of unwonted geniality in the old man's voice, which Max sought in vain to match. "I could ask the same of you," he calmly murmured, or tried to.

"So go ahead and ask," said his father, unruffled, patting his thick sides: "I'm here, aren't I?"

"So'm I," said Max. "Is that what we're talking about, degrees of substance on the reality scale? I thought you meant things like washers, dryers, automobiles."

Yet his father failed again to rise to the bait; he shrugged, looked off pensively, shook his head. "There's a middle level," he said. "A connection. You call that a job you got, sitting on a stool in a hippie bookstore? Where you live, is that a home? Anybody care here if you fall over dead? Would you like me to go on?"

The quite obvious political objections to be raised here fluttered away. Instead Max stared at the brown merry eyes under the raised brows, violet shreds of broken capillaries splayed across cheeks and nose. He himself was gasping for air, mind snapping like a windowshade released in cartoons. He forced himself to look away and found they were already past Bryant, nearly downtown, moving through a fringe area of gas stations, Burger and Pizza Huts, suck-it-up desert belt of interchangeable parts backlit by the day's last light. He thought of the beer waiting for him at the Roost, how good it would taste in a moment, and, bolstered by this thought, began his reply.

"I believe," he said, "a brief review is in order. We can start by agreeing you did indeed work your butt off. And that you did so at least partly to give us a good life. And since this made you unhappy much of the time, you made other people miserable at work, came back home to the suburbs miserable, and made us miserable as well. Let me remind you that we lived in a lousy tract house, my mother your wife had no fun for years at a stretch cooped up with us, the TV and an infinitely-refillable scrip for Elavil. And now you come back wanting to talk ontological security? Don't make me laugh."

But Max's father was not laughing; just the opposite. The brown eyes whose gaze in real life had been always opaque now shone with clear trembling tears, forcing the realization that it was he, Max the Rad, who was yelling, waving his arms, being a crud. Then, to his own further astonishment, he was stretching out his arms, drawing his father into something like an embrace. Beneath his hands, through the layers of clothing, he could feel his father's body shudder regularly as if hiccuping, sense the obdurate bones afloat in his dead flesh. With a twinge of shame he realized just how glad he was the street lay as still as a pond. Maybe now, with no one else around, was the time to ask questions, get some information: how the old man got here anyway, ins and outs of life after death, whether this appearance was a special or the first of a series. On the other hand, that seemed like so much male chitchat on stats and techniques, right down there with sports and cars. What you really want to know is what happens next.

No sooner asked than answered: already, with a fresh dapper smile, his father was pulling away from Max's hold. "What you were wondering there a minute ago," he said, brushing his front smooth, "think of it like graduate school. You finish up, you graduate, in your particular case you get so hot to change the world you just drop out, whatever—you think that means you have to stop learning too? Same with dying. Or put it another way—you stop growing you're already dead. It's the truth of the capitalist world."

And with that, stepped jauntily back the way they came, leaving Max staring after with the evening breeze a chill gale force against his stricken face, scarecrow body, bereft self. "Dad!" he cried out. "Dad! Dad!"

A block away, no more than that, beneath a used-car lot sign blinking off and on, he waggled his hand. "See you later, boy," Max's father was calling. "Take care."

Though the Roost was no more than another dank woody bar of
students, hippies, misfits and the slightly crazed, there were at least
other people, people he knew, who knew him, sitting around the
scarred wooden tables smoking cigarettes, drinking beer, talking
whenever they could pry their eyes away from the TV over the bar. For
a while he talked with silver-toothed Soni in her bedraggled peasant
blouse; later, bony Ryland, blinking watery blue eyes; later still, dark
moonfaced Eva, chainsmoking as always, booming out her harsh
clanging laugh. Those three, and then a few others, people he had
worked for, seen at demonstrations, tried to organize. It was hard not to
recall this as they talked, having pretty much the same conversation
every time. How's it going, what are you up to these days; then, a few
minutes later, You still living over on 14th, how's that working out, still
at the bookstore too? Not a word about politics past or future, local or
world; nor did Max display any interest in their exciting personal lives.
It got to be a kind of stalemate, he would just sit there at whoever's
table, let the conversation drop, watch their eyes drift back to the TV
until they figured out that was what you were doing, watching them, at
which point they generally left you alone to rummage through your
own movies from long ago. Working in McMinnville with the migrants,
preaching La Raza, talking union at the nail factory in Culver until you
were canned, proletarianizing yourself but still taking acid, back when
any minute it could still come down, how many years ago now? And
still there, after all, was Johnny Carson over the bar with his first guest
the Lovely So-and-So, the cackle of Ed McMahon. At some point Max
the Rad looked around him at the other tables and chairs, recognized
nary a soul, tried and failed to count the pitchers he'd consumed. It was
time, he figured, to get on back.

So then outside he was making his way back past a litter of
storefronts and houses, beneath a chaos of stars. In his head a numb
buzzing like a fluorescent light, his rangy body a carcass of wet wool.
Under the light on his mind's floor were odd scraps of words he could
pick up and put down as he pleased. *Pessimism of the intelligence,
optimism of the will, el pueblo unido jamas será vincido, you lose till
you win. It stands to reason,* he was thinking—only in his present state
it was neither thought nor exactly what he meant—*the problems of
three little people don't amount to a hill of beans . . .*

In his house—home?—the front room was empty, unlit except for
the fish tank in one corner, the Agrolite in the other over Jill's small
shelf of potted herbs. It would have been Angela, though, who before

the meeting came in and picked up the place the way it looked now, like a goddamn leftie *House and Garden*, folding the afghan on the battered couch, piling the magazines and papers on the packing crate beside the armchair. Good old Angela, getting things done. Aspects of this her ordered world swam toward him as large heavy motes through which you have to chart a path upstairs to the place where you sleep, a.k.a. your room, across from Carol's and Jill's. Dirty clothes fermenting on the floor, sheets and blankets twisted on the futon, bookshelves of paint cans and pine boards holding beat-up paperbacks whose every cover he can see without looking, whose titles he knows by heart. *The Whole World is Watching. The Wretched of the Earth.* The problems of three little, five little, million little. While out on the airstrip Bogie touches Ingrid Bergman's smooth warm face. And down the hall beyond the living room, past the staircase, a bright seam of light edges Angela's door.

"You seen the movie *Casablanca*?" he said, pronouncing with as much care as he could.

When he'd first knocked and walked in she'd looked up startled from the clothbound book she'd been writing in. Now she set down her pen and slid her chair back from the small walnut desk. She was wearing her brown robe, he had seen it, her in it around the house a thousand times.

"It's after one, Max," she said. "I don't want to discuss movies now."

"Okay, sure," said Max. "Right. Fine." He did not feel at all drunk any more. Angela was shelving her journal in place atop the desk, amongst a short neat row of her canonical works, Simone de Beauvoir, Marge Piercy, etc. She was standing up, pushing her chair in, on her way to something else. Her expression remained severe but her cheeks were rosy. Long as they had known each other, after how many years and a kajillion meetings, it only struck him now, the effect of that sharpness together with that very nice skin.

So when she looked back over he tried to thoughtfully furrow his brow. "I'm feeling bad," he said.

"I'm not surprised," said Angela, smiling, folding her arms across her chest. "Tonight was not your finest hour. But I don't think anyone's permanently upset."

"It's not that," Max said. "Not just that, I mean. It's where that came from, why I did it." Yet now, even looking away from her scrutinizing eyes and smooth skin, down at the patterns of her rag-rug on the floor, he could not go on explaining, this new need had opened up so crazy strong and fast. "Angela," he said—astonished by the forcing of his gaze back up to hers—"could I just be with you tonight? Would that be okay?"

A whole lot of time seemed to pass. She stared at Max so hard, with such a steep frown on her face that her look was like a glare. Could it be she was seeing him now as he had just seen her? Was she trying to figure repercussions for the household, implications for their Bread and Roses group? Or trying to see in your face, through your own eyes, what you mean/feel/want? Finally she moved two steps forward with her expression basically unchanged, bare forearms extending straight out from the level of her waist.

"You should know I'm nervous," she said as her fingertips touched his elbows. "Not to say scared. Are we talking about really just sleeping together and that's all?"

She was holding him, he was holding her. It felt wonderful even if they were both shaking some, the way their bodies were just like that. "I'm not sure," he whispered dry-mouthed, eyes still shut. "It's been a long time for me too."

But now already she was pulling away, leaving only a soft murmur behind. "So what was that about *Casablanca*?" she said, tapping his butt. Then she was moving around the old iron-frame bed, yanking down the sheets. "How about if you go wash up—you smell like a brewery—maybe get yourself a shave as well? Then when you come back you can get right in here and tell me all."

Which was no doubt how a part of her—a part of them both—must have wanted it to be. Only it did not happen like that. What happened instead, that night then three times more in the following week, was that he came back to her room from washing up and got into bed and they went at it staring at each other as if it were anger, that intense. Age and weight dropped away, even names; then afterwards, whenever he remembered that he ought to say something, start getting things clarified, sleep closed over him before he could think of word one. Next morning he would wake at first light, long body feeling loose and wonderful, head jangling, still entangled with Angela Patillo, no idea what it meant. While he tugged and slid himself loose she would sleep on, her lips parted open, soft, making dreaming sighs of ease and protest so unlike her official waking self he was both moved and shocked as he threw on pants and shirt, grabbed his boots and went up to doze another hour or so on his own mattress, in his own room, dreaming light uneasy dreams. In the one he remembered most clearly afterwards, he was sitting across a table from her—a kitchen table, it seemed—and in response to some indication or request from her, raised his forearms up from the table surface where they had been resting, and felt her terror and amazement with his own at the sight of the dark cool subsoil dotted with green liverwort along the white undersides, entrenched in his skin. Meanwhile, at the real kitchen table a real hour or so later, the four of them got through breakfast same as always, reading the paper, listening to the radio, mumbling to each other on the news and weather, this and that until it was time for Carol and Jill to go off to school, Angela to her job at Community Services, Max his stool at the Rainbow Bookstore. Then as the week wore on he began to sense a problem. First it seemed as though she was having trouble looking at him when they met with the others around the table; then it became unmistakably clear she was looking away. Finally, Thursday morning, after their most recent night together, he brushed her side as they stood together at the stove—his oatmeal, her scrambled eggs—and felt her flinch, watched her face go hard and blank.

"What is it with you people," said his father, "you don't date any more? Why not take her out, spend a little money on her, have a good time?"

Though the bookstore was a tiny one, Max had been too engrossed in the new Murray Bookchin to have seen him come in. He simply looked up at the sound of the voice and there he was again, dead Dad across the counter, his cane neatly hooked over the wrist of his right hand, a French intensive gardening paperback in his left. For a second Max toyed with absurd possibilities, either going back to his own book and hoping he would leave, or something more drastic—shutting off the background tape of mellow sounds, sea and synthesizers and dreamy neo-folk, informing everyone, his father and, over by the Mysticism section, the brown-haired girl and her overalled friend, that the store was closed as of right now.

Instead, though, like a good boy, he shut his book and sought to calm his double-timing heart while composing his reply. No sense playing into the old man's hand, letting him get you all freaked out. "It's not like that," he said, explaining with a patient smile. "I tried pulling anything like that, she'd eat me alive."

His father gave a little shrug and snort. "What'd be so bad about that?" Then quickly raised the hand with the cane: "All right, just kidding, just kidding."

They paused, both uneasy, Max still trying to keep down the—what?—*irritation* he felt unfolding inside him. As if, were he to consent to it, let it grow, it might blossom into something utterly different, something else. "What's with the cane?" he said finally, randomly, trying to keep the heat down off his face.

"The cane," said his father. "What's with the cane." Softly, musingly repeating it, the dumb question they both knew it was. "Just an affectation, I guess," he said. "All my life I wanted some kind of class."

"Is that right?" said Max. "I never knew that."

"Neither did I," said his father. "In those terms." He snapped the gardening book shut like a wallet, smacked it against his other palm. "Besides," he said, "we never talked, you know that. I yelled at you, you took off, I died."

Another pause. The brown-haired girl and her hulking friend nodded at them on their way out, Max and his father sent back identical vacant smiles, then lapsed into sad shyness again.

"So tell me about the girl," his father said finally. "Angela. What's she like?"

"Well—" Max tried honestly to think. "She's from Lawrence, Massachusetts, where they had the big famous strike in 1912. By the time her parents were grown, the place was a wreck, all the industry was gone. She grew up in some of the first projects ever, living there with her folks, who were basically unemployed most of the time, and her brother and sisters, and her Grandma, who was in on the actual strike, she found out later, but who wouldn't even—"

"Hey," said his father. "I'm not asking for credentials. I want to know what you think of her, who she is to you."

"That's what I'm trying to tell you," said Max. "She's political too, it's important to her too. I'm trying to tell you how and why that is."

His father shook his head. "Not interested," he said. "That is not what I'm here for."

It was like old times, almost. They could almost have been back in the tiled kitchen or out on the patio, Max could see himself, his young and confident self in jeans and the old R. Crumb t-shirt, Keep on Truckin', standing on the grotesque green plastic lawn they'd put in sometime since he'd left for school, his crimson pudgy father in one of those white wrought-iron chairs yelling at him as he stood there hardly listening, easily living in the truth. All the advantages, our hard-earned money, just throw it down the drain. Only now he was no longer yelling. Now he just stood there waiting, dead.

"All right," said Max. "I don't know what she's like. We've worked together three, four years, we get along, we live together with a couple other people in this house. But I don't know what it means, our sleeping together. I don't know what she's like. And that does bother me, yes it does."

Like reciting a confession, a prepared statement, looking down at the all-weather carpeting on the floor. Like being old and heavy and a little kid again, all at once. When he looked up again his father had stepped over to the Handyperson section to reshelve the book. Dully, as depleted as if watching TV, Max watched the slender cane bow under his father's weight and snap straight again until the old man, half-turning, looked off and up as if sniffing the air.

"This stuff you got on here," he said, "how come it never changes?" He was smiling, albeit a smile mixed with rue, as he headed past the counter, register, and Max, moving for the door. "You used to tell us our music was boring. Now you listen to this?"

"My boss wants it on," Max said. "It's for sale. Don't accuse me of liking this stuff."

"Okay," said his father on his way out. "So what do you like?"

As an exit line, infuriating. Yet Max found himself thinking it over, ticking off his options long after the store door tinkled shut. At the moment, for obvious reasons, anything Latin American was hot, from Peruvian flutes to demo sing-along; there was women's music, okay to like if you were non-patronizing; reggae or rap if it was non-sexist, selected New Wave. But the last music he had really liked, the last made for him. . . . He had to admit it went back to the Stones. Stones and Beatles. Nasal snarling Dylan, too cool to live. Moby Grape, for Christ's sake. Phil Ochs before he lost it, the Doors before Morrison died. And The Airplane, of course. *Look what's happenin' out on the street . . .*

The next night, at the meeting of his Bread and Roses group, he was still flashing on it, feeling how far it was from there to here in Harry's apartment where they met week after week, month after month, trying to think of something possible that might matter, bigger than just holding tight, more effectual than nudging the other ragtag groups— anti-nuke, anti-interventionist, that was just about it—along. Partly given this impasse, partly because it was still late summer, not yet fall when things might once again pick up, the group was down to its hard core, Angela, Carol, Jill, Harry and Max himself, lounging on the batik pillows, stained and faded, thrown on the floor. It was Harry talking now, Harry, Carol, then Jill sharing announcements which were virtually zilch. To Max's left knelt Angela, frowning down at the bare wood.

Carol announced running into Dale from the Freeze who was trying to put up a phone tree, did people want their numbers on too? Jill and Harry both said something, Harry took a piece of paper from his shirt pocket and took something down, Max looked away from Angela who would not return his gaze, and went back to Harry instead. What had Harry been into back then—back somewhere in Michigan, Lansing or Ann Arbor, Max seemed to recall. These days Harry was nearly bald on top, with a little belly pushing his ragged jeans' waist, red eyes from staying up too long, too many days making the rounds with posters, fliers, exhortations after working nights as janitor of the Tidee Town laundromat. At this very moment, in fact, he was talking again, sad impeccable Harry, in the absence of other new business expounding his favorite schemes and themes concerning the old vexed question of how to make contact with the Real Working People of the town.

"Door-to-door canvassing," Harry was saying, stubby fingers poking stale air. "Find out what the workers want and need in their own words, then bring them together to go out and get it." What music would Harry like now? Max wondered, then realized what without looking he'd known all along. There was no stereo, no tape deck, no records in this small dark studio. Only a hand transistor on the counter by the sink, and that most likely for the news. Nor had old Harry ever been known to have a lover. Nor did anyone know what old Harry's parents were like.

"What we need," Harry said in his flat fervent twang, "we gotta have a good survey instrument. And that means we can't, I mean shouldn't, make it up ourselves." To his right Carol was listening, nodding encouragement, next to her Jill was practically asleep. When Max shut his own eyes he saw his dead father smiling and shaking his head. When he opened them once again they were on Angela's bowed figure and then for a sharp, shocking instant he was with her, in her all opened up, but she still would not look back. There was no air moving in here, it was almost foul. The clock on the bookshelf said 8:45. The posters on the walls, Harry's single indulgence, matted, framed and glassed at no small expense, said day-glo Viet Nam, khaki Wounded Knee, pastel Three Mile Island, black-and-white Greensboro massacre, blue and red and gold Nicaragua and El Salvador.

"We can't look patronizing," Harry said, and now at last Angela was looking up and over at Max, the hurt open question flashing to anger passing from her eyes to his along with what he realized to his terror might be tears.

The Angel of Dad

"We've got to avoid class bias at all costs. So the first step is to *find* some workers, *talk* to them, *ask* them—"

"Harry," Max said, "how bout if tonight we cut it a little short? I'm tired. I want to go home."

Harry stopped talking. At first his mouth stayed open, then it turned into a sneer. Everyone by now was sitting up straight. "Max, I think that's very bad process, interrupting like that," Carol said to his right.

"Really, Max," said Jill, wiping her long hair from her face. "I was really listening. I want to hear what Harry has to say."

All this time, with contemptuous indolence, Harry's small hands scratched his belly under the faded brown t-shirt. "Max the Rad," he said softly, sneer still on. "Max the big Rad. Where are your big ideas now?"

Now Angela was indeed crying, making no effort to conceal the fact. Tears slid down her face and dropped to the streaked pillow, their landings audible in the awful silence. Then, swiftly, Max was standing, joints cracking, stepping over to her, kneeling down. He put his arms around her; she neither flinched nor relaxed; her skin was hot to the touch on her shoulders and arms.

"I don't have any big ideas, Harry," he heard himself say with astonishing ease. "Except the Revolution seems a long ways away. And spending my whole damn life trying to find it, crack it open, isn't making it for me any more."

He could have gone on, told them all about his dead father, taken them too into his arms to hold and be held. But Angela was tearing herself loose. Flustered, he made a soothing noise, then saw the fury on her face and let go instead. In another second she was standing stock-still in the doorway, turned back to the four of them, lips quivering, not as though crying but seeking the words to make a statement through the confusion on her face. Then, with Max behind her, she was out the door, tripping down the porch steps.

"Angela!" he called and, when she just went faster, broke into a lope. Within a block he had reached her, put his arm around her waist.

"Get your meathooks off me," she said, shaking it away. "I'm not your property."

"I know you're not," said Max.

She stopped and turned to face him, hands on hips, jaw set square. The pupils in her eyes were flat black discs. "Sure you do," she said. "That's why you sneak in and out of my room, so nobody knows. Then, when I break down at a meeting, come on over and stroke down my hide. Hey," she said, "it's a great relationship. I understand it perfectly, and like it a whole lot."

"That's not who you are to me," Max said. "Not what I mean."

His voice so low it was almost a whisper, aching all along his limbs. They were stopped at the corner of 5th and Cooper. Angela's face darted up and down the street as if checking the traffic, though there was not a moving car in sight.

"I'll tell you what," she said, again turning away, her own voice choked and harsh. "When you do have it figured out, let me know. Until then, just stay the hell away."

M ax the Rad watched her figure growing smaller, moving off under streetlights which had just now winked on. When it was clear she would not turn around, would not beckon within any pool of light, he turned away too, heading randomly westward, toward the better side of town. For a time he moved through census tracts of blue-lit boxes inside which pale faces floated, across from their sets. Then bent his steps southward, cutting across campus, past black windows of brick classroom buildings, students drifting to and from the computer center's bright humming hive. On Fraternity Row he paused on the sidewalk to gaze in on a chugging contest, young smoothfaced managers-to-be stomping and chanting and swilling down beer. Somewhat later, brushing past other young blank faces glued to video gamescreens, pressing buttons to blow things up, he went up to the counter of a nearby 7-Eleven, squinting in the hard flat brightness of its lights, assailed by all the goods on their shelves. On the sidewalk outside with his Monster Cookie he was approached by a three-coed squadlette in designer jeans, with Walkmans clamped to their heads. One of the three, with short blonde hair, a flash of dazzling teeth in perfect line, tilted her bright face towards his cookie as they passed, said *Mmmmmmmm* and rolled her eyes. Then they were beyond him, the glass and silver of their carefree laughter already faint as if far away.

By the time he reached downtown the traffic lights were all blinking yellow, and a stiff wind, the first lick of winter, had begun to blow. Max groped through the streets, feeling his limbs becoming heavy aching stone. Finally he stopped to rest and after some further passage of time came to understand he was staring through the window of a men's store at the smooth hard eyeless faces of the dummies in their blazers, sportshirts, hats. *The point*, he told them, *is not to understand the world but to change it. The personal is the political. If you're not part of the solution, you're part of the problem. Yankee, come home.* They did not respond.

Later still, he was down by the river at the east edge of town. A light rain had started to fall. Its drops reached through the leaves and branches of the ghostly sycamores and birches over his head until his shoulders were damp, ginger hair misted, face and hands stiff with cold. From down the bank and out beyond the trees came the ceaseless rushing noise of the river, glimmering wherever its currents eddied and swirled. Back in his head—way back in his head—Janis Joplin was singing a blues he couldn't have named. In the corner of his eye, a sense of movement up the footpath. The murkiness took shape, suitably attired in a warm wool herringbone coat. He took his place beside Max, so close their shoulders touched. They stared at the invisible river without speaking a word.

I'm not surprised, said Max. *I knew you'd show.*

Bright boy, said his father. *Always were. Tell me what you see, bright boy, when you look out there.*

It took a while to answer; the words came slow and hard. As if not words at all, but pieces of the stone inside him, cracked and levered up to light. Even then, at the moment of their silent utterance they seemed to change, lose their colors, be no longer what they meant. *Nothing,* said Max the Rad. *Babble. Waste of motion. Murderous rush.*

His father lowered his head and tucked in his chin, rolling slight jowls up around his jaw. *And that's all?*

No, said Max. *Also death. I see death too.*

This, said his father, *is what I would call a very depressing view. And undialectical, if I might add.*

Come off it, Max said. *Remember who you are. An objectively unpleasant person living at best a useless life. What do you know about dialectics?*

You keep forgetting, said his father. *I'm dead now. I'm in you now, I know a lot more. Theory is gray, my friend,* he said quoting Lenin quoting Goethe, *but green is the tree of life. What do you think that was you felt, back then when it was so exciting and awful and you woke up every morning thinking Today's the day? That thing so much larger than you, that was just the Revolution? What you think you were tapping into, boy, what power is that?*

For a while Max looked down at the dark ground and said nothing, not even in his head. Then, slowly, he drew his wet hands to his mouth and blew them warm.

All right, said his father. *Don't say it. You don't want to lose, but you know what it is.*

Max the Rad closed his eyes, listened to the rain's music, heard the river run.

Got it? said his father. *Okay, then, I'm taking off. Call your mother sometime, why don't you? She'd be real glad to hear from you.*

The cold rain had settled into a drizzle whose steady hushing soon subsumed the river's sounds. He moved purposefully now over the grid of streets. In no time at all he was coming down the sidewalk towards the house, whose bright front windows stood out like a ship's lights. Two cats broke yowling from the shrubs on his way up the steps to the porch; then he was standing in the living room, completely drenched, looking back at them: Jill glaring from the armchair, Carol from one end of the couch; on the other, Angela staring simply, stonily, at the TV set from Carol's room. On the tube was poor dead Belushi running rampant, bouncing antennae atop his head, *Best of Saturday Night Live*; around the living room, not a flicker of amusement on a single face.

"Angela?" he said, wiping rain from his brow and cheeks, smoothing wet hair against his skull. "May I speak with you?"

Her eyes flitted up and over him, then back to the TV. "Sure. What do you want?"

From the middle of the room, where he still stood dripping, he raised his eyebrows first at one, then the other, Carol to Jill. They looked back like unfriendly scientists. "Alone?" he said.

Jill and Carol looked over at Angela. Angela's hand scrabbled in the bowl beside her for a few last kernels of popcorn. On the TV now was a Diet Coke commercial. Angela brought the popcorn up to her mouth.

"You've done enough talking for one night, don't you think?" Carol said. "Angela's been very upset—"

Max the Rad paid no attention. He waved his hand to shut Carol up, took another step forward, towards the couch, and squatted down. "Angela?"

Angela stopped chewing, swallowed, looked back into his eyes. In another minute she sent a shaky smile left and right. "You can take off now," she told Carol and Jill. "I'll be okay."

History, it is written, *is what hurts, what refuses desire*; so what happened from the time Jill and Carol left the living room remains unknown, at least in its details. We know that outside the rain continued; inside, in the tank across the room, the little fish swam round and round; on the unattended TV the channel signed off, leaving roaring snow behind until next morning's *Good Morning America*, the resumption of the bloody craven song. By that time they had agreed to have a relationship; agreed to consider, if things went well, sharing bedroom space or more, depending how that went. By that time Max the Rad had moved up to the couch, snuggled beside her beneath the afghan. Their conversation turned into sleepy murmurs, then gradually stopped. By that time through the snow on the tube, in Max's mind, beyond the steady rain his father walked off whistling and spinning his cane, thinking to himself *Good enough, good enough for now.*

■■■■■■■■■■■

Eating in Berkeley

Naomi Shihab Nye

When I think how gently the waiter placed
the plate of lettuce on our table,
how it was creamy Boston
and the next couple leaned over jealously
to count our olives, I think
this is where the word *monument* comes from,
the small tight eggplant lodged in the glistening cheese.

All day we had hiked, my mother and I,
speaking of artichoke flowers and earthquakes
to women who said their greatest fear in life was
mud. Now the night stretched out from us
like a pause between two sentences
as he brought and brought, coffee,
a slope of chicken salad crackling with almonds,
our table became a city of plates.
I watched my mother eat
as if we were two people just meeting,
something in us almost shy.
And he stood by saying Take more,
there is more to be taken.
The rest of California was a stone,
was a sea.

We had taken tea with a swami.
We had slept on a futon bed in a house
overlooking the bay.
We were full, he brought almond tart.
Two pale hills of ice cream—
I wanted to say how everything with an edge
finally softens, how nothing hard we ever said
to one another would remain.
But I said, politely, it was good you came so far
to see me again. Good to see each other
in a new place. Good we were born to one another
in this world nobody understands.
One hand over another on the table.
I would have given every dollar I had
for that meal but he wouldn't let me pay.

Outside the streets were stitched together with moonlight.
It is never too late to listen harder.
We climbed the hills so patiently
we could have been anchors tied to the stars.

■ ■ ■ ■ ■ ■ ■ ■ ■ ■

The Stars Like Minstrels
Sing to Blake

Lloyd Van Brunt

A wire strung with starlings, all
fluffed and bobbed in a stormy wind
black as their shako tails.
They seem to be squeezing that electric wire.
They seem to be playing it with their feet,
the stops pitched higher than human hearing,
like some kind of music of the hemispheres —
like 24 hands at the same piano.
When they leave together
the way a school of bait-fish jump
from shallows when a shadow
veers into view
the wire that hums volts to this studio
swings like a jump-rope — about to explode
and snap through the window. If you were holding me now
a current of fear might light up your bones like mine.

My grandmother said never to help
man, woman, or child that's been struck by
            lightning. Leave them there
on the ground, by a tree, or a tractor. The current remains
live long after the scorched heart
stills in the blazed body
and if you even touch them
you'll light up once and turn dark forever.

Though the stars like minstrels sing to Blake
I don't woo death any more than those birds
that ignorant of science rest
clef feet on a singing wire.
But it's necessary to touch death sometimes.
It's necessary to reach out for bodies
struck by lightning
slumped on city streets these days—
superstitious bodies
lying there all exposed
blazed with the mark of Cain—
bundles that might explode
like the corpses of Viet Cong.

■ ■ ■ ■ ■ ■ ■ ■ ■ ■ ■

The Legacy of the Sixties

Milton Mankoff

I t began with the 1960 sit-ins by black college students seeking to force an end to segregation at Woolworth's lunch counters in Greensboro, North Carolina and the 1964 Free Speech Movement at Berkeley. It peaked with the massacres at Jackson State and Kent State in 1970 and the massive nationwide student strike in the aftermath of President Nixon's invasion of Cambodia that same year. With Richard Nixon's defeat of George McGovern in 1972 it effectively passed into history. In between there were assassinations, riots, challenges to virtually all American institutions and values, as well as the establishment of new sensibilities in popular culture, a revolution in sexual norms, gender behavior and drug consumption. Ever since, amnesia has warred with nostalgia in framing the era of the Sixties in the consciousness of both the individuals who witnessed, or participated in, its upheavals, and the public.

Amnesia, while robbing a people of a usable past, obviously serves critical protective functions. It permits, for example, politicians and the media to harken back to a mythic "golden age" when life may have seemed more harmonious, without having to acknowledge that whatever harmony existed was at the price of ignoring festering social pathologies and suppressing justifiable rage. For individuals, amnesia allows the reconstruction of autobiography to allow parents to dismiss their own children's rebellion with the self-righteous invocation of traditional values they once flaunted. It enables political leaders to fabricate their past positions and policies to avoid condemnation in the contemporary milieu.

Nostalgia has its own attractions. Not the least of these for aging baby boomers is that glancing backward to days of drugs, sex, rock and roll and demonstrations may be far more appealing than worrying about layoffs, mounting credit card debt, passionless marriages, bypass surgery and early Alzheimer's. But if amnesia can lead to reproducing the errors of the past, nostalgia does not automatically preclude this. It is not just what is retrieved from the dustbin of history but who retrieves and the meaning they assign to it.

The Sixties has become an orphan decade, rejected, of course, by conservatives, who bore the brunt of its disrespect for authority and tradition, but also to some extent by liberals still inclined to speak of misguided idealism and excesses. The Sixties has even suffered abandonment at the hands of a significant number of its erstwhile heroes. Many middle-aged radicals seemed, during the 1980s, to view their earlier incarnations with ambivalence.[1] The late Abbie Hoffman, still proud to be an activist but not an anarchist, and Jane Fonda, then Tom Hayden's wife as well as an actress and former activist, chose to receive secular absolution on prime time from America's Mother Confessor, Barbara Walters. (In 1993, Katherine Ann Powers, a radical bank robber and fugitive for over twenty years, followed the same path to redemption.) Mr. Hayden has himself attempted a political makeover in the hopes that the burdens of being a founder of SDS would not permanently limit him to the status of a California assemblyman.

Then there are those who are embarrassed by their youthful actions: Jerry Rubin, the born again entrepreneur, and Eldridge Cleaver and former *Ramparts* editor David Horowitz, who have developed new careers as reformed political sinners, trying to follow in the footsteps of the "God that failed" ex-Communists who played such a critical role in making anti-Communism a central component of contemporary American political life for four decades.

Several prominent radicals like William Kunstler and Noam Chomsky have stayed the course. But many in this group were well beyond thirty in the Sixties and already had long established political commitments and careers.

Perhaps it is best not to seek the legacy of the Sixties in the memoirs and post-mortems of those who have always self-consciously defined themselves as public figures and who feel they must account for their thoughts and actions of nearly a generation ago. Such witnesses must always be suspect, not only because they have an agenda which colors their analyses, but because they were and are celebrities who invariably are insulated from the ways in which social and cultural movements impact the rank and file citizenry. For the Hoffmans, Rubins, and Horowitzes, there will always be a Sixties. In some parts of America, maybe where Slim Whitman sells all those records, there might never have been one.

Between these two extremes we find the bulk of the *non-college student* white adult population who took note of the turmoil on the 7 o'clock news, but failed to comment on it except as an occasional adjunct to small talk, unless one of the decade's more dramatic manifestations. . . changing hair length, erotically and politically charged music, sexual experimentation, psychedelic drugs, a draft notice or bust. . . touched a child or sibling. As for being moved by the "revolution" to transform one's personal life, this rarely happened to those who weren't already ripe to divorce or quit a job.

The celebration of personal freedom of expression in the pursuit of happiness, which was the hallmark of the decade's cultural revolution, may have sensitized some ordinary Americans to think more deeply about whether they were truly content with their lot. The divorce rate did accelerate, for example, but more so after the Sixties Thermidor than when the political critique of bourgeois lifestyles was most pronounced. Despite popular conceptions, almost 70 percent of married couples continued to describe their marriages as "very happy" in national polls throughout the Seventies.[2] The vast majority of married Americans continued to remain in that state. The same was true for work. Although many social critics decried alienated labor, most Americans enjoyed their work and wanted only more pay for it. Similar positive sentiments were consistently found when people were asked to evaluate their communities, neighborhoods, and friendships.

Americans have always sought to realize bourgeois dreams, not transcend them. Personal unhappiness has typically been rooted in material deprivation and failure to achieve or maintain a loving domestic situation. It may be different in other societies, but observers of the American scene have never detected any significant mass desire to revolutionize our social institutions. Radicals were often tilting at windmills when they sought to politicize private troubles. Our tradition is the opposite. . . to reduce social problems to individual psychopathology.

If the Sixties had little measurable effect on the personal lives of non-students, it unquestionably affected their feelings about government. The notions that it had grown too big, that politicians cared little for the average citizen, that they lied or were crooked. . . all became far more commonly held after 1966 than before. The source of the growing alienation from government was disillusionment with its policies (Vietnam in the Sixties, Watergate in the Seventies, Iran-Contra in the Eighties) and changes in the way the mass media reported government activities. A number of studies have demonstrated significant changes in the stance of mainstream media toward social institutions and political leadership from the mid-to-late 1960s to the present. Whereas the press and broadcast media once had a protective and supportive orientation, beginning in the late Sixties an adversarial style emerged which continues to this day.[3] It is important to note, however, that political alienation has not by any means meant endorsement of the political values of the Left. Rather it has been the Right which has typically captured the hearts of those suspicious of government during the past twenty-five years or so, though not because Americans are basically more conservative on the gamut of foreign policy and domestic issues than they once were. The Right's forte has been an ability to allay economic anxieties and fears of disorder that have grown in this age of national decline.

Although most white non-students were only peripherally affected in their daily lives by the spirit of the Sixties, this was not true of blacks, for whom the era brought major victories and lasting achievements: the end of *de jure* segregation, the development of black political power, the creation of a substantial professional class, and growing racial pride. These cannot be minimized because of the failure to overcome more subtle forms of racism and a persistence of widespread poverty. Unlike whites, who could be unaffected by protest, it would be difficult to find blacks whose lives were not deeply transformed. Nor can one find ex-civil rights leaders willing to disavow their earlier activism.

As for students, much has been said of what occurred in colleges and universities from 1964 to 1971. Suffice it to say that for a few years several million students lived through a revolutionary atmosphere. Old beliefs and aspirations were shed. Fear of authority withered. There was indeed power to the imagination.

Even if state power wasn't overturned, there were profound accomplishments. First and foremost, student protest was essential in crippling the Vietnam War effort. In historical terms, there has never been a case in which students played such a central role in stopping a war their government was determined to pursue. This showed, as did civil rights marches, sit-ins, and ghetto riots, that politics need not be confined to the voting booth. Indeed extra-parliamentary politics, however unpopular with the silent majority, may have been more effective than electoral strategies in terminating Vietnam and promoting black gains. The lessons of the anti-war movement have not been forgotten to this day. One of the major considerations which no doubt inhibited Ronald Reagan's military options in Nicaragua was the fear of waking the sleeping giant of student activism. Even with no student movement on the horizon,

George Bush recognized, as did his predecessor in Grenada, that military operations in Panama and the Persian Gulf must be both successful and short-lived to avoid political fallout. President Clinton's premature departure from Somalia, and fear of engagement in Bosnia and Haiti, testify to the continued reluctance to use armed force even in those rare situations which might generate support from those significantly *left* of center.

Another achievement of the protest generation was an end to university paternalism. Anachronistic curfews, dress codes, etc., were swept away when students demanded control over their personal lives. Those who were graduate students at the time also opened up a great many academic disciplines to a refreshing pluralism which still thrives. Before the Sixties, American students rarely read Marx beyond the Manifesto, knew nothing of women's history and little of social history. Their understanding of the American experience was confined to the doings of Great White Men. The current debate over the content of undergraduate core curricula is rooted in the challenges to pedagogical orthodoxy of the Sixties. In many instances, ex-student activists cum professors are leading the movement to broaden contemporary students' appreciation of the contributions to civilization of non-Westerners, minorities and women.

Although student activists had their most significant impact on government policy, and university political culture and institutional practices, one must also acknowledge that the culture of protest which was passed from southern blacks to college students did not end there. The women's and gay rights movements borrowed theory, tactics, and above all spirit from the struggles of the Sixties. This despite the fact that sexism and homophobia were not absent from a movement that still left many questions unasked in its confrontation with mainstream culture.[4]

Finally, sexual and pharmacological experimentation cannot be ignored when one assess the legacy of this period. Although the dark side of the quest for sexual pleasure has received most attention in the present decade, it would be foolish to say that there were not heavy psychological burdens and social costs in the sexually repressive neo-Victorian Fifties and substantial gains in the wake of the "sexual revolution" which began in the mid-Sixties.

Regarding drugs, there has never been any scientific evidence that marijuana, mescaline or LSD have more deleterious effects than the alcoholic beverages they were replacing on American campuses. Those who attempt to connect psychedelics with heroin addiction polemicize at the expense of sociological reality. The social groups which opted for psychedelics were rarely drawn to heroin or vice versa. Students sought drugs which promised to stimulate inner exploration or allowed them to feel, hear and see more intensely. Ghetto dwellers had more of an interest in blunting the negative feelings regarding self and their limited horizons.

Cocaine is a more complex case. It didn't become popular during the Sixties and may owe its appeal more to the Yuppie sensibility which emphasized workaholism and performance as much as hedonism. Crack, the poor man's cocaine, once again appeals to those who wish more to escape from a depressing reality than embrace life more fully.

I f the legacy of the student activists involves militant confrontation of illegitimate authority, relentless questioning of conventional wisdom, and the pursuit of happiness, what has become of the vast majority of those that left the legacy? Are they nostalgic or do the Sixties represent values which no longer move them?

It has been fashionable during the past twenty years to argue the Sixties rebellion was youthful folly at best and that veterans of the era had turned in their long locks and oppositional ways for three-piece suits. Jerry Rubin's personal odyssey from Yippie to Yuppie was seized upon by the media as representative of an entire generation's rapprochement with Middle America. The influential 1983 film, *The Big Chill*, ironically validated the once famous Sixties generation's cry, "Don't trust anyone over thirty." Yet, if we look beyond the experience of celebrities (and even among them, Rubin's path has been atypical in its embrace of the capitalist ethic) and the offerings of popular culture, evidence suggests far more fidelity to past commitments than is commonly believed.

A nationwide study tracing 1965 high school seniors to 1973 and 1982 found that those who had participated in protests among the college-attending group could still be differentiated from non-protesting college students in a number of respects.[5] Those who were activists in the mid-to-late Sixties were significantly more likely in 1982 to believe the U.S. erred in becoming involved in Vietnam than those who were not protesters at the time. Similar differences exist when questions designed to tap feelings about support for blacks and civil liberties are considered. In other words, the protest generation, or at least a significant segment of it, has not repudiated the values associated with their "political baptism."

When more recent political positions are considered, like voting behavior in the 1980 election, there has been some movement back to the mainstream. Nevertheless, the protest veterans, though not as politically distinct from non-activists as in a 1973 follow-up, still are decidedly more liberal across a broad range of issues than those who never protested.

The above research was limited insofar as it identified as protesters many people who may have participated only marginally in the events of the time. Fortunately, other research has followed Sixties activists who showed an unusual sense of political commitment and never became media celebrities: nearly 150 white civil rights workers who volunteered in the summer of 1965 to aid black voter registration in the South under the auspices of the Southern Christian Leadership Conference.[6]

The researchers who contacted the activists in 1983-84 were as interested in examining lifestyles as politics. When compared to Americans of comparable age and with at least some college education, the activists differed quite markedly. They have been unusually geographically mobile, with large numbers living in New York and the Bay Area, and indicate a clear predilection for residing in areas adjacent to liberal university centers. More significantly, they have a tendency to remain unmarried or at least marry several years later than the comparison group. Those who have married are more likely to divorce and less likely to have children.

Regarding educational and occupational histories, the cohort is distinct too. They have more formal education, with more than half earning post-graduate degrees, twice as many as the controls. Those working full-time, the vast majority, are far more likely to work in law, as college or high school teachers, or in other professional service occupations. They are also disproportionately self-employed, though not as entrepreneurs. There seems as well to be a greater tendency for the former activists to change jobs and to be engaged in part-time employment rather than pursue stable careers. Given this pattern, the Sixties activists generally earn less than would be expected.

In regard to political values, the ex-civil rights workers showed considerably more stability over time than the nationwide study of 1965 high school seniors. This is not surprising given the more selective nature of this group. For example, less than two percent of the sample voted for Ronald Reagan in 1980, compared to 19 percent of the class of 1965 activists and 62 percent of the non-activists.

What is striking in some of the interviews with veterans of the voter registration drive is the extent to which they are still living out the culture and politics of the Sixties. Many of them seem to have remained activists, either by participating in political struggles directly, or more commonly, choosing occupations which reflect their political values. For example, one interviewee observes: "I consider teaching to be a political activity, especially since I teach U.S. history in an area with an active Ku Klux Klan."[7] Another, a YWCA executive, says: "Since 1977, employment and volunteer work have consumed the majority of my working hours, 95 percent of which are devoted to social and racial equality."[8]

In April of 1988 I attended a reunion of about two hundred participants in the 1968 Columbia University strike. The large turnout testified the spirit of the Sixties was not extinguished for this group either. Not only were there more Jesse Jackson for President buttons than one might ever expect to see at an Ivy League alumni gathering, but a significant number of speakers eloquently described their continued involvement in local organizing projects, union activities, or the provision of professional services to the poor. No doubt those at the reunion were self-selected and there were certainly people who chose to stay away because the events of 1968 no longer held a positive meaning for them. Still, it was extraordinary to see an assemblage of men and women in their forties wearing tags with the name of the building they once occupied as opposed to their corporate affiliation. Another amusing aspect of the event was the way in which celebrants seemed embarrassed and apologetic for any material success they currently enjoyed. Once again, the contrast with the typical reunion in which people wear their resumés on their sleeves was extraordinary.

All this is not to say that the Columbia strike veterans had not evolved for twenty years. Reaffirmation of earlier commitments was accompanied by expressions of regret for arrogance and the use of counterproductive tactics. Mark Rudd, a strike leader and eventual Weatherman, was particularly moving in a lengthy address which embodied both pride and self-criticism. There were also acknowledgements of the rampant sexism which reduced female strikers either to "go-fers" or, for those with upward mobility in mind, bedmates of movement "heavies."

The Reagan-Bush years clearly did not destroy the spirit of many former student radicals. But they made it difficult for them to sustain movements for social change. Conservative regimes often seem to lower expectations rather than stiffen resistance to social injustice. Liberal ones, on the other hand, even if offering more rhetoric than substance, frequently have an energizing effect by raising aspirations and making activism seem more viable.

But what of the next generation and its legacy? Since the end of the 1980s the offspring of the activist cohort have begun to attend colleges and universities in increasingly larger numbers. Although certainly not all baby boomers were activists themselves, and among those who were there are no doubt politically apathetic or conservative youths, there is reason to believe that parental transmission of values might be contributing to a more liberal campus culture than existed during the period between 1980-1990.

Even in the mid-to-late 80s, with the very first wave of activist offspring entering college, there was a modest revival of militancy on a number of campuses which were the scene of anti-apartheid demonstrations that urged universities to divest themselves of investments in South Africa. An attempt was even made, with "New Left" diaper babies in leadership roles, and oldtimers in attendance, to reconstitute a national student movement. The conservative or apolitical character of the vast majority of students proved a major obstacle to such an ambitious undertaking. The balkanization of the small number of activists into status groups based on race, gender and sexual orientation, which were either unwilling or unable to merge their demands into a common program, also doomed this effort. The token resistance to the Persian Gulf war testified to the impotence of students faced with the first threat of a major war since Vietnam.

With the election of President Bill Clinton, if the belief that liberal regimes foster activism is correct, one might be more hopeful of a renaissance of student activism. The President himself is a former anti-war activist and liberal reformer and a number of his associates have similar credentials. However, either the President's political ideology has moved toward the center or even the moderate right during the course of his career or, for strategic reasons, he presents himself in such a fashion. Tactically, he searches for consensus rather than seeking to confront the political opposition to liberal reform. And he prefers to back off when opposition is stiff, or the public recalcitrant, instead of using his position to elevate political consciousness.

The consequence of the President's approach is seemingly to confuse rather than inspire by both raising and lowering expectations in quick succession. Moreover, the major crusade of the Clinton administration, health care reform, was both too complicated for students and others to comprehend and not an issue those in their late teens and early twenties, typically in robust good health and feeling invulnerable to all but sexually transmitted diseases, would go to the barricades for.

What might mobilize students? Without a military draft it seems doubtful foreign crises will arouse political passions. Worries about shrinking economic opportunities are not likely to generate compassion for those victimized by various forms of discrimination. These days nearly all students feel victimized by the erosion of opportunities for high wage employment. But this is a reality, with its resultant frustration and anger, students will not fully comprehend until after graduation, and is a problem facing the entire industrial capitalist world. Political solutions have escaped right-wing, centrist, and social democratic regimes to date.

The collapse of states which embraced a Marxist perspective, however perverted in practice, has also robbed the younger generation of any inspirational intellectual framework to seek answers for their insecurities. This will inhibit the growth of student activism if it seeks to do more than address single issues. It factor has also reinforced the balkanization process which has splintered attempts to organize a common political response to social problems facing society as a whole.

Perhaps then the legacy of the Sixties will live on in a certain admiration for the skeptical and rebellious, in a greater tolerance of deviation from social norms, and in a continued demand for participation in the institutions that affect our lives. But the unique set of historical circumstances that brought about the Sixties *per se* might not be repeated in the foreseeable future. Of course in 1959 no one anticipated what was to come soon after.

Notes

1 Some important recent memoirs by former activists include Todd Gitlin's *The Sixties: Years of Hope, Days of Rage* (New York: Bantom, 1987), Tom Hayden's *Reunion: A Memoir* (New York: Random House, 1988), and, edited by John Bunzel, *Political Passages: Journeys of Change Through Two Decades, 1968-1988* (New York: The Free Press, 1988).

2 See Richard F. Hamilton and James D. Wright, *The State of the Masses* (New York: Aldine, 1986) for a use of polls to explore American personal and political concerns from 1970 to 1980.

3 See David Halberstam's *The Powers That Be* (New York: Random House, 1979) for a description of this development at four major news organizations.

4 See Sara Evans, *Personal Politics* (New York: Vintage, 1980); John D'Emilio, *Sexual Politics, Sexual Communities: The Making of a Homosexual Minority in the United States, 1940-1970* (Chicago: University of Chicago Press, 1983).

5 M. Kent Jennings, "Residues of A Movement: The Aging of the American Protest Generation," *American Political Science Review* 81 2 (June 1987), 367-382.

6 See Gerald Marwell, Michael Aiken and N.J. Demerath III, "The Persistence of Political Attitudes Among 1960s Civil Rights Activists," *Public Opinion Quarterly* 51 (1987), 383-399; and Marwell and al., "The present lives of 1960s Civil Rights Activists: The Dreamers Turn Forty," mimeo (1988).

7 Ibid., 10.

8 Ibid., 10.

9 See Milton Mankoff, "Rutgers, DSA and the Revival of the New Left," *Tikkun* 3 (May/June 1988, 85-88).

■■■■■■■■■■■

Notes on Contributors

Terry Adams was Top Secret Control Officer for Strategic Air Command Headquarters in 1971-72, and left the service as a conscientious objector in 1972. His poetry has appeared in *College English, Midwest Poetry Review, Washington Review,* and *Ironwood.*

Rosellen Brown's novel *Civil Wars* (Knopf, 1984) focused on Mississippi. Her most recent novels include *Before and After* (Farrar, Straus & Giroux, 1992) and *Tender Mercies* (Dell, 1994).

David Caute is a journalist and historian of the post-World War II era. His most recent books are *The Year of the Barricades* (Harper & Row, 1988) and *Fellow Travellers: A Postscript to the Enlightenment* (Yale University Press, 1988).

Richard Currey spent four years as a combat medic with the Marines in Vietnam. He is the author of a novel, *Fatal Light* (Dutton/Lawrence, 1988), and two collections of short stories, *The Wars of Heaven* (Houghton Mifflin, 1990) and *Crossing Over: the Vietnam Stories* (Clark City Press, 1991).

Todd Gitlin is a professor of sociology at the University of California, Berkeley. He is the author of *The Whole World Watching* (University of California Press, 1980), *Inside Prime Time* (Pantheon, 1985), and a novel, *The Murder of Albert Einstein* (Bantam, 1994).

Duane Hall worked as a staff news photographer for the *Chicago Sun-Times* for twelve years, before moving to North Carolina. He freelances for *Time, Newsweek,* and other major magazines worldwide.

Casey Hayden worked with SNCC from 1963 to 1965 in Atlanta and Mississippi.

Tom Hayden was a founder of SDS and co-authored *The Port Huron Statement* in 1962. His books include *The American Future: New Visions Beyond Old Frontiers* (South End Press, 1980) and *Reunion* (Random House, 1988). He is presently a California state assemblyman from Santa Monica.

Maxine Hong Kingston is the author of *The Woman Warrior* (1976), *China Men* (1980), and a novel, *Tripmaster Monkey: His Fake Book* (1989), all published by Knopf.

Danny Lyon was a SNCC photographer. His most recent published work is *Merci Gonaives: A Photographer's Account of Haiti and the February Revolution* (Bleak Beauty Books, 1988).

Milton Mankoff teaches sociology at Queens College, City University of New York, and is a columnist for *Tikkun*.

Elaine Mayes teaches photography at the Tisch School of Arts, New York University. Recipient of a NEA Fellowship, she has exhibited her work many places, including the Museum of Modern Art and the Metropolitan Museum of Art in New York City.

Jim Miller is the author of *Democracy is in the Streets* (Simon & Schuster, 1988), *Fluid Exchanges: Artists and Critics in the Age of AIDS* (University of Toronto Press, 1992), and *Convergence: A Futuristic Thriller of Environmental Intrigue* (Shapolsky, 1994).

Peter Najarian is the author of three novels, *Voyages* (Pantheon, 1971), *Wash Me on Home Again, Mama* (Berkeley Poets' Workshop and Press, 1978), and *Daughters of Memory* (City Miner, 1986). He lives in Berkeley, California.

Naomi Shihab Nye's most recent books of poetry are *Dream Bottle* (Macmillan, 1994) and *Red Suitcase* (BOA, 1994).

P.J. O'Rourke was the foreign correspondent for *Rolling Stone*. His most recent books are *Bachelor's Home Companion* (1993) and *All the Trouble in the World* (1994), both from Grove/Atlantic Press, and *Give War a Chance* (1994) from Random House.

Fred Pfeil is the author of two novels, *Goodman 2020* (Indiana University Press, 1986) and *Shine On* (Synx House, 1987). His short stories have appeared in *TriQuarterly*, *Social Text*, and *The Georgia Review*.

Paul Silas is the pseudonym of a writer currently serving a federal prison sentence because of protest activities during the Vietnam War.

Louis Simpson was a professor of English at Berkeley from 1959 to 1967, when he left to teach at Stonybrook. His latest books include *The King My Father's Wreck* (Story Line, 1994) and *Ships Going into the Blue: Essays & Notes on Poetry* (University of Michigan Press, 1994).

Gary Snyder's latest book is *No Nature: New and Selected Poems* (Pantheon, 1993). His *Turtle Island*, which received the Pulitzer Prize for Poetry in 1975, was reissued from Shambhala in 1993.

Jay Stevens is a writer who lives in northern New England.

Peter Stine has published in *The Threepenny Review, Boulevard, Modern Critical Views, The New York Times* and elsewhere. He is the editor of *Witness*.

Diane Wakoski is writer-in-residence at Michigan State University. Her latest book, *Emerald Ice: Selected Poems 1962-1986,* appeared from Black Sparrow Press in 1990.

Lawrence Wright lives in Austin and is the author most recently of *Peace Report* (Harper/Collins, 1991) and *Remembering Satan* (Knopf, 1994). His articles have appeared in *Rolling Stone, Vanity Fair* and *Texas Monthly.*

Lloyd Van Brunt has been involved in the underground and alternative press movements since the early Sixties. His latest books of poems are *And the Man Who Was Traveling Never Got Home* (Carnegie-Mellon Press, 1980) and *Working Firewood for the Night* (The Smith, 1990).

Cover photos:

Allen Ginsberg	Marilyn Monroe			
Vietnamese peasant	John F. Kennedy			
Martin Luther King, Jr.	Richard Nixon	Bob Dylan	Jackie Kennedy	Lyndon Baines Johnson
Haight-Ashbury hippie	Angela Davis	American infantryman	Malcolm X	Mario Savio
Robert F. Kennedy	Tom Hayden	Charles Manson	Civil Rights activist	John Lennon